Theatre, Sacrifice, Ritual

D1145615

'Erika Fischer-Lichte's new book is a groundbreaking and compelling study of the theatre of the 20th century and its performance cultures.

Masterfully combining the century's obsession with sacrifice and its utopian ideologies, Fischer-Lichte analyses in detail how they were reflected and shaped in the mass-spectacles of Reinhardt, the early Soviet revolutionary street performances, the Nazi Tingspiels and American Zionist Pageants, concluding with a fascinating analysis of the liberating forces that formed the theatre of the 1960's and on. This book presents a radically innovative reassessment of the theatre of the last century.'

Freddie Rokem,
Tel Aviv University; author of *Performing History*

In this fascinating volume, acclaimed theatre historian Erika Fischer-Lichte reflects on the role and meaning accorded to the theme of sacrifice in Western cultures as mirrored in particular fusions of theatre and ritual. *Theatre, Sacrifice, Ritual: Exploring Forms of Political Theatre* presents a radical re-definition of ritual theatre through analysis of performances as diverse as:

* Max Reinhardt's new people's theatre
* The mass spectacles of post-revolutionary Russia
* American Zionist pageants
* The Olympic Games

This innovative study of 20th century performative culture boldly examines the complexities of political theatre, propaganda and manipulation of the masses, and offers a revolutionary approach to the study of theatre and performance history. In offering both a performative and a semiotic analysis of such performances, Fischer-Lichte expertly demonstrates how theatre and ritual are fused in order to tackle the problem of community-building in societies characterized by loss of solidarity and disintegration, and exposes the provocative connection between the utopian visions of community they suggest, and the notion of sacrifice.

Erika Fischer-Lichte is currently Chair of the Institute for Theatre Studies at the Free University Berlin, Germany. She was President of the German Association for Theatre Studies (1991–1996) and the International Federation for Theatre Research (1995–1999). Among her numerous publications are *The Semiotics of Theatre* (1992; in German 1983), *The Show and the Gaze of Theatre* (1998), and the *History of European Drama and Theatre* (2001; in German 1990).

THE UNIVERSITY OF WINCHESTER

Theatre, Sacrifice, Ritual
Exploring forms of political theatre

Erika Fischer-Lichte

Routledge
Taylor & Francis Group

LONDON AND NEW YORK

First published 2005
by Routledge
2 Park Square, Milton Park, Abingdon, Oxon OX14 4RN

Simultaneously published in the USA and Canada
by Routledge
270 Madison Ave, New York, NY 10016

Routledge is an imprint of the Taylor & Francis Group

© 2005 Erika Fischer-Lichte

Typeset in Baskerville by Wearset Ltd, Boldon, Tyne and Wear
Printed and bound in Great Britain by Biddles Ltd, King's
Lynn

British Library Cataloguing in Publication Data
A catalogue record for this book is available from the British
Library

Library of Congress Cataloging in Publication Data
Fischer-Lichte, Erika.
    Theatre, sacrifice, ritual / Erika Fischer-Lichte.
        p. cm.
    Includes bibliographical references and index.
    1. Pageants. 2. Theater. I. Title.
    PN3203.F57 2005
    791–dc22

                                        2004019539

ISBN 0-415-27675-6 (hbk)
ISBN 0-415-27676-4 (pbk)

Contents

Preface

'Nine Eleven' shocked the world. It had seemed inconceivable that anyone would be capable of sacrificing thousands of innocent people and themselves for the sake of a so-called holy cause. The very idea was absurd. And yet, it happened. In an attempt to explain the inexplicable, a 'clash of civilizations' was proclaimed. This implied that the ideas, beliefs, impulses and cultural patterns underlying terrorist acts are totally alien and incomprehensible to members of enlightened Western culture. In view of the century just passed, however, the suggestion appears somewhat strange and certainly inappropriate. As Eric Hobsbawm (1994) has shown in a pioneering study *Age of Extremes: The Short Twentieth Century 1914–1991*, this was a century of war, catastrophe and all kinds of violence; an age of crime and madness. Secular religions such as socialism and nationalism spread across Europe, igniting the masses. Those who opposed their omnipotence or, for whatever reason were not counted among the members of their 'congregation', were denounced as Evil incarnate which was to be persecuted mercilessly, tracked down and sacrificed for the final victory of the forces of Good embodied in that particular movement. The latter also demanded self-sacrifice from their own followers whenever it seemed vital for the movement.

Thus it is small wonder that Western cultures in the twentieth century were haunted by, if not obsessed with, the idea of sacrifice. Even from the turn of the nineteenth century on, scholars of religious studies and the classics, anthropologists and sociologists were caught by the subject and developed various theories. The theatre was enraptured by it. In 1893, Maeterlinck's *Pelléas et Melisande* premiered in the Théâtre des Bouffes in Paris, followed by the first performance of Oscar Wilde's *Salome* in the Théâtre de l'Œuvre in 1896, starring Sarah Bernhardt as Salome. In 1902, Debussy's opera

Pelléas et Melisande (by Maeterlinck) premiered in the Opera Comique. A whole series of plays dealing with sacrifice was performed in Max Reinhardt's theatres in Berlin from 1902 until the outbreak of World War I. In the 1902/03 season these were: *Salome*, Frank Wedekind's *Erdgeist* (Earth Spirit – Lulu) and *Pelléas et Melisande*, in 1903/04, Hugo von Hofmannsthal's *Electra* (following Sophocles) and Strindberg's *Miss Julie*, in 1905/06 Hofmannsthal's *Oedipus and the Sphinx* and the following season Wedekind's *Frühlings Erwachen* (Spring's Awakening). Almost all of these productions were veritable box office successes. The subject of sacrifice obviously proved to be highly attractive.

My study is devoted to the topic of sacrifice in theory and theatre of the twentieth century. It does not deal with secular religions, though I shall touch upon the 'religious' plays performed in their context as mass spectacles. It does not claim to explain the role and meaning of sacrifice in social and political life nor in the related discourses in twentieth-century Western cultures. However, by restricting its investigations to various theories as well as carefully selected theatre performances, I hope it will be able to shed some light on the hopes, beliefs, expectations and desires of the intellectuals before World War I, of the larger masses between the two wars, and of all those who, since the late 1960s, strove for a 'cultural revolution'.

Although, at first glance, it might seem that a parallel could be drawn between the secular religions between the wars and fundamentalist Islamism today, no conclusions can be drawn from my study regarding the evolution of terrorism, which threatens the whole world today and seems to have become the plague of the twenty-first century. The aim of this study is to reflect on the role and meaning accorded to the topos of sacrifice in twentieth-century Western cultures as mirrored in theatrical performances which fuse theatre and ritual in order to deal with the problem of community-building in societies characterized by loss of solidarity and disintegration. The heart of my study is the provocative connection between the utopian visions of community which such performances devised and tried to realize and the idea of sacrifice.

Acknowledgements

There are a number of people who have contributed significantly to the evolution of my study whom I would like to thank. For many years, the German Research Council has generously supported my research on this topic, and The Free University of Berlin granted me a sabbatical to finish it. Jo Riley translated all the German quotations and also looked after my English. Renate Schlesier and Matthias Warstat critically read an earlier version and gave inspiring advice. Ursula Schinke took upon herself the trouble of typing my handwritten manuscript into the computer. Dominik Walther prepared the manuscript for print. Sabine Krüger and Nina Tecklenburg provided bibliographical data and other useful information. During seminars on the subject of my book, I took the opportunity of discussing selected problems with my students. I am deeply grateful for all the support and help I received. For the remaining errors and faults only I am to blame.

Prologue
Electra's transgressions

Approximately one hundred years ago, at the Kleines Theater Berlin, a memorable performance took place: the première of Max Reinhardt's production of Sophocles' *Electra*, adapted by Hugo von Hofmannsthal, on 30 October 1903. The part of Electra was played by Gertrud Eysoldt. Since the opening of the season 1902/03 at the Kleines Theater, Eysoldt had played Henriette (in Strindberg's *Ecstasy*), Salome (in Oscar Wilde's play), Lulu (in Frank Wedekind's *Earth Spirit*) and Nastja (in Maxim Gorki's *The Lower Depths*). In all these productions, she both enchanted and shocked audiences and critics alike by an intense display of corporeality which seemed to express and create something which had never been expressed or created on stage before, something which had evaded any kind of language, or conventional, standardized, formalized movements, gestures, postures or attitudes till then. It was after having seen Gertrud Eysoldt as Nastja when the Kleines Theater toured to Vienna that Hugo von Hofmannsthal promised, at a breakfast he had together with Reinhardt and Eysoldt a few days later, to rewrite Sophocles' *Electra* for both.

The performance – which lasted about one and a half hours – and in particular, Eysoldt's acting, had an incredible impact on the audience. At the end, one critic reports that the spectators were 'numb for a few moments from sheer nervous exhaustion' and remained completely still, before 'they gave the poet and the actors a standing ovation'.[1]

What was it that so deeply affected the spectators and transposed them into a very particular state? The playwright and critic Hermann Bahr traces it back to the exceptional acting of Gertrud Eysoldt:

Here, the world has stopped, the breath of mankind skips a beat. A woman, entirely drained and hollowed out with suffering and all the veils which otherwise tradition, friendly custom and shame draw around us are torn to shreds. A naked body reduced to its last. Thrown out in the night. Become hateful [...]. Screams from some primitive past, footsteps of wild beasts, a look of eternal chaos in the eyes. Horrible, say the people, shuddering.

(Bahr 1907: 276)

However, from Bahr's words alone, we can hardly guess what Eysoldt actually did to perform Electra. He does not describe her bodily postures, the gestures she performed, the facial expressions she employed, how she modulated her voice while speaking, or any other concrete elements of her acting. It is not a report of what he perceived but rather an attempt to revive in words the impression and the impact her acting made on him. It seems that it allowed him to experience a dimension otherwise forgotten, hidden and locked: 'screams from some primitive past, footsteps of wild beasts, a look of eternal chaos in the eyes'. What Bahr seeks to describe in words seems to evade verbal expression. It cannot be overlooked that he articulates a sensation that Eysoldt had transgressed certain boundaries which were considered invulnerable. Through her transgression of such boundaries, she had ventured into an unknown land, from which others retreated, shuddering.

Neither Bahr nor other critics at the première elaborate clearly which boundaries. It is also striking that the reviews hardly ever provide precise or concrete descriptions. It gives the impression that the critics do not possess an adequate vocabulary to provide a clear account of what they perceived. However, the information is sufficient to allow an intelligent guess as to which boundaries Eysoldt had transgressed. It seems that more than anything, the critics were drawn to the particular use the actress made of her body and the relationship between stage and audience, actors and spectators.

From the reviews, whether positive or negative, it can be concluded that Eysoldt used her body in a way which had not been witnessed on the stage up to then – that she created a new kind of acting. Above all, the critics emphasize the excess of her acting and its enormous intensity. With these characteristics, as one critic notes, Eysoldt violated the norms of 'strength', 'dignity' and 'sonorous tone of voice', valid at the time for performances of Greek tragedies in particular. Instead, the critics noticed her 'nervousness', 'unrestrained passion' and 'hoarse roaring'.[2] Those who felt repelled by this claimed that the boundaries between the 'healthy' and the 'abnormal', the 'pathological' were thereby transgressed. In the view of many a critic, the 'screams and the fidgets, the exaggeration of the dreadful, distortion and degeneration all along the line',[3] the 'passion growing into absurdity', were 'only to be explained by recurring to the pathological'.[4] Accordingly, they rejected Eysoldt's movements as 'unbearable', without 'measure' and 'restraint', and her transgression to the 'pathological'[5] as dissolution of the self. How far the critics differed in their assessment of this excess is highlighted by their judgement on the 'nameless dance' at the end of the performance in which Electra collapses and dies. The critic quoted above felt it to be perverse and was deeply shocked by it: 'The final scene, in which Electra dances in the yard as if her mother's blood went to her head like wine, belongs to the most abominable I have ever seen on stage.' Another critic, however, only expresses his considerable astonishment:

> The final scenes in which she ran up and down before the gate like an excitable guard dog, then watched the gate in a convulsive crucifix pose and, finally, in a grotesque-dreadful dance acted out her wild excitement at the success of the deed, belonged to the most peculiar of the art of acting I have ever witnessed.
>
> (A.K., probably Alfred Kerr, *Vossische Zeitung*, 31.10.1903)

A third critic, on the contrary, regards Eysoldt's dance as the artistic climax of her play: 'No one will ever be able to imitate the way she stared into space in visionary rapture, her head thrown back.'[6]

From such comments, we can at least conclude that some of Gertrud Eysoldt's movement patterns – such as the crucifix pose or the bowed back – were similar to drawings by Charcot and Richer of different stages of hysteria or like the images of maenads on Greek vases. For the contemporary spectator, such patterns pointed to a loss of individuality and personality, either as hysteria, investigated and demonstrated by Charcot (1991), Breuer and Freud (1991), or ecstasy as postulated in Nietzsche's *The Birth of Tragedy out of the Spirit of Music* (1872; 1995). In this way, they could be understood as signs of either something 'pathological', something related to hysteria, or a new vision of Greek culture, which was no less alarming. For the image of Greek culture which the performance and, in particular, Eysoldt's acting conveyed, differed completely from the image so deeply cherished in German and all other European cultures of the time. It was not 'noble simplicity' and 'quiet greatness', as Winckelmann suggested, that characterized what the spectators witnessed in the scene, but wild ecstasy 'from some primitive past'. Such an image of ancient Greece could not be taken as exemplary, as a model of one's own culture; it was instead simply appalling.

The critics who passed a positive judgement on Eysoldt's acting particularly emphasized the contrast between her tiny, delicate body and the enormous power of her passionate, forceful movements. 'In the lead, Gertrud Eysoldt who played Electra with the eerie impulsiveness of a fanatical revenge demon: simply in the bare contrast between her tiny physical stature and the great power of her temperament.'[7] This power also came to the fore in acts of violence which Eysoldt performed on her own body when, with 'chopped hurried movements'[8] and 'convulsive spasms'[9] or other kinds of movements, 'which were taken to the highest level of ecstasy from the very first scene'[10], she forced her body into extreme exertions.

Whether the critics condemned Eysoldt's play as a transgression verging on the pathological and as an aberration from the current image of Greek culture, or whether they celebrated it as a significant artistic innovation, their reviews all lead to the conclusion that Gertrud Eysoldt had stepped over a boundary which had been drawn by the theoreticians of acting in the eighteenth century that had hardly ever been touched or questioned since then. The boundaries which the actor has to draw through acting should differentiate more or less clearly between the violence that is done to the character being played and the actor's own body that does not actually suffer from such violence. In his book on *Mimic Art* (1784/85), Johann Jakob Engel, a philosopher and some years later the director of the Royal Theatre at Berlin, expressly forbids the actors – and particularly the actresses – a form of acting which draws the attention of the spectators to their bodies by doing violence to them as in the case of 'falling' or 'plunging', 'as if they wanted to shatter their skulls'. Such acting would make the spectator concerned for the physical integrity of the actress/actor. And 'such a concern, inevitably, disrupts the illusion; we should only sympathize with the character and we start sympathizing with *him*' (Engel 1804: 58–9). Accordingly, a good actor has to develop techniques and skills that enable him to create the illusion that the character he plays suffers from physical violence – caused by an external or internal effect – without actually doing violence to his own body. That is to say, Engel draws a clear boundary between the semiotic and the phenomenal body of the actor. It is the semiotic body which brings forth the expression of suffering, while the phenomenal body does not actually suffer.

In and through her acting, Eysoldt permanently transgressed the boundary between the semiotic and the phenomenal body. The movements she performed not only expressed the unspeakable violence that the character Electra suffers to her body. By performing such movements, she also did violence on her own body. It was no longer possible to draw a clear borderline between the semiotic and the phenomenal body, the bodily being-in-the-world of the actress. Even if one would not go so far as to state that, here, the boundary between the semiotic and the phenomenal body disintegrated, the impression is created that the particular use Eysoldt made of her body shifted back and forth – oscillated – between her semiotic and her phenomenal body. She did not embody the character in the sense that she lent her body to a character which already exists in another world, namely, the script of the play, by transforming her phenomenal body completely into a semiotic body, into a 'text' composed of signs which exclusively point to the character embodied, as the theoreticians of embodiment since the eighteenth century would have it. Instead, Eysoldt embodied Electra in a way that incessantly directed the attention of the spectators to her phenomenal body, her bodily being-in-the-world, to the simple fact, so often overlooked, that the character Electra was rooted in her phenomenal body, that her phenomenal body was 'the existential ground' (Csordas 1994: 6) of the character, that without or beyond this very particular phenomenal body the character does not exist.[11]

That it is to say, Eysoldt's phenomenal body did not disappear behind her semiotic body. It also came to the fore and could not be overlooked or forgotten by the spectator. While it is the semiotic body that creates the illusion in the mind and imagination of the spectator, it is the phenomenal body, i.e. the vital, organic, energetic body whose sensuousness works directly on the phenomenal body of the spectators.

Thus, it is small wonder that no illusion was created for the spectators. The relationship between stage and audience, actors and spectators changed significantly. This change is addressed by most critics, although they seem to have great difficulty in describing and defining it clearly. They all agree that the performance had an incredible and, in many respects, absolutely unique impact on the spectators – notwithstanding the fact that they differ immensely in their assessment of such an impact. They repeatedly take recourse to dream in order to characterize more precisely the particular modality of the impact: 'The events stormed past us like a dream fantasy created by Maeterlinck, a single uninterrupted Furioso which began with the first scene and increased in power until the very end.'[12] The recourse to dream entailed and pointed to the impossibility of following the stage events by interpreting and understanding them. What happened there exceeded any human understanding. At the same time it should give an idea of the strange impact of the performance evidently unknown up to then: 'What happens to Electra, is enacted like a terrible dream with its wildly alternating and flickering images.'[13] Such images were not to be grasped. Rather, they triggered 'emotional associations of compelling power'.[14] The events were not to be understood but to be experienced: 'In all, an atmosphere which it is impossible to describe briefly in these lines. One has to have felt it.'[15] Since the boundary between the semiotic and the phenomenal body of the actress was blurred, the stage events were not experienced as an illusion of a fictional world but as 'tortuous reality',[16] which worked on the senses of the spectators and strained their nerves. 'It raves, storms and whimpers incessantly. One watches the raging like the fight of wild beasts in a cage, with nerves lashed.'[17]

This is the reason why some critics reproached such an impact as inartistic: 'The shock [. . .] was certainly enormous, but not remotely artistic and as worthless as the excitement of the audience at the circus.'[18] The comparison with wild beasts in a cage and the circus recall the fair booth into which Engel wanted to ban the concern for the physical integrity of the actors. In fact, when perusing the reviews, it becomes clear why the performance was incapable of creating an illusion in the sense of Diderot, Lessing or Engel. It worked first of all on the body of the spectators, on their senses and nerves and not so much on their imagination, their mind, via empathy. This is exactly what some critics complain about: 'The effects of this art are exclusively created by physiological stimulation and are a long way from having any value.'[19]

While it is the clear demarcation line drawn by the apron stage between actors and spectators which, beside the focus on the semiotic body of the actors, allows for any illusion to appear, Gertrud Eysoldt's acting stepped even beyond this line. 'Then, however, it was the nervous force of Eysoldt which one sensed, literally, glide over the apron stage and reach for the throats of the listeners' (Bahr 1907: 277). Thus, suggestion did its work in place of an illusion. The spectators were 'fixed to their seats by a basilisk-glance, by hypnotic magic powers'.[20] The performance spellbound them in a way that they were seemingly incapable of distancing themselves from its immediate impact, which whipped up their nerves and, at the same time, completely wore them out. They were caught in a kind of hypnotic state, from which they were only able to detach themselves by 'freely breathing again'[21] and by frenetic applause some minutes after the end of the performance, after remaining seated and 'numb' at first.

It seems that it was not only the actress who suffered from a loss of self while acting but also the spectators in the act of looking on. By working on their senses and nerves, Eysoldt's play induced a kind of hypnotic state in them. According to contemporary beliefs and understanding, being transposed into a hypnotic state implied a dissolution of the self, a loss of one's own free will which was synonymous with a loss of individuality and personality.[22] That is to say, not only the actress underwent a process of transformation in the course of the performance but also the spectators. This transformation implied a temporary annulment of the principle of individuation as it can be determined in terms of both an ecstatic and a hypnotic state. A community consisting of spectators and the actress emerged in which the boundaries separating individuals were dissolved. This was not entirely the same way Nietzsche characterizes the dancing and singing community of satyrs in ancient Greek theatre[23] but it is, nonetheless, comparable. Such a community, however, could not be regarded as a stable, long-lasting community – it disintegrated after the end of the performance the very moment its 'members' awakened from their 'hypnotic' – or 'ecstatic' – state, i.e. it was a community which one could call an 'aesthetic community'. Now it seems quite extraordinary that a community could emerge, even on a temporary basis, in which the boundaries separating individuals were dissolved in the course of a theatre performance for a bourgeois audience which made a cult of the individual. Even more so since it was a community that was based on a shared experience and not on common beliefs, values, convictions, interests and so on.

Even more striking is the fact that this happened in a performance which dealt, on different levels, with the subject of sacrifice. Electra addresses the topic almost right at the beginning. Every night, at the hour of Agamemnon's death, she conjures up his ghost and promises him a great feast of sacrifice. It will cost the lives of Clytemnestra and Aegisthus as well as Agamemnon's horses and dogs and will be celebrated with a wild ecstatic dance:

> All time shall fall
> down from the stars, just as the blood
> of a hundred slit throats shall pour on your grave!

Flowing as if from pitchers smashed to the ground
so it will flow out of the murderers' bound bodies,
and in the tumult,
of a swollen river
the vitality of their lives will
gush from them [. . .]
And we, we,
your blood, your son Orestes and your daughters
we three, when this is done
enthroned in purple from the steam of warm blood
which the sun sucks up to itself,
then we shall dance, your blood, in a ring around your grave:
Passionately, with pathos
And I shall step over the corpses
one foot after another [. . .]

      (von Hofmannsthal 1979a: 191; translated by Jo Riley)

When Clytemnestra asks Electra for the appropriate sacrificial ritual to free her of the nightmares that torture her every night, Electra suggests that Clytemnestra herself should be the sacrificial animal that has to be hunted and slaughtered in order to placate Agamemnon's ghost and free her of her nightmares. After Orestes has done the deed, killing Clytemnestra and Aegisthus, and after all those who hated Aegisthus have killed the others there is, in fact, a great feast:

CHRYSOTHEMIS [. . .] all,
who live, are stained in blood and have
wounds themselves, yet they all smile, all
embrace each other and cheer, a thousand torches
have been lit.

      (Ibid.: 232)

And Electra starts her promised dance.

*Electra steps down from the doorway. Her head is thrown back like a
Maenad. Her knees are bent, her arms stretched out, it is a nameless
dance in which she takes forward steps.*
CHRYSOTHEMIS [. . .] Electra!
ELECTRA *stands immobile, staring at her*
Be silent and dance. All must
come! Join with us! I shall bear the burden

of joy, and I shall dance before you.
Whoever is filled with joy can do one thing:
be silent and dance!
She takes a few more steps in this most intense dance of triumph and collapses.

(Ibid.: 233–4)

Thus, in the course of the tragedy, two sacrifices are performed: the sacrifice of Clytemnestra and Aegisthus, which should mitigate Agamemnon's ghost, and Electra's self-sacrifice at the end by which she completes the series of all that which 'I was made to sacrifice for my father' (ibid.: 225).[24] During the performance, it is not only these two sacrifices which are represented. One sacrifice is actually performed: the self-sacrifice of the actress Gertrud Eysoldt.[25]

After first reading the play which Hugo von Hofmannsthal sent to her at the theatre, Eysoldt replied in a letter dated 9 September 1903 that the pain and the agony which the reading caused her felt like a kind of ordeal:

> This evening I brought Electra home and read it through. I am broken by it – I suffer – I cry out against this extreme violence – I am afraid of my own strength – of this torment which awaits me. I think I could only play her once. I feel the need to escape from myself.
>
> (cited Fiedler 1996: 9)

Eysoldt revived this experience of reading the play in her acting. The violence that was done to her as she read was repeated in the acts of violence which she performed on her own body when playing Electra. By transgressing the boundary between her semiotic and her phenomenal body, Eysoldt sacrificed her own physical integrity. Her 'chopped hurried movements', her 'convulsive spasms', her gestures and movements 'which were taken to the highest level of ecstasy from the very first scene', her 'screams from some primitive past', her 'footsteps of wild beasts', her 'look of eternal chaos in the eyes', did not leave her phenomenal body untouched and unchanged. She sacrificed its integrity for the sake of the impact of the performance. And it was this sacrifice which transposed the spectators into a hypnotic state.

Thus, in her play Eysoldt transgressed yet another boundary – that which separated theatre from ritual.[26] Not only was a ritual of sacrifice represented on stage but, moreover, a ritual was actually performed. The performance was realized as a kind of ritual – the ritual of the actress's self-sacrifice which created a temporary community of actors and spectators.

What we have gathered so far from the documents on Reinhardt's production of *Electra* allows two general conclusions. First, that the performance offended current ruling concepts and ideas of theatre, at least in terms of the use of the actor's body and the relationship between actors and spectators, as well as insulted the dominant, generally accepted image of Greek culture which saw Greek culture as a powerful model of modern European culture. Second, it paralleled or even foreshadowed and anticipated new developments which appeared in the fields of theatre theory, theatre studies, religious studies, anthropology, sociology and the classics in the time between the turn of the century and World War I. These were developments which ultimately changed the view of European culture and its relationship to non-European, mainly 'primitive' cultures in a fundamental way.

In German theatre at the turn of the century, two paradigms of acting prevailed: the 'realistic' and the 'idealistic' style. The realistic style was typical of naturalistic theatre, while at the court theatres the idealistic style dominated, particularly when staging the 'classics'. Naturalistic acting had been developed in private, newly founded theatres such as Otto Brahm's Freie Bühne in Berlin (1889), which was foreshadowed by André Antoine's Théâtre Libre (1887) in Paris and followed by the Moscow Art Theatre, founded by Konstantin S. Stanislavski and Nemirovich-Danchenko in 1898. In 1894, Brahm took over the Deutsches Theater Berlin and succeeded in turning it into the leading 'modern', i.e. naturalistic, stage in German speaking countries. Here, plays by Ibsen, Björnson, Strindberg, Hauptmann, Wedekind, Gorky, Tolstoy, Galsworthy, Wilde, Shaw and other contemporary playwrights were performed. According to Brahm, the new, naturalistic acting style continued and developed the realistic-psychological, so-called 'natural' acting as it had been elaborated in the second half of the eighteenth century. That is to say, naturalistic actors transformed their vital, organic body into a 'text' composed of signs that could be read and understood as expressions of the character as well as of the psychic and mental states of the part being played. This was even to a greater degree than in the eighteenth century, for in naturalistic plays, the *dramatis personae* are unable to express adequately their feelings, emotions, sensations, wishes, intentions, thoughts, ideas etc. through words – either because they evade their own consciousness and/or their linguistic ability. In this case, the body of the actor was the only means of expression. At the turn of the century, language was generally no longer thought of as a sufficient instrument for expressing the innermost self – as is impressively manifested in Nietzsche's complaint (1876; 1960: 387) that language is 'diseased', its strength 'exhausted', that it is incapable of expressing 'strong emotional feelings', and in Hugo von Hofmannsthal's *Letter of Lord Chandos* (1902; 1979b: 465) where Lord Chandos describes the inability of language to function as a tool which structures and controls perception, knowledge and action: 'the abstract words, which the tongue must naturally serve in order to bring any kind of pronouncement to the light of the day, crumbled in my mouth like rotten fungus. It all crumbled into bits and the term came to describe nothing at all.' This being so, the body was believed to give the only true, authentic, reliable account and expression of what was going on in the mind of a person. So it is small wonder that in naturalistic theatre the most important theatrical means became the complete transformation of the actor's body into a semiotic body.

The idealistic style of acting favoured by the court theatres, on the other hand, reverted to the 'classical' style which Goethe developed whilst he was director at the Weimar Court and National Theatre (1791–1817). This style was intended to be 'an open and honest declaration of war on naturalistic art', as Schiller proclaimed in the introduction to his play *The Bride of Messina* (1803; 1980), which revived the ancient chorus. Since art should not be an imitation of reality but a symbol of what is real, the characters of a play are not to be understood as imitations of real people but as 'ideal persons and representations of the human species' (ibid.: 14). In *Rules for Actors* (1803) Goethe laid down the principles of acting which follow from this prerequisite. They govern the internal communication of the *dramatis personae* on stage as well as the external communication between actors and spectators. These principles unmistakably reveal the anti-illusionist drive of the Weimar theatre. The guiding maxim governing the relationship between actors and spectators postulates: 'the actor must never forget that he is there for the sake of the spectators' (Goethe 1901: 154). Unlike Diderot's demand for the fourth wall, which is the necessary precondition for any kind of illusion, the actor is not asked to play as if there were no audience, but be constantly aware while on stage that everything which happens on stage happens, 'because of the audience', that the performance takes place for the audience. Thus, the internal communication between the characters cannot be carried out as if it were communication in everyday life:

§39 [. . . The actors] should therefore not play to each other out of a misunderstood sense of what is natural, as if there were no third person present; they must never act in profile, nor turn their back on the audience. If it should happen through their character or as necessity requires, then only with great care and gracefulness.

§40. Also, one should particularly remember never to speak towards the back wall but always towards the audience. For the actor must always divide himself between two things: the person with whom he is speaking, and the audience.

(Ibid.: 54)

From such general 'laws' of the stage follow the guiding principles of acting: '§35. First, the actor must reflect that he is not only to imitate Nature, but he should also represent Nature in an ideal way, and that he must therefore unite both Truth and Beauty in his performance' (ibid.: 153).

This principle not only determined the demand for a speech free of dialect, for an art of declamation as a 'prosaic art of music' and a rhythmic recitation appropriate to verse, but it also demanded gestures and poses whose artificiality can be regarded as programmatic. The fingers of the actor, for example, should 'be held half curled, half straight, but never in a forced position. The two middle fingers should always remain together; the thumb, index and small finger should be slightly curled' (ibid.: 156). That is to say, the actor must completely transform his phenomenal body into a semiotic body. Such a semiotic body, however, not only serves as a sign for a particular *dramatis persona*, but also as a sign of the particular demands of the theatrical performance as a work of art which fundamentally distinguishes itself from nature as well as from social reality. Therefore, the actor's body as part of a work of art is not allowed to retain any detail, feature or trace that might remind the spectator of his sensuous, organic nature: '§74. The actor should not allow even a handkerchief to be seen on stage, let alone blow his nose, or spit. It is terrible to be reminded of such aspects of Nature in a work of Art' (ibid.: 164).

This style of artificial acting did not allow the spectator to empathize with the character or to identify with him, as did the realistic style. The spectator was supposed to adopt an attitude of aesthetic distance, 'detached pleasure', to use a Kantian term. Looking on was conceptualized as a hermeneutic process which required deciphering, understanding and reflecting on the symbolic meaning of everything displayed as well as recognizing and appreciating the harmonious, balanced relationship between all the elements – a mainly cognitive process.[27]

Despite the enormous differences between the realistic and the idealistic style of acting, they shared two characteristics. Both demanded that the actor completely transform his body into a semiotic body and avoid anything that would draw the attention of the spectator to his vital, organic body, his own bodily being-in-the-world. Both wanted the act of spectating to trigger mental, not physical processes, i.e. processes which any spectator performs individually and consciously – as an autonomous subject.[28]

In *Electra*, as we have seen, quite the contrary was the case. Gertrud Eysoldt seemed to be in an ecstatic state while performing. Thus she not only blurred and transgressed the boundaries between her semiotic and her phenomenal body in a permanent way that drew the attention of the audience to her bodily being-in-the-world – but she also lost her self, her individual identity. Such acting worked directly on the senses and the nerves of the spectators, exciting in them physiological effects. Eysoldt's ecstatic acting, her self-sacrifice, transposed the spectators into a kind of hypnotic state, so that they even experienced a dissolution of their selves. The actress and the spectators, i.e. all those participating in the performance, stepped over the threshold to a new state, a state of 'betwixt and between', as Victor Turner (1969: 95) would call it, a state of liminality.[29] As they underwent this transformation, they experienced the time of the performance as liminal time.

Thus, according to the ruling concepts and ideas of theatre of the time, *Electra* cannot simply be regarded as a theatre performance. It adopted traits of a ritual; moreover, theatre and ritual seem to have merged. In this way, the performance appears as a kind of focal point where new ideas of theatre and ritual arising and developing between the turn of the century and World War I met and converged. And these ideas not only referred to theatre, ritual and the relationship between them, but also, if not foremost, to the relationship between individual and community in modern society, to the role and function of the human body with regard to culture, to the European/Western notion and understanding of culture, and the newly recognized need to revise them which was just bubbling under the surface at the turn of the century.

This is what makes *Electra* such a fascinating point of departure for my study. Here, in a nut-shell, the problems and questions I want to address and to pursue are posed and dealt with performatively, not discursively, which makes it all the more interesting. In the following study, I shall proceed from the non-controversial assumption that in retrospect, the twentieth century can be regarded as an age of transition – not only because of the second and third industrial revolutions and their consequences, or the transition from an industrial and colonial to a post-industrial and post-colonial era, but in many other respects, too. Among the many changes brought about in different cultural fields it is particularly the various redefinitions which two relationships underwent in this course of time which interest me here: the relationship between mind and body and that between individual and community. These redefinitions went hand in hand with a search for new cultural identities, with the transition of Western culture from a predominantly 'textual' to a prevailingly 'performative' culture. Such redefinitions were also closely connected to political upheavals, revolutions, catastrophes and repeated outbreaks of violence throughout the twentieth century.

I am trying to shed light on the particular contribution which different ways and forms of bringing theatre and ritual together, of fusing them, made to these redefinitions. As we shall see, it is strikingly often the cultural paradigm of sacrifice which plays an important part in this process – from the turn of the century until its close. For good reasons, which will be explained in the course of the investigation, I shall proceed chronologically. Part I deals with the period from the end of the nineteenth century until World War I, Part II is dedicated to the years between the two great wars and Part III starts with the 1960s and covers the time span up to the end of the century. It is not my purpose or ambition to consider all theories or concrete forms of fusion between theatre and ritual that arose in the course and wake of the twentieth century. Rather, I have chosen my material primarily with regard to its suitability to reveal the almost hidden, sometimes more obvious connections between a particular kind of fusion of theatre and ritual to which it refers, and the redefinitions of the two relationships in question brought about by such a fusion; and second, in terms of the relevance the various redefinitions have from today's point of view in search of a new cultural identity in earlier times.

Thus, it might well be that the reader will miss one theory or another, one performance or another which s/he counts among the fusions of theatre and ritual which, for whatever reason, s/he holds to be particularly important. I do hope that the course of my argumentation will make up for such a disappointment and reconcile the reader with my choice.

The prologue, thus, is over and the curtain may rise for the first act of my historical play entitled, *Theatre, Sacrifice, Ritual.*

Part I

The search for origins to outline a utopian vision of the future

1 Reconceptualizing theatre and ritual

Between text and performance

The search for origins and the construction of genealogies was high on the agenda of science and the humanities in the nineteenth century. The climax and most influential model, after Charles Darwin's *The Origin of Species* (1859), was his study The *Descent of Man* (1871). In the field of Classics, in particular, the question of the origin of theatre – which at that time meant European theatre or, more precisely, ancient Greek theatre – featured most prominently. Philologists and archaeologists alike pursued it thoroughly and with great enthusiasm. In 1839, the Greek Archaeological Society began excavations at the Dionysus Theatre in Athens, and there was enormous anticipation and excitement about the results. Not only the scientific community but also the public at large, the educated middle classes, waited impatiently for any study dealing with the origins of ancient Greek theatre, and greedily devoured every new publication on the subject.

In 1872 (i.e. one year after Darwin's most successful study) a new book appeared on the subject written by a young Classical scholar, Friedrich Nietzsche, who hoped it would help him qualify for a Chair in philosophy. The book, entitled *The Birth of Tragedy out of the Spirit of Music*, was not greeted with enthusiasm, however. It did not qualify its author for the professorship for which he had hoped; instead, it cost him his reputation as a philologist and all his students at Basle University (except for one Law student and another of German Literature). It was the greatest failure imaginable.

What can have been so scandalous about a book which, in its very subject matter, would seem to have fitted perfectly into mainstream contemporary issues? First and foremost, it was the statement that ancient Greek theatre originated in the Dionysian principle, which was manifested in and enacted by a chorus of satyrs, the original dithyrambic chorus. It is this principle which annuls individuation, transposes individuals into a state of ecstasy, and transforms them into members of a dancing, singing community – a community in which the boundaries separating individuals are dissolved. This idea was a total contradiction in an age in which there was a cult, a cele-bration of the individual. The shock it caused was not even softened by another concept Nietzsche formulated in the study – the idea that tragic theatre only comes into being as long as the Apollonian prin-ciple, the principle of individuation, is also included: it is from the collision of both principles that tragic theatre arises.

This collision not only strives to annul individualization. It pre-supposes and entails another scandalous statement:

> Greek tragedy in its oldest form dealt only with the sufferings of Dionysus [. . .] all the celebrated characters of the Greek stage – Prometheus, Oedipus and so on – are merely masks of that ori-ginal hero [. . .] this hero is the suffering Dionysus of the myster-ies, the god who himself experiences the suffering of individuation [. . .] This suggests that dismemberment, the true Dionysiac *suffering*, amounts to a transformation into air, water, earth and fire, and that we should therefore see the condition of individuation as the source and origin of all suffering and hence as something reprehensible.
>
> (Nietzsche 1995: 51–2)

That is to say, Nietzsche traced back the origin of Greek tragic theatre to a ritual, a very particular ritual, in fact: a sacrificial ritual, the ritual of dismemberment. Such an idea was unacceptable to his contemporaries. It not only equated Greek culture with 'primitive' culture, and negated the value of the individual, moreover, it also completely disregarded the role and significance of the great texts handed down to us. In nineteenth century Germany, theatre was predominantly defined by its capacity to convey or mediate literary works of art. A theatrical performance was only awarded the status as a work of art if it fulfilled this function. Otherwise it simply served to entertain the audience. The idea was raised, albeit sporadically, that a theatrical performance as such might be seen as an autonomous work of art as, for example, Goethe suggested of opera in *On the Truth and Plausibility of Works of Art* (1798), an idea which Richard Wagner took up and developed even further when defining the performance of a musical drama as the only conceivable and valuable artwork of the future (*The Artwork of the Future*, 1848). (Besides, it was Richard Wagner's music theatre, which Nietzsche hailed and celebrated as the resurrection of the temporarily dismembered, tragic theatre in *Birth of Tragedy*.) The majority of Goethe's and Wagner's contemporaries, however, believed that only the performed dramatic text could secure the status of a work of art for a theatrical performance. Even as late as 1918, the critic Alfred Klaar wrote: 'Theatre will only succeed in maintaining a position of great importance when dramatic poetry adds its substance.'[1]

Considering the importance that was accorded to the text, it is small wonder that Nietzsche's vision of the origin of Greek theatre in ritual aroused an upsurge of indignation and open hostility among his contemporaries. Meanwhile, however, times had changed. Klaar's statement provoked contradiction. Max Herrmann, a professor of German literature, specializing in the fields of German and Latin literature of the late Middle Ages and Renaissance Humanism, and early German theatre history, refuted it by taking recourse to the origins of theatre: 'In my view, theatre and drama were [...] originally opposites, whose differences are so vast that the symptoms continually reappear: a drama is the word-based artistic creation of an individual; theatre is the product of an audience and those who serve it.'[2] While Herrmann connected the dramatic texts to individuals as their creators, he related theatre to a collective, citing some vague origin.

Max Herrmann (1865–1942) was one of the founding fathers of German theatre studies as an academic discipline. Because theatre was considered as something based on dramatic texts, until the beginning of the twentieth century it was regarded as a suitable subject of literary studies. Max Herrmann was preoccupied with early German theatre history and so came to a different understanding of theatre. More than twenty years of research in this subject led him to the conviction that it is not literature which constitutes and secures theatre as art, but performance. In the book that comprised and mediated the results of his research published in 1914, he states: 'The most important aspect of theatre art is the performance' (Herrmann 1914: 118). Since none of the current academic disciplines took performance as the object of their study but rather different kinds of texts and monuments, Herrmann called for a new discipline to be founded. Thus, in Germany, theatre studies were established as an academic discipline devoted to performance – not to text.

The redefinition of theatre that led to the foundation of a new discipline can be regarded as a symptom of a change in terms of the cultural self-understanding of the elite which occurred at the turn of the century. It had huge repercussions not only in the humanities and the ruling concepts of theatre but also in the whole culture. At the end of the nineteenth century, modern European culture understood itself prevailingly as a 'text' culture. That is to say, it articulated itself and saw itself adequately represented in texts and monuments (such as buildings, statues, paintings and the like) which formed the objects of the different humanities. Alongside this notion of a modern European culture as a 'textual' culture, there also circulated the idea of a 'performative culture', although it was labelled differently.[3] This comprised and exemplified all those features and qualities which did not define modern European culture and thus helped to shape and define it *ex negativo*. Performative culture was understood to be that which was called 'primitive': medieval, 'exotic' or native popular culture which abounded in display, spectacle and excess.

This argument is *not* based on the assumption that European culture from the end of the Middle Ages until the end of the nineteenth century actually *was* a prevailingly 'textual' culture. Quite the contrary, there are good reasons to believe that it was not only medieval culture which was performative. Even after print was invented,[4] forms of cultural performance still existed and played an important role in European culture, even determining the self-image and self-understanding of its members to a great extent, right up to the late eighteenth century. Quite a large proportion of texts were actually exposed to performative means first – as, for instance, when they were read aloud in the circle of the family or of friends. Even as late as the nineteenth century, there were a considerable number of cultural performances in which the *élite* participated as, for instance, weddings, funerals, religious services, national festivals and so on. Moreover, new genres of cultural performance such as circus performances, colonial exhibitions, striptease shows and the like were being invented. These were undoubtedly important for modern European culture for various reasons, as will be explained, but by the end of the nineteenth century they did not determine the self-image and self-understanding of its members. Performances such as these were created to represent and embody 'the other', i.e. that which the modern (male) European excluded from his own self-image. In these performances, it was exposed and displayed before his controlling gaze.

In the circus, wild animals which man can control and tame were the focus of observation as well as human beings who were defined by and through their bodies, such as acrobats, tight-rope walkers, trapeze artists, horse-riders etc. on the one hand and all kinds of freaks, on the other. The different kinds of show put on in the market place and at fairs were created as a new genre of cultural performance which exposed either the wild, strong nature of man and beast under control, or all kinds of deviation from the 'normal' human body.[5]

The colonial exhibition also drew on different kinds of shows from the fifteenth century which exhibited 'savages' in fairgrounds, taverns, gardens and the like. In the course of the nineteenth century, this kind of exhibition moved into new arenas: to the World and Colonial Exhibitions as well as zoological gardens. Their character also changed. It was now claimed that they served primarily scientific and educational goals and purposes. At first, the exhibition consisted of the everyday lives of the people on display. Later, it was 'enriched' by shows including prayers, singing, dancing, wedding processions and even theatrical plays. In most cases, the 'authenticity' of such performances was emphatically stressed. The purpose and aim of such exhibitions/performances was, among others, to reveal and demonstrate to the European audiences the inferiority of the 'uncivilized', 'primitive' people on display in order to legitimize their colonization by 'civilized' Europeans.[6] Thus, it is small wonder that *Electra*, by equating Greek culture with the culture of such 'uncivilized', 'primitive' people in some respects caused an outrage among some 'civilized', 'educated' critics.

The striptease show embodied, represented and confirmed a particular relationship between male and female: it was the male gaze which defined and controlled the norms of femininity; and however these were determined, the female was denied the status and rights of a speaking subject. The female was defined purely by and through her body.[7]

It is characteristic of the newly invented genres of cultural performance that the roles of performer and spectator were clearly defined and regarded as irreversible. It was the (male) European individual who, defined by 'mind', was in the position of the external, superior observer while the performers – the acrobats, the so-called primitives, the women – defined by the body, represented and embodied his inferior 'other' – an 'other' whom he desired as well as feared and whom he attempted to exclude not only from power but also from his own self-image. Thus, it was appropriate for them to be represented by/in performances and not in texts. For texts were meant to represent the self-image of the (male) middle class

European. Textual culture and performative culture were thought of as extreme opposites.

It must not be overlooked, however, that modern European culture was never monolithic, i.e. exclusively 'performative' or 'textual'. Rather, it was characterized by the prevalence of certain tendencies, which, even if they gained temporary cultural dominance, still left room for other cultures to contradict, counterbalance, or simply offer an alternative.[8] Accordingly, the performative turn which I diagnose at the turn from the nineteenth to the twentieth century – as is manifested in a performance such as *Electra* or the theories under investigation in this chapter[9] – can be described as a shift of focus from 'text' to 'performance', which allowed and even encouraged a 'return' to other, more performative epochs in European culture and, above all a change in focus towards so-called primitive cultures in search for models.

Redefining 'theatre'

In German culture, theatre was traditionally held in high esteem. At least, from the eighteenth century onwards, it was generally considered to be part of the *élite* culture, i.e. the culture of the educated middle classes – and something that greatly contributed to the shaping and stabilization of their cultural identity. Accordingly, theatre, as we have seen, was thought of and defined as textual art. Thus, it is small wonder that Herrmann's definition of theatre as performance came close to sacrilege.[10] However, as a direct consequence of the performative turn, this concept gained the status of a key term which begged thorough theoretical definition and reflection. Herrmann elaborated and provided it in different works between 1910 and 1930 in terms of (1) the particular medial conditions of theatre, (2) its materiality and (3) aestheticity.

The particular medial conditions of the theatre

Most interestingly, it is the relationship between actors and spectators from which Herrmann proceeded as he developed his concept, arguing by citing some vague, never explained origin of theatre:

> The original meaning of theatre was derived from the fact that it was a social game – played by all for all. A game in which everyone is a player – participants and spectators [...] The spectator

is involved as co-player. The spectator is, so to speak, the creator of the theatre. So many participants are involved in creating the theatre as festive event that the basic social nature of its character cannot be lost. Theatre always involves a social community.

(Max Herrmann, 'Über die Aufgaben eines
theaterwissenschaftlichen Instituts', Lecture held on
27 June 1920, cited Klier 1981: 19)

It is the bodily co-presence of actors and spectators constitutive of a performance which allows it to come into being. For a performance to occur, it is necessary that actors and spectators assemble for a particular time span at a particular place and do something together. By defining it as 'a game played by all for all', Herrmann also redefines the relationship between actors and spectators in theatre. The spectators are no longer conceived of as distant or empathetic observers of the actions unfolding in the scene, making sense of what they perceive, or as intellectual decipherers of a message formulated by the actions of the actors. It is not a subject–object relationship which comes into existence, in the sense that the spectators turn the actors into objects of their observation, nor in the sense that as subjects, the actors confront the spectators with messages that are authoritative, non-negotiable. Rather, bodily co-presence implies a relationship of co-subjects. The spectators are regarded as co-players, as participants. It is they who also contribute to the creation of a performance by participating in the game, i.e. by their physical presence, their perception, their responses. The performance comes into existence by way of and resulting from the interaction between actors and performers. The rules according to which it is brought forth can be regarded as rules of a game which are negotiated by all participants – actors and performers alike – and which are complied with or violated. That is to say, the performance is taking place *between* actors and spectators; it is brought forth by both parties. Thus, the performance is not to be regarded as a representation or expression of something which already exists elsewhere – like the text of a play – but as something which is brought forth by the actions, perceptions, responses of both actors and spectators alike. The performance calls for a social community, since it is rooted in one, and, on the other hand, since in its course it brings forth a social community that unites actors and spectators. Theatre, thus, appears to be an important community-building institution.

Theatre's materiality

In line with his insight that a performance happens here and now *between* actors and spectators, that it cannot be fixed or handed down, that it does not dispose of an artefact but is ephemeral and transitory, Herrmann did not analyse the texts being performed nor include artefacts such as the set when he elaborated his concept of performance. He even wrote a polemic against naturalistic and later expressionist stage painting because he regarded it as 'a fundamental and decisive mistake' (Herrmann 1931: 152–3), though in some cases, he did accord it an artistic value. In his view, all this is somewhat arbitrary in terms of the 'essence' of performance. Instead, it is the bodies of the actors who move in and through the space which bring about and characterize the particular – ephemeral – materiality of the performance by bringing forth an ever changing corporeality. For, 'the greatest theatrical achievement lies in the art of acting'. It alone brings forth 'the genuine, the purest work of art which theatre is able to create' (ibid.). In this sense, Herrmann seems to be less interested in the fictional character of a fictional world which the actor creates through his art. It is the 'real body' and the 'real space' (ibid.), which he is talking about, i.e. he does not regard the body of the actor in the stage space as a mere carrier of meaning, as a semiotic body – a text composed of signs for the character played – but understands body and space in their particular materiality. It is these which most of all constitute the performance and not just the fictional characters and fictional spaces which they might signify. Herrmann seems to be less interested in the body as signifier, in the semiotic body, and more in the 'real' body, the phenomenal body of the actors, their bodily being-in-the-world.

Critics of theatre performances at that time – and, to some extent, critics of today – proceeded from the assumption that the actor in the performance has to represent and to express the meanings conveyed in the text by means of his body and, in this way, to transmit them to the audience, thus affirming the priority of the text over the performance. But Herrmann does not deal with the question of representation at all, i.e. the particular reality which is represented on stage and the possible meanings that could be attributed to the outward appearance of the actors and their actions. These are not included in his concept of performance. This may be because these were the only criteria which contemporary theatre critics and literary scholars were willing to accept as relevant, so that the semiotic dimension of a performance could be taken for granted. Or, it may be that Herrmann – as Judith Butler some decades later – understood expressivity and performativity as opposites, one excluding the other. The concept of performance which he developed seems to suggest such an understanding. For he declares the bodily co-presence of actors and spectators to be the fundamental, essential defining factor, between and through which the performance happens, as well as the bodily actions which both parties perform. This dynamic and, in the end, unpredictable process, during which unplanned and completely unforeseen things arise, excludes the notion of representing, expressing and mediating given meanings from elsewhere. Meanings that emerge during this process are to be conceived as having been brought forth, primarily, in and through this very process. However, Herrmann did not reach such a conclusion, at least not explicitly. In his concept of performance, any reflection on the particular semioticity of a performance remained irrelevant.

Aestheticity

By understanding performance as a 'festival' and a 'game', as something that happens between actors and spectators, by describing its materiality as ephemeral, as a dynamic process and not as an artefact, Herrmann annulled the condition for applying the term 'work of art' – even if he himself used the term 'work of art' with regard to acting, as we have seen. This resulted from his intention to have theatre accepted as an autonomous and not as a derivative art. For, at the beginning of the twentieth century, the ruling concept of art included the notion of a work of art. Read from today's perspective, however, Herrmann's conceptualization of theatre, his concept of performance, excluded the possibility of addressing theatre as a 'work' at all. The performance's status as a piece of art, its aestheticity, is not due to a 'work', an artefact which it creates, but to its particular eventness. For in the performance, as Herrmann explains, a constellation arises that is unique, unrepeatable, something which can only partly be influenced and controlled, from which something emerges that can only ever occur this once. This is the case when a group of actors come together with a crowd of spectators who, coming from different cultural, social, biographical and situational backgrounds, assemble with certain expectations, in a particular mood, a specific temper. What interested Herrmann most at such events were the activities and dynamic processes in which both parties become involved, the creative processes which they perform,

their actions as well as the impact which participating in the performance may have on them, the kind of community that the performers
and spectators may create. Herrmann argues that the 'creative' activity
which the spectator develops is realized 'in a secret re-enactment, in a
shadowy repetition of the actor's performance, in a perception which
occurs not just through the visual senses but far more through bodily
sensations, in a hidden urge to execute the same movements, to
produce the same sounds in the throat' (Herrmann 1931: 153).[11]

Herrmann emphasizes that for the aesthetic experience to occur
during the performance, 'the most important theatrical aspect' is
'the shared lived experience of real bodies and real spaces' (ibid.).
The activity of the spectator is understood not only as an activity of
the imagination, as it may appear at first glance, nor as a production
of meaning, i.e. as a cognitive process. Rather, it is conceived as a
physical process, set in motion by participating in the event, by perceiving not only through the eyes and the ears, but through bodily
sensations which affect the whole body. Thus, it is the bodies performing in space which constitute theatre – the bodies of the actors
moving in and through the space and the bodies of the spectators
experiencing the spatial dimensions of their common environment,
the particular atmosphere of the space they share and their response
to the bodily presence of the actors that articulates itself in particular
physiological, affective, energetic and motoric impulses.

In this process, the spectators not only respond to the actions of
the performers but also to the behaviour displayed by other spectators. Herrmann points to the fact so often observed that

> there will always be certain parts of the audience incapable of
> empathy with the actor's performance. The psychic contagion
> which happens between members of the audience is usually
> favourable, but in this case, it is unfortunate. For, a small group
> infects other members of the audience and lowers their ability to
> feel empathy.
>
> (Ibid.)

The metaphor of contagion once more emphasizes that in a
performance, aesthetic experience does not refer to a 'work', but
springs from what is emerging between the participants, from their
bodies. It seems that the emergence of what happens is more
important than what happens, and in any case more relevant than
any meanings that may be attributed to it. *That* something happens
and *that what* happens affects everybody participating in the

performance, even if in different ways and to a different degree. In the course of the performance, energy is exchanged, forces are unleashed, activities triggered. Whether and to what extent Herrmann has in mind a simultaneous transformation of the spectator which his participating in the performance brings about, when he uses such terms as 'inner re-enactment', 'shared lived experience', 'psychic contagion', he does not explain. But it does seem a highly plausible theory in line with his argumentation.

The concept of performance which Max Herrmann developed corresponds, in many respects, to the theories of performativity elaborated by the philosophers John L. Austin (1975) and Judith Butler (1990a) in the middle and end of the twentieth century. They all agree that performative acts/performances do not express something that pre-exists, something given, but that they bring forth something that does not yet exist elsewhere but comes into being only by way of the performative act/the performance that occurs. In this sense, they are self-referential – i.e. they mean what they bring forth – and, in this way, constitute reality. They are capable of doing so not because of some magic power they contain, but because of some additional conditions that must be fulfilled. While Austin (1975) deals with institutional and social conditions on which a performative utterance succeeds or fails,[12] Butler (1990b) discusses particular conditions of embodiment. In Herrmann's view the conditions needing to be considered are partly institutional – it is the social and artistic institution of theatre which entails particular conditions and possibilities – partly, however, they stem from some internal elements of the performance – from the spectators and their particular disposition towards and ability to re-experience the actors' performance. For this factor will determine what kind of 'contagion' will spread, i.e. whether or not a community comes into being through/with the performance. Having such correspondences in mind, Herrmann's concept of performance seems to entail a theory of performativity *avant la lettre*, which, in terms of its fundamental aspects, agrees remarkably with later theories developed in anticipation (Austin) or as an aftermath (Butler) of another performative turn which took place in Western culture in the 1960s.[13]

Herrmann's concept, no doubt, appears highly appropriate when applied to *Electra*. It justifies Gertrud Eysoldt's acting which did violence to her own body and thus, drew the attention of the spectators to her phenomenal body, her bodily being-in-the-world by its focus on the 'real body' in 'real spaces'. It explains the impact it had on the spectators because it relied on a 'perception which occurs not just through the visual senses but far more through bodily sensations' which affect the whole body; the hypnotic state which it induced in the spectators is somewhat clarified by way of the metaphor of contagion. Eysoldt's ecstatic state infected the spectators and the symptom which arose as a direct consequence of such infection, was the hypnotic state. Herrmann's concept of performance understands the impact of acting on the spectators as a physical process which, primarily, affects their bodies. Thus, the community between an ecstatic actress and hypnotized spectators came into being by way of physical processes. Ultimately, *Electra* can be understood as one of the first articulations of the new concept of theatre to be developed later by Herrmann. In this context it should be considered that it is most likely that Herrmann did not only elaborate his new concept on the basis of purely theoretical reflections or by researching early German theatre history. He was a frequent visitor to Berlin's theatres and highly enthusiastic about Max Reinhardt's productions. He even invited Reinhardt to join the board of the 'Society of Friends and Supporters of the Institute of Theatre Studies at Berlin University' (which Reinhardt accepted). One can, therefore, assume that the performances of contemporary theatre in which Herrmann participated as a spectator greatly contributed to the development of his ideas on theatre.

Herrmann's redefinition and explanation of the 'essence' of theatre – an issue he addressed far more than its 'origins' – shifted the emphasis from the words of the text originating in the mind of an individual creator to the bodies of the actors and to the community of actors and spectators brought about by the performance. In the concept of theatre as textual art, the relationship between mind and body entailed the unrestricted dominance of the words/the mind over the body and the relationship between individual and community presupposed an undisputed supremacy of the individual author, actor, spectator over any kind of community. But Herrmann's concept seems to imply a reversal of these positions, or at least a remarkable shift. Without considering ritual – which immediately comes to mind when regarding *Electra* and in particular Eysoldt's self-sacrifice – without even mentioning it, but instead, insisting uncompromisingly on theatre as art, Herrmann defined theatre in a way which incorporated features into his concept of theatre that, as we shall see, contemporary ritual theory attributed to ritual, even claimed to be constitutive of ritual: the prevalence of bodily acts and the coming into being of a community as a result.

Herrmann, however, was well aware that such a definition was not only at complete variance with the ruling concept of theatre as textual art, but also the ruling concept of culture as 'text'. He declares theatre to be a 'cultural factor' (Herrmann 1931: 17), not only in view of the 'deeply histrionic nature of modern man' (Herrmann 1914: 13), but first and foremost because contemporary culture experienced 'times of radical change' (Herrmann 1931: 17). What kind of change this was and what a theatre as reconceptualized by Herrmann could contribute to them, however, he does not elaborate.

We learn more about the changes occurring in the time between the turn of the century and World War I from *Émile Durkheim* (1858–1917), the leading French sociologist of his time and an eminent scholar of religion and ritual. As early as his *thèse*, *The Division of Labour in Society* (1898), Durkheim dealt with the problem of how individual and community are related to each other in a society which is slowly disintegrating because of the growing division of labour. He posed the question as follows:

> This work had its origins in the question of the relations of the individual to social solidarity. Why does the individual, while becoming more autonomous, depend more upon society? How can he be at once more individual and more solidary? Certainly, these two movements, contradictory as they appear, develop in parallel fashion.
>
> (Durkheim 1933: 37)

The problem Durkheim confronted was how something like a moral bond can come into being among competing members of societies with division of labour. The mere fact that Durkheim posed such a problem seemed new and innovative in the view of bourgeois intellectuals. For it was common belief among them that an individual is to be regarded as a kind of monad, for whom society is of subordinate significance. Durkheim, however, proclaimed the overriding importance of society:

> Collective life is not born from individual life, but it is, on the contrary, the second which is born from the first. It is on this condition alone that one can explain how the personal individuality of social units has been able to be formed and enlarged without disintegrating society.
>
> (Durkheim 1933: 339)

At first glance, the problem posed by Durkheim appears to be a problem each and any society must face. Perhaps; yet it becomes obvious in the light of his further explanations that he is tackling a very modern problem that arose at the end of the nineteenth century. In modern Western societies at the turn of the century, two opposing developments could be observed. On the one hand, there was a growing individualism to the extent that, as Durkheim expressed it, 'the individual becomes the object of a sort of religion' (Durkheim 1933: 172). On the other hand, increasing industrialization and urbanization meant the development of anonymous masses that expanded daily. The constant and intensifying opposition between individuals who made a kind of cult of their personality and the anonymous 'masses' threatened to undermine and to blow up society. Thus, new forms of integration and social bonding had to be found.

This was the situation that made a performance like *Electra* possible and led to reconceptualizations of theatre and ritual. Herrmann's new concept of theatre as performance responded to this situation. Here, theatre appeared to be capable of transforming individuals into members of a community, albeit only temporarily, by focusing on the bodily co-presence of actors and spectators, on the physical acts of the actors and their capacity to 'infect' the spectators as well as on the 'contagion' occurring among the spectators. The shift from text to performance which Herrmann accomplished here had already been undertaken by ritual theory some years earlier and no less radically.

Redefining 'ritual'

In the nineteenth century it was common belief in religious studies that there was a clear hierarchy between myth and ritual. Myth was regarded as of primary importance and ritual merely a kind of illustration of it. The Scottish bible scholar *William Robertson Smith* (1846–94) deeply shocked his contemporaries by reversing this hierarchy (he was even sued for heresy because of his non-dogmatic interpretation of the Old Testament). In *Lectures on the Religion of the Semites* (1889) he argues that myth only serves as an interpretation of the ritual and is, therefore, to be regarded as secondary. Instead, it is the ritual to which primacy has to be accorded:

> So far as myths consist of explanations of ritual, their value is altogether secondary, and it may be affirmed with confidence

that in almost every case the myth was derived from the ritual, and not the ritual from myth; for the ritual was fixed and the myth was variable, the ritual was obligatory and faith in the myth was at the discretion of the worshipper.

(Smith 1957: 18)

Hence it follows that the religious scholar must primarily deal with rituals. For the fundamental principle of religion is action, or practice, rather than scripture or theological doctrine. The supremacy of religious texts, the Holy Scripture, which up to then was undisputed, particularly in Protestant cultures, thus, was seriously challenged. Moreover, such a shift from myth to ritual, from text to practice simultaneously entailed a shift of interest from the individual to the community. 'To us moderns religion is above all a matter of individual conviction and reasoned belief, but to the ancients it was a part of the citizen's public life, reduced to fixed forms, which he was not bound to understand and was not at liberty to criticise or to neglect' (ibid.: 21).

That is to say, investigating ritual promised a clearer insight into the means and mechanisms of integrating individuals into a community and the emergence of social bonds between them. In this way, ritual could become a model for solving the problems at stake at the turn of the century as outlined by Durkheim. This conclusion was not drawn by Smith, however, but quite explicitly by Durkheim. He confessed that he owed his insight into the functioning of religion to Smith's *Lectures*. He was convinced that the study must be based on the most 'primitive' people in order to gain insight into the unconscious world of the collective. Through this, he hoped to elaborate an advanced solution to the problems at hand for the future; his findings were published in a pioneering study *Elementary Forms of Religious Life* (1912) which heavily relied on Smith's theory of sacrificial ritual.

Smith regarded the sacrifice as the fundamental and oldest ritual of all ancient, even archaic, religions whose significance is still preserved in the highest forms of religion. He dealt in particular with the ritual of sacrificing a camel, which according to an author named Nilus (the so-called Pseudo-Nilus) from the fourth century, was common among Arabic tribes and Jewish rituals as they are described in the Old Testament. While in those days, a sacrifice was commonly interpreted as a gift to the gods in order that they are benevolent, Smith explained it as a meal shared by men and gods as a communion that is brought about by the common eating of the flesh and blood of the sacrificial animal. The sacrificial meal not only serves as an act of communion between men and gods but also establishes a community of those men who take part in it. '[...] the act of eating and drinking together is the solemn and stated expression of their fact that all who share the meal are brethren, and that the duties of friendship and brotherhood are implicitly acknowledged in their common act' (ibid.: 265). The community that comes into being among the participants of a sacrificial meal, thus, is due to the shared consumption of the 'flesh and blood' of the sacrificial animal. The bond uniting them results from the physical act of eating and drinking. Such a bond of union, 'strictly speaking lasts no longer than the food may be supposed to remain in my system. But the temporary bond is confirmed by repetition, and readily passes into a permanent tie' (ibid.: 270). Such a bond is even stronger when the sacrificial animal is regarded as a deity in the sense of totemism, as Smith assumed with respect to the sacrifice of the camel by the Arabic tribes on which Nilus reports. It is not only the act of common consumption which establishes the bond, but also the consumption of a particular animal which is worshipped as ancestor that makes it even stronger. In either case, it is the sacrificial meal which turns a ritual religious group into a social and political community.

The parallels between Smith's reconceptualization of ritual and Herrmann's redefinition of the 'essence' of theatre are striking. The shift from myth to ritual corresponds to the shift from text to performance. The physical act of eating and drinking together are echoed in the physical actions of the actors and the physical sensations they excite in the spectators. The political community which comes into being by and in the sacrificial meal can be equated to the theatrical community that comes into existence in the course of the performance. Bodily acts and actions that had been previously held to be insignificant – only receiving any kind of meaning from being related to the myth or to the dramatic text – were accorded meaning to the extent that they were thought able to constitute a meaningful structure such as a community. Ritual theory and, somewhat later, theatre studies, thus, re-evaluated the traditional opposition between a textual – European – and a performative – 'primitive' – culture. On the one hand, the performative was given attributes that had previously been held to be characteristic of texts alone, such as the notions of meaning and sense. On the other, emphasis was laid on the potential of a collective to execute performative acts that create, bring forth, culture whereas before, creativity had been conceived of only in connection with the mind of the individual and the artefacts which were brought forth (ignoring the physical acts of writing, painting, sculpturing that were necessary for their production). Thus, the way was paved for bridging the gap between *élite* (textual) and popular (performative) culture, between European and non-European, so-called primitive cultures, that was characteristic of the beliefs of nineteenth century middle class Europeans, and so persistently cherished.

Beliefs of this nature, however, were harshly attacked by another book which took up the subject of sacrificial ritual: *The Golden Bough* by *James George Frazer* (1854–1941). It first appeared in two volumes in 1890 and expanded to the twelve volumes of the third edition (1906–15), and a supplement which Frazer added in 1936. Considering the subject of the study and the fact that it fiercely defied ruling beliefs, it seems almost incredible that it was an overwhelming success from the start. His contemporaries commented,

> from the very beginning, Frazer's book possessed a shady reputation [...] In its time, *The Golden Bough* was the sort of book to read beneath the bed-sheets by the light of a torch. When the first edition appeared in 1890, a little *frisson* seems to have gone round the literary world. People sent one another letters, phrased in an urgent whisper.
>
> (R. Fraser 1994: IX)

It was undoubtedly a scandalous book, like Nietzsche's *The Birth of Tragedy*, but nonetheless, read with enthusiasm and much discussed – even if this was not public.

Victorian and post-Victorian society was convinced of its fundamental otherness with regard to all other societies, cultures, human beings. Frazer's book was so scandalous because it stressed the sameness of all societies and cultures. Frazer applied a new method – to which the subtitle of his book 'A Study in Comparative Religion' points – and this method is still in agreement with the basic principles of evolution. Through this, Frazer tried to show that the base on which modern civilization is founded exists in all cultures whether they are exotic, popular or primitive.

The fundamental idea underlying and structuring Frazer's study was the idea of the slain and reborn god, an idea which Frazer confessed in the foreword to the first edition he owed to his friend William Robertson Smith.[14] On the basis of rich material collected by others in most diverse cultures – non-European as well as popular European cultures – the armchair anthropologist Frazer made a bold attempt to prove his theory that a sacrificial ritual of death and rebirth was common in all cultures, that it was a universal rite performed everywhere for the sake of the welfare and well-being of the community concerned. The examples Frazer cited stemmed, for instance, from the African Shilluk as well as from Cambodia and Thailand, from contemporary German grain-harvest traditions – which the German anthropologist Mannhardt (1875/76) had researched extensively – as well as from Babylonian and Egyptian sources, from the Maori as well as from ancient Greek and Roman cultures. First, he refuted the idea of the uniqueness of Greek culture – already challenged by Nietzsche – as a culture which Victorians and other Europeans liked to refer to as the model of their own culture. He did this by comparing the rituals, myths and customs connected with Greek gods like Dionysus or Persephone to those related to gods of other cultures – as, for instance, Tammuz or Osiris or the Shilluk kings – and, in particular the ritual of sacrifice, of death and rebirth. He also refuted the principle idea that modern European culture is fundamentally other in comparison with non-European and, especially, so-called primitive cultures. Frazer wanted to show that European civilization has evolved from a culture based on sacrificial ritual which can be regarded as a universal rite; that it originates in a type of culture common to all human beings all over the world that still exists packed away in the basement somewhere.

For the rationalist Frazer, this insight legitimized him to reveal, challenge and uncompromisingly put down any kind of 'superstition' he came across in contemporary society. This approach did not even leave Christianity untouched. But Durkheim drew the opposite conclusion. As he explains in his final work, *The Elementary Forms of Religious Life* (1912), recourse to so-called primitive cultures that practise totemism[15] demonstrates that religion can be socially productive. He was not interested in any particular religion or in religion as such, but in religion as the source of collective life in a society which is slowly disintegrating because of the division of labour. Thus, it is wise to read his comments on totemism not only as explanations on this topic but also, and foremost, as reflections on the state of contemporary society at the time.

Totemism, according to Durkheim, is based on social facts and the expression of things experienced by the individual in and with collective groups. The totem, whether animal or plant, represents such a group. The worship of it is socially productive in that it transforms many individuals into a community which has a supernatural reality of its own. This experience can be applied to contemporary societies:

> There are circumstances where this strengthening and revitalising activity of society is particularly clear. Within a crowd moved by a common passion, we are moved and become capable of actions of which we are incapable if we rely on our individual powers. And if the crowd disperses and we stand alone again, then we sink back onto our usual level and only then can we measure the incredible heights which we had reached [...]. That is the reason why all political, economic, or religious parties call regular meetings at which their members can revitalise their shared beliefs by bearing witness together.
>
> (Durkheim 1912: 209–11)

What happens in such meetings, accordingly, corresponds to what happens at a sacrificial meal.

With regard to the two relationships under investigation here, it seems interesting, if at first glance somewhat confusing, that Durkheim performs a kind of reversal in *The Elementary Forms* – and even more explicitly in an article written two years later (Durkheim 1914). He claims human existence is twofold: in terms of the body, man is a sensuous, individual, egoistic being; in terms of the soul/mind, man is a moral, social, rational being. Up to this point in our study, it seemed that at the turn of the century a correspondence was conceived between 'mind' and 'individual' as well as between 'body' and 'community'. But in Durkheim's view it is just the other way round: 'mind/soul' corresponds to 'community' and 'body' to the 'individual'. For Durkheim, this re-evaluation was the basis from which he could state that the structure of moral autonomy is anchored in the religion of elementary societies. This, in turn, implies that modern society only filled a form already moulded by primitive religion. This reversal now made it feasible to explain sacrificial ritual and totemism in terms of the problems arising in modern societies from the disintegration brought about by the division of labour. It opened up the possibility of looking for completely new solutions to the problem. Searching for 'origins' was less oriented towards the past than towards the present and, more importantly, to the future. The findings of such studies might spark new visions of the future.

Amongst all the theories of sacrificial ritual summarized so far – the most influential theories of their time – the concept of transformation plays a central role. By sharing the flesh of the sacrificial animal and drinking its blood, those who participate in the sacrificial meal are transformed: they are no longer simply isolated individuals but form a community together. Thus, they acquire a new status and a new identity. In terms of the modern problem formulated by Durkheim – how to find new paths towards integration and social bonding in a society disintegrating because of the division of labour – it is vital to get a clearer insight into the functioning of such a transformative process. Surprisingly enough, Smith, Frazer and even Durkheim seem to have been more or less satisfied with stating such a transformation exists without explaining it any further. In Durkheim's *Elementary Forms* it appears as a kind of miraculous transubstantiation that turns a number of individuals into a moral community.

It was these processes of transformation to which the French/ Dutch anthropologist *Arnold van Gennep* (1875–1957) devoted many years of research. He not only examined sacrificial rituals but all kinds of ritual in the course of/through which a transformation takes place. In his seminal study, *The Rites of Passage* (1909) he embarked on the enterprise of analysing the process of transformation in detail.[16] Van Gennep proceeds from the notion of borderline, of boundary. It is the transgression of a marked, visible spatial boundary which he takes as a model for all passage. To transgress a boundary always entails a risk – for the individual concerned as well as for the whole community. In order to minimize the risk, to secure a safe passage, particular rituals must be performed. Van Gennep calls them rites of passage. It is their purpose to secure a safe passage from one place or state to another when individuals or social groups are going through changes of their state and identity – have to undergo a transformation – as in life crises, such as birth, puberty, marriage, pregnancy, illness, famine, war or death – or in seasonal cycles. Van Gennep took a closer look at the process and found that it always follows the same scheme. This scheme consists of three phases: (1) the separation phase in which those who are about to undergo a change are alienated from their everyday life and their social milieu, i.e. are removed from their former place, time, social status; (2) the threshold or transformation phase, in which the people concerned are transposed between and betwixt all possible realms, between different worlds which allows for completely new, partly rather disconcerting experiences – the phase, Turner later would call 'liminal'; and (3) the integration phase, in which the newly transformed are reintegrated into society and socially accepted in their new status.

In all three phases, a boundary is transgressed – this not only means abolishing an existing boundary but also drawing a new boundary. While in the separation phase a boundary is crossed which closes the former everyday life from the particular event that is to take place and the usual social milieu from others, in the integration phase, a new boundary is drawn. The threshold and transformation phase, in its turn, allows for most diverse kinds of transgression, and may even be experienced as a total dissolution of all boundaries. It is the dangerous phase, between the old and the new state, the phase in which the transformation that should take place may fail.

Although such a three-phase structure is to be found in all cultures, it may well be the case that the structure of the ritual is even more complex. Sometimes one of the three phases is more organized than the others or stretches in time to an extent that it has to be structured in different sub-phases. Nonetheless, the underlying scheme remains, in principle, always the same.

Following this method of taking the transgression of a spatial boundary as the model for all rites of passage, van Gennep demonstrates that the passage of a spatial boundary is often an important element of other kinds of rites of passage (as, for instance, in birth, initiation, wedding, funeral, seasonal rites); moreover, in fact, rites of passage are generally based on a spatial conception: a newborn has left the world of the unborn and is integrated into the world of the living; an adolescent is separated from the world of children and passes into the world of adults; the dead must dissolve from the world of the living and be incorporated into the world of the dead. As van Gennep shows by referring to a wealth of material taken from different cultures, such passages are understood as an analogy of the process of dying and being reborn. Whoever transgresses a boundary in order to be transformed dies in the former world only to be reborn in another. That is to say, those who undergo a rite of passage will experience what, for the sake of the community's well-being, Frazer's year-god or year-spirit went through when slain or dismembered and later reborn.[17] Here, ritual transformation is explained as a symbolic death which must be experienced in order to be reborn in a new state. In exposing the three-phase structure underlying and organizing all kinds of rites of passage, van Gennep actually sheds light on how transformation processes function.

This exposition can be fruitfully applied not only to the rituals Smith, Frazer and Durkheim were dealing with,[18] but also to *Electra*. The performance can be regarded as a kind of threshold and transformation phase. After having been removed and alienated from their everyday lives, the participants enter a new state: the actress an ecstatic and the spectators a hypnotic state. They have all transgressed the boundary separating the 'normal' state from the ecstatic and hypnotic one. This new state means living in-between different worlds – in a state of liminality, to use Turner's term – which allows for many other kinds of transgression and, accordingly, for new, sometimes shocking, confusing, horrible, in short, unbearable experiences. The moment of 'breathing freely' and of frenetic applause marks the beginning of the incorporation phase. The actress and the spectators have left behind the particular state of ecstasy or hypnosis and awaken to new lives, in another world. Thus, the reintegration into everyday life and the social milieu is initiated. In this way, recourse to van Gennep's scheme contours the ritualist features of the performance to which I have pointed even more distinctly. Apart from that, an important difference regarding the state of liminality in rituals and in theatre performances can be found. While in ritual, the liminal phase leads to a new status or identity, which, later on, is accepted by the community, in theatre the transformation brought about by the liminal state is reversible and does not ask for public acclaim.

Ritual and theatre

The comparison of Smith's and Herrmann's redefinition of ritual and theatre outlined above shows that the reconceptualizations carried out by them both focus on similar aspects. First, on the reversal of the hierarchy between text (myth and drama) and performance (ritual, theatrical performance), and second, on the importance of physical acts which bring forth a community. While all ritual theories considered here emphasize the process of transformation which the individuals participating in the sacrificial meal undergo in order to form a community together – even though they do not elucidate how such a process functions – Herrmann's theory of theatre only implies such a transformation. Thus, it follows from such reconceptualizations that it was these that brought to light, even brought about, significant affinities between ritual and theatre.

Nietzsche had already analysed and stressed such affinities in his essay on *The Birth of Tragedy*. Here, he identified them in the presumed origin of Greek tragic theatre in ritual. Like Smith, who sees a bond established not only between humans participating in the sacrificial meal, but also between the gods and humans, Nietzsche proceeded from a union between man and nature in the tragic chorus:

> Not only is the bond between man and man sealed by the Dionysiac magic: alienated, hostile or subjugated nature, too, celebrates her reconciliation with her lost son [...]. Now, with the gospel of world harmony, each man feels not only united, reconciled, and at one with his neighbour, but *one* with him, as if the veil of Maya had been rent and now hung himself in rags before the mysterious primal Oneness. Singing and dancing, man expresses himself as a member of a higher community: he has forgotten how to walk and talk, and is about to fly dancing into the heavens. His gestures express enchantment.
>
> (Nietzsche 1995: 17–18)

And, as in the theories on ritual, the idea of transformation is at the core. For Nietzsche, it seems to be the fundamental idea underlying tragic theatre which is applied not only to the chorus but also to the spectators:

> [...] the Dionysiac Greek [...] saw himself transformed into a satyr. The ecstatic horde of Dionysiac votaries celebrated under the influence of such moods and insights, whose power was so transformed before their very eyes that they imagined they saw themselves as reconstituted geniuses of nature, as satyrs. The later constitution of the tragic chorus is the artistic imitation of this natural phenomenon, which required a separation between Dionysiac spectators and Dionysiac votaries who are under the god's spell. But we must never forget that the audience of the Attic tragedy discovered itself in the chorus of the orchestra, and that there was no fundamental opposition between the audience and the chorus: for everything was simply a great, sublime chorus of dancing, singing satyrs, or of those whom the satyrs represented.
>
> (Ibid.: 41)

In stark opposition to the Aristotelian concept of theatre which focuses on mimesis, at the heart of Nietzsche's concept is the performative act of transformation which is only possible because theatre originated in the Dionysian ritual of dismemberment.

What Nietzsche claimed without, however, providing the slightest evidence – which incidentally sealed his academic career – was picked up by another Classics scholar approximately thirty years later who was bold enough to make a further attempt to find concrete evidence that Greek theatre actually originated in a ritual of death and rebirth. This scholar was *Jane Ellen Harrison* (1850–1928). She was the head of the so-called Cambridge Ritualists which also included *Gilbert Murray* (1866–1957) and *Francis MacDonald Cornford* (1874–1943) who actively supported her research and even contributed chapters of their own to her book *Themis*. Early in her research, Harrison came to the conclusion that ritual precedes myth – whether independent of Smith or not is hard to decide.[19] The foreword of her third book *Mythology and Monuments of Ancient Athens* (1890), provides an explicitly ritualistic view:

> My belief is that in many, even in the large majority of cases *ritual practice misunderstood* explains the elaboration of myth. [...] Some of the loveliest stories the Greeks have left us will be seen to have taken their rise, not in poetic imagination, but in primitive, often savage, and, I think, always *practical* ritual.
>
> (Harrison 1890: iii)

Accordingly, she regarded 'the myth-making Greek as a practical savage rather than a poet or philosopher' (ibid.). Thus, it is small wonder that the search for evidence of such rituals in Greek religion and the examination of relevant documents, whether texts or vases or whatever, became the centre of her research. In her study *Prolegomena to the Study of Greek Religion* (1903, i.e. the year of *Electra*) she tried to show that under the layer of the world inhabited by the Olympian Gods lies buried another religion which she understands and explains as the chthonic pre-history of the Olympian Gods as well as a later victory over them. It is the rituals of this other religion which she contrasts to the myths of the Olympians.

On the basis of these studies, in *Themis. A Study of the Social Origins of Greek Religion* (1912; 1962) Harrison developed a theory of the origin of Greek theatre in ritual. Among her extensive readings other than Nietzsche were also Smith, Frazer, Durkheim and van Gennep, whose theories she considered while pursuing her project. She drew heavily not only on Nietzsche but also on Frazer, in particular on his idea of the death and rebirth of a god or a spirit underlying *The Golden Bough*. Harrison proceeded by assuming a pre-Dionysian ritual in which a year-demon, the so-called *eniautos daimon* was worshipped. An ancient ritual of this kind seemed to explain why similar structures of death and rebirth of a god corresponding to the annual cycle of the seasons could be found in most diverse cultures, as Frazer had demonstrated. The Dionysian ritual, accordingly, was assumed to be an off-spring of the ancient ritual to the Spring Demon.

In this context, Harrison defines ritual as a *dromenon*:

> A δρώμενον is [. . .] not simply a thing done, not even a thing excitedly and socially done. What is it then? It is a thing *re*-done or *pre*-done, a thing enacted or represented. It is sometimes *re*-done, commemorative, sometimes *pre*-done, anticipatory and both elements seem to go to its religiousness [. . .] the thing done, is never religious; the thing *re*-done with heightened emotion is on the way to become so. The element of action re-done, imitated, the element of μίμησις, is, I think, essential. In all religion, as in all art, there is this element of make-believe. Not the attempt to deceive, but a desire to *re*-live, to *re*-present.
>
> (Harrison 1962: 43)

I have quoted this passage in almost full length because it contributes two interesting features particularly relevant to our context: on the one hand, the physical, performative acts are stressed, the doings by which the ritual comes into being; on the other, the extract emphasizes that a ritual is not only a thing done, but a thing re-done or pre-done, which is to say that the acts performed are meaningful mimetic acts which are intended to re-present and not to represent something: regarding this latter aspect, ritual is compared to art – which includes theatre. In this respect, Harrison clearly deviates from Nietzsche in assuming a more Aristotelian position when connecting art with mimesis.

There are two ideas arising from the research done so far which underpin her argument in *Themis*: '(1) that the mystery-god and the Olympian express respectively, the one *durée* [a term Harrison borrowed from Bergson, whose works she had also studied], life, and the other, the action of conscious intelligence which reflects on and analyses life, and (2) that, among primitive peoples, religion reflects *collective* feeling and *collective* thinking' (ibid.: XIII). While, according to Harrison's beliefs, the Olympians are to be regarded in the context of patriarchy, the mystery-god is characteristic of a matriarchy.

In setting out to show that Greek theatre has its roots in the *eniautos daimon* ritual Harrison proceeds from Aristotle's statement in *Poetics*, in her view undisputed, that Greek theatre originates in the dithyramb. Thus, her task is to find evidence of a connection between the dithyramb and such a ritual. She found this evidence in a recent archaeological discovery of the *Hymn of the Kouretes* in Crete in the temple of Dictaean Zeus at Palaikastro. The Hymn appeared to Harrison as providing the 'missing link' between the dithyramb and the *eniautos daimon* ritual. For, since 'the Hymn sung by the Kouretes invoked a daimon, the greatest Kouros, who was clearly the projection of a thiasos of his worshippers' (ibid.: XIV), it promised the results needed in order to substantiate her argument. In a meticulous analysis of the Hymn, Harrison applied a comparative method, i.e. she connected the different findings of her analysis not only to other Greek texts and archaeological material but also to anthropological material collected in most diverse cultures in Africa, Australia and the Americas. In her extensive and thorough analysis, Harrison came to the conclusion that

> the Dithyramb [. . .] is a Birth-Song, a δρώμενον giving rise to the divine figures of Mother, Full-grown Son and Child; it is a spring-song of magical fertility for the new year; it is a group-song, a κύκλιος χόρος, later sung by a *thiasos*, a song of those who leap and dance rhythmically together.
>
> (Ibid.: 203)

On the basis of such findings, she attempts to create a new etymology of the word 'dithyramb', an attempt that can be regarded as the keystone in the construction of her argument:

> The word *Dithyramb* now speaks for itself. The first syllable Δῖ for Δῖϊ is from the root that gives us Ζεύς and Διός. The ending αμβοζ is probably the same as in ἴαμβος, σήραμβος. We are left with the syllable θυρ, which has always been the crux. But the difficulty disappears if we remember that [. . .] the northern people of Greece tend, under certain conditions, to substitute υ for o, which gives us for Δῖ–θῦρ–αμβοζ Δι–θορ–αμβοζ – Zeus-leap-song, the song that makes Zeus leap or beget. Our Hymn of the Kouretes is the *Di-thor-amb*.
>
> (Ibid.: 204)

One is tempted to add: *Quod erat demonstrandum.*

Gilbert Murray contributed a chapter to *Themis* entitled 'Excursus on the Ritual Forms Preserved in Tragedy'. Here, he takes up Harrison's argument and tries to elaborate and substantiate it further.

Proceeding from a myth reported by Herodotus, he lists the elements that seem to be typical and characteristic of various Year-Daimon celebrations: an *agon* or contest, a *pathos*, generally a ritual or sacrificial death, a messenger, who announces the death, a *threnos* or lamentation, an *anagnorisis* and a *theophany*. Referring to different Greek tragedies and, in particular, Euripides' *The Bacchae*, Murray attempts to show that these elements in the tragedies fulfil similar functions as in the *eniautos daimon* ritual. Emphasizing the difference between the ordinary year-daimon and the never dying Dionysus, he concludes:

> An outer shape dominated by tough and undying tradition, an inner life fiery with sincerity and spiritual freedom; the vessels of a very ancient religion overfilled and broken by the new wine of reasoning and rebellious humanity, and still, in their rejection, shedding abroad the old aroma, as of eternal and mysterious things: these are the fundamental paradoxes presented to us by Greek Tragedy.
>
> (Ibid.: 362–3)

Two years later, Cornford's Study on *The Origin of Attic Comedy* (1914) appeared, in which a corresponding pattern for comedy was laid out.

The theories of the Cambridge Ritualists and, in particular, of Jane Ellen Harrison shattered the views and beliefs of her contemporaries, even more so than Frazer's *Golden Bough* had done. According to them, the much-admired texts of Greek tragedies and comedies could ultimately be deduced from – if not reduced to – a ritual celebrating Dionysus as a kind of year-daimon. First came the ritual and from it developed the theatre and texts which were written for performance. Such theories could lead to the conclusion that if Greek culture, which was regarded as the epitome of human civilization, a model of an ideal civilization, exemplary in almost every respect, articulated its self-image and self-understanding not only in texts but also in different kinds of performances as, for instance, rituals, and if the much-admired texts of Greek tragedy and comedy originated in such rituals, then Greek culture could no longer be regarded as a prevailingly textual culture but as a performative culture as well. Such a conclusion contained a vision of the future. For, if the ideal culture was, at least in part, if not to a great extent, a performative culture, then modern European culture could also change into a performative culture where necessary to solve particular problems, without, however, running the risk of losing its high aspirations, level of achievement and standards.

I have not cited the theories of ritual from the turn of the twentieth century because I hold their arguments to be sound. That would undoubtedly prove foolish, considering the fact that most of them have been more or less reliably refuted.[20] What makes them interesting, even fascinating, though, and worth closer examination, is the fact that they betray a particular mentality which, in some respects, seems to be typical of the *élite* in European culture of the time. True, they did not close their eyes to the problems of the day. However, they hoped to find a solution for the future by searching for origins, by going back to a distant, mostly misty past which it was by no means possible to illuminate sufficiently. Thus, the past was treated as a kind of plane of projection for their visions of the future. It was the brutal violence, the atrocities, the senseless 'sacrifice' of youth in World War I that revealed this kind of solution as utopian. It is small wonder that, after the war, Harrison did not return to her pre-war research. The new performative culture which her theory entailed had taken a turn which she had not foreseen, let alone expected. This is even truer with regard to the developments between the two wars. Marcel Mauss, a prominent disciple and nephew of Emile Durkheim, wrote in a letter of 6 November 1936 to S. Ranulf:

> Durkheim and after him we others, are I think, the founders of the theory of collective representation. That great modern societies could be so moved by suggestion as the Australians in their dance, and could be so activated as a group of children, is something that we could not foresee. This return to the primitive was not the subject of our considerations. We were satisfied with vague references to the state of the Masses [...]. We were simply satisfied to prove that the individual can find the basis for and nourishment for his freedom, his independence and his critical awareness in a collective spirit.
>
> (Cited in Lepenies 1989: 107–8)

In any case, after World War I, the utopian vision lay shattered in pieces. Nevertheless, the reconceptualizations of ritual and theatre as proposed between the turn of the century and World War I revealed a cultural change, which was actually underway and, in some respects, would haunt European/Western culture until the end of the twentieth century. The shift from text to performance which entailed a shift from individual to community and from mind to body challenged the supremacy of the mind over the body and the individual over the community that had been undisputed in European culture for approximately three hundred years. Such a performative turn, upon which the reconceptualizations addressed here reflected as well as helped to bring about, was the initiation of a process in which the relationships between mind and body, individual and community would be constantly redefined.

Between the turn of the century and World War I, however, it was not only the field of humanities which took part in this process of reconceptualizing ritual and theatre – or the much more visible new body culture as proclaimed by the *Lebensreform* movement. It was also, if not foremost, the invention of new forms of theatre and ritual that contributed to this process. The most effective and successful forms were those which were passed off for ancient Greek theatre and ancient Greek ritual, or which were understood as a rediscovery, reinvention or revival of them – Max Reinhardt's new peoples' theatre, his Theatre of the Five Thousand, and the Olympic Games, 're-opened' on the initiative of Pierre de Coubertin in 1896.

2 Re-inventing a people's theatre

Max Reinhardt's Theatre of the Five Thousand

It was not only Max Herrmann who claimed that theatre is brought forth as a 'festive event'. At the turn of the century, the idea of theatre as a festival was widespread among theatre reformers. In 1899, the playwright and theatre theoretician Georg Fuchs – a disciple of Nietzsche – elaborated it in an article which hailed theatre as a celebration of life. He repeated and rephrased the same idea later in two very influential books on the revolution of theatre that appeared in 1905 and 1909 and were translated into various European languages. In 1900, a book appeared on the subject written by the architect and designer Peter Behrens.[1] And two years later, in a conversation with friends and colleagues which took place at the famous Café Monopol in Berlin at a late hour, Max Reinhardt explained his plans regarding the function of classical plays in his theatre of the future by referring to this very idea.

> The classics must be performed in a new way; they must be performed as if they had been written by playwrights of today, as if their works were alive today. [...] New life will arise out of the classics on the stage: colour and music and greatness and splendour and merriment. The theatre will return to being a festive play which was its original meaning.
>
> (cited in Kahane 1928: 118–19)

Of course, the idea of theatre as a festival was not new at all. In nineteenth century Germany it had been proclaimed and propagated by Richard Wagner. Wagner felt appalled and disgusted by the attitude of the bourgeois audience towards theatre. He felt the audience consumed theatre as a kind of 'industrial institution' and the performances were a reproducible commodity which can be devoured at any time rather like any other industrial product.

Wagner's uncompromising critique of performance as a commodity – as well as his wish to 'revitalize' the ancient Greek theatre – led him to the idea of theatre as a 'democratic festival' to which he wanted to invite 'the people'.[2]

At the turn of the century, it was not only the idea of performance as a commodity at the centre of the critique of contemporary theatre which provoked the idea of theatre as a festival. Rather, it was also the widely felt inability to create an opportunity for any kind of communal experience. Naturally, each different reformer upheld a different concept of festival. While Fuchs celebrated the 'state of ecstasy' induced by participating in a festival, Behrens directed his attention to the 'surplus energy' accumulated by everyday culture to be consumed by the festival. Finally, Reinhardt emphasized the 'splendour and merriment', the particular mood and atmosphere of a festival. However, they all agreed on certain points. First, on the opposition between everyday life or labour and the festive occasion which they regarded as liminal time, and second, on the communal experience opened up by festival. In a festival, there is no separation between actors and spectators; those who arrive as spectators are transformed into participants, and together they form a community. That is to say, it is the transformational force of a festival, the communal experience it provides – in short: its ritualistic aspects, which these reformers all had in mind when proclaiming that theatre should turn into a festival. Thus, theatre as festival implied a particular fusion of theatre and ritual.

Reinhardt proceeded from the assumption that theatre as festival in this sense could only come into being when both parties joined forces – actors and spectators alike. For he was convinced that

> the best theatre is not only performed on stage. Actually, the most important players are sitting in the auditorium [...]. One day, the two-way flow which passes from the stage to auditorium and from auditorium to stage will be scientifically researched. The moment when one who creates receives at the same time and the receiver becomes one who creates, is the moment when the precious and incomparable secret of theatre is born.
>
> (cited in Fetting 1973: 61)

Such a moment occurred in *Electra*, as we have seen. But the audiences did not always turn out to be as responsive. Reinhardt complained about the bourgeois audiences (not unlike Wagner, who called them 'lounging spa tourists'): 'The so-called "best" audience is actually the worst audience – insensitive and not naïve. Inattentive, self-important, used to being at the centre of attention [...] the best audience is up in the gallery' (cited in Adler 1964: 43). Reinhardt felt challenged to look for new audiences that would be able to join forces with the actors and, thus, to create the performance as a festive event. This was the birth of the idea of a new people's theatre.

In 1908, the Munich Artist's Theatre was opened, founded by Georg Fuchs and built by Max Littmann. Fuchs propagated the idea of *Volks-Festspiele*, of a theatre festival for the people who, because of the exorbitant price of theatre tickets, were excluded 'from the most artistically significant and pioneering performances of the stage'. It was to be a theatre '[...] for those workers, craftsmen and employees who are open to art and reaching for the sky' as well as for the 'broad masses of professionals' (Fuchs 1911: 78–9).

When Fuchs organized the first Munich *Volksfestspiele* in 1909, he asked Reinhardt to collaborate. Reinhardt seized the opportunity to develop and, ultimately, to realize his idea of a new people's theatre, a Theatre of The Five Thousand, as he called it, a theatre-for-the-masses. The music festival hall on the Theresienhöhe was rebuilt in such a way to include an arena stage. In 1910, Reinhardt staged Sophocles' *Oedipus Rex* here and in 1911, Aeschylus' *Oresteia*. Both productions later moved to Berlin, into a 'real' circus, the Circus Schumann. After the festival season was over, Reinhardt took *Oedipus Rex* on tour through Europe to London, Stockholm, Moscow, St. Petersburg, Vienna, Budapest and Brussels among other places. In some cities, such as Budapest, Moscow and London he restaged it with local actors and amateurs (the chorus). Wherever Reinhardt presented the production, it was an overwhelming box office success. It seems that this new theatre strongly appealed to pre-war audiences all over Europe and that it found deep resonance. What happened at these performances where the spectators were given the opportunity to undergo unusual but, obviously, eagerly sought for experiences? What was it that attracted the spectators so much?

Given the high esteem shown to ancient Greek culture by all Europeans at the time, it seems significant that Reinhardt chose ancient Greek tragedies for his first experiments with the new people's theatre. Reinhardt was well aware that the theatre in Athens was part of a festival and that it was a people's theatre in which all citizens were not only allowed, but also expected to participate. Both his chosen tragedies deal with the problem of how to acquire a new identity. In *Oedipus Rex*, it is the question of an individual identity which is at stake; the trilogy of the *Oresteia* explores the passage from a clan identity to a political identity (i.e. an identity which refers to the *polis*, the city). In *Oedipus Rex* as well as in the *Oresteia* the problem of identity is closely related to the topic of sacrifice. Oedipus acts as a kind of scapegoat (following Frazer's model); the crimes of patricide and incest which he unknowingly committed have brought a *miasma* upon the city, have infected it with the plague. In order to cleanse the city, i.e. for its sake and welfare, he has to be sacrificed. In the trilogy of the *Oresteia*, the clan identity of the members of the house of Atreus is confirmed through sacrifice, through acts of violence done to other members of the house. Agamemnon sacrifices his daughter Iphigenia on the altar of Artemis to guarantee fair winds for the journey of the Greek army to Troy; to avenge her daughter's death, Clytemnestra kills Agamemnon in the bath with an axe when he returns from Troy; Cassandra is directly addressed as sacrificial animal by the chorus: 'how can you, serene/walk to the altar like a driven ox of God?' (*Agamemnon*, line 1297 f.), and finally Orestes sacrifices his mother in compliance with Apollo's order to revenge his father's death.[3] In contrast, in the third part of the trilogy, *The Eumenides* (which was performed in Munich but omitted in Berlin), the political identity of the Athenians is brought forth and strengthened through an act of agreement by which the Athenians, following the order of Athene, established their legal system.[4]

Most critics[5] expressed dismay that neither the production of *Oedipus* (translation by Hugo von Hofmannsthal) – nor the *Oresteia* (translation by Carl Vollmoeller) one year later – could be called a representation of the tragedy's meanings. Even though not all went as far as to state that Reinhardt proceeded 'from the principle that the director is everything, the poet nothing',[6] they all question the production's 'truth' to the text and complain – as already some critics did of *Electra* – that the performance worked more on the 'senses' and the 'nerves' of the spectators than on their 'souls'. Nonetheless, they all admitted that the impact of the performance was 'powerful' and that this was due to particular 'modern scenic devices'[7] which Reinhardt elaborated and applied.

From perusing the reviews, the impression arises that most of the devices which the critics mention have to do with a new relationship that seems to have been established between actors and spectators. This is all the more surprising since the audience, unlike the audience that frequented the Deutsches Theater, was far from being homogeneous. As most reviews report, the spectators came from all social classes and strata. School classes and students attended as well as union workers; ladies and gentlemen from the elegant West of the city as well as scholars who were not in the habit of visiting theatre; members of Parliament and even – something almost every review mentions – members of the imperial family with their entourage. Members of the workers' theatre organization, the *Volksbühne*, could purchase their tickets at special rates. So this was, in fact, a people's theatre as far as the attendance of all social groups, classes and strata is concerned. Bearing in mind that at the beginning of the twentieth century it seemed difficult, if not impossible, to turn a homogeneous audience made up of the bourgeoisie into a community, it is most unlikely that Reinhardt succeeded in transforming the members of such a highly heterogeneous audience into members of a community. However, this is what the reviews suggest.

The devices mentioned by most critics refer either to the particular use made of the space or the performers' bodies. In *Oedipus Rex* (stage by Franz Geiger, costumes by Ernst Stern), the arena at the side of the stables was defined by a huge entrance to a palace building from which a flight of steps projected. The circus ring remained empty. On a special enclosure which had been added to it, two altars with 'sacrificial flames'[8] were placed. The nearly five thousand spectators were seated all around the circus ring in a kind of amphitheatre arrangement. A cloth of reddish-brownish colour was put up under the roof that stretched over the whole huge space of the circus – covering the ring as well as the auditorium. The beginning of the performance was announced by

> long drawn-out fanfares. Blue light falls in the ring that has become the orchestra: bell-like sounds clang, swell, voices moan, becoming louder, surging, and the people of Thebes swarm in through the central entrance opposite the built-up stage. Running, stampeding, with raised arms, calling, wailing; the space is filled with hundreds of them and their bare arms stretch to the sky.
>
> (Norbert Falk, *BZ am Mittag*, 8 November 1910)

The opening already reveals the dominant devices characteristic of the performance as a whole: (1) the occupation of the space by the masses; (2) the way a particular atmosphere functions; (3) the dynamic and energetic bodies moving through the whole space.

(1) The occupation of the space by the masses

Partly confused and irritated, if not disgusted, all critics remark on the fact that the chorus did not consist of a mere fifteen members but rather hundreds. The chorus members not only moved and acted in the orchestra, i.e. in the ring, overcrowding it, though still neatly separated from the spectators; they also occupied the space otherwise 'reserved' for the spectators. They had entrances which took them right past the spectators; they even acted among them. They were everywhere, they occupied the whole space. In the *Oresteia*, where Reinhardt also used this device, the critic Alfred Klaar felt most uncomfortable because of

> the division of the action into the space in front, between, beneath and behind us, the eternal exertion to change our viewpoint, the actors flooding into the auditorium so that the figures in their glittering costumes, wigs and make-up jostle against our bodies, the dialogues held across great distances, the sudden confusing shouts from all corners and directions of the house which startle us – it all helps to distract; it does not help create the illusion but tears it apart instead.
>
> (Alfred Klaar, *Vossische Zeitung*, 4 October 1911)

The critic not only felt uncomfortable because as a spectator he had to change the position of his body if he wanted to see and hear what was going on in the space (see below), but also because the performers moved among the spectators, because they even occupied the space of the auditorium and, thus, 'jostled against' the spectators' bodies, i.e. they did not respect the boundaries separating one individual body from others. The occupation of the whole space by the performers, on the other hand, cancelled the difference between performers and spectators. The performers moved among the spectators, they seemed to be one with them. Thus, they drew the spectators into the action and made it difficult to distinguish between actors and spectators. All together they formed one mass.

This point is made by another critic. First, he mentions the presence of Prince August Wilhelm and Prince Oskar. Then, he continues:

> But the individual has no impact here. In this half light, only the crowd has an impact. One begins to understand what 'the public' means. This is what Reinhardt needs [...] He believes

the crowd is everything, subject and object. He rewards five thousand spectators by presenting a company of almost ten thousand. He presents the masses to the masses. He shows them themselves in the exaggerated form of passion and costume.

(Fritz Engel, *Berliner Tageblatt*, 8 November 1910)

It seems significant that the critics who adhere to bourgeois individualism do not use the term community but the term 'the masses' instead, which has a negative connotation. What we can gather from their remarks, however, is the idea that through Reinhardt's special devices, not only was a community of hundreds presented and represented in the orchestra to the spectators but also a community was brought forth in the course of the performance, a community of thousands, comprising performers and spectators alike. In fact, it was a temporary community only. It may not even have lasted the whole duration of the performance and it may have been that not every spectator sensed a kind of communal experience – it seems to have been a matter of pride for most critics that they resisted it. In any case, whatever kind of community it was, it finally dissolved, at the latest, when the cheers stopped and the spectators left the Circus Schumann. Because the community that came into being during the performance was temporary, it was not able to change the relationships between members of the different social groups, classes and strata on a longer lasting basis. However, from the reviews we can gather that the performance brought forth a kind of community and established a bond of sorts between performers and spectators. One of the devices that made this possible was undoubtedly the particular use made of the space – a device which we will find being applied to different kinds of mass spectacle in the 1920s and 1930s.

(2) The way a particular atmosphere functions

The opening of the performance in the above quotation lists a number of elements which created a particular atmosphere. The blue light, the sounds of the fanfares, the bell-like sounds, the moaning voices, the particular rhythm of different noises as well as the movements of the performers, all contributed to the creation of a particular atmosphere. As we learn from the reviews, some of the recurring elements in the performance which had an effect on the spectators included constant lighting changes (blue, violet, green, greyish, reddish-brownish, bright like sunlight and so on), the orchestration of music and sounds, the changing rhythm of movements, sounds and music. By the time Reinhardt produced *Oedipus Rex*, he was already famous for the ways in which he created and used atmosphere. (The reviews of all his productions mention the atmosphere.) It was not only the use of light, colour, music, sounds and rhythm of movements which contributed to the atmosphere but often smell too. His famous *A Midsummer Night's Dream* (1904) was regarded as sensational because it used a revolving stage which was covered in fresh moss that emanated a bewitching fragrance in the space giving the spectators an intense physical sense of the presence of the woods.

Reinhardt applied this sophisticated use of atmosphere – something he had developed over the previous ten years – to *Oedipus* as well as to the *Oresteia*. Whether this created 'a magical effect'[9] and 'wild excitement'[10] as in *Oedipus*, or a 'barbaric' atmosphere, which was 'circus-like in the most vulgar sense' as in the *Oresteia* when Agamemnon made an entrance to the clash of circus music, with 'four snorting, stamping' – and one is tempted to add: stinking – 'horses' (Jacobsohn 1912: 51); it seems that in all cases, it was the particular atmosphere which succeeded in involving the spectators and making a strong impact on them.

As the philosopher Gernot Böhme explains, a particular atmosphere is not bound to space, although it does permeate space. Atmosphere belongs neither to the objects or persons who seem to radiate it, nor to those who enter the space and sense it physically. In a theatre space, atmosphere is usually the first element to seize the spectator and open him to a particular experience of that very space. This experience cannot be explained by referring to single elements in or of space. For it is not single elements that create atmosphere, but the interplay of all these elements together. Böhme (1995: 33) defines atmosphere as 'spaces that are "tinted" by the presence of objects, humans or environmental constellations [...] They are spheres of a presence of something, of its reality in space.' Böhme goes on to argue that atmosphere is

> not something that exists by itself in a vacuum, but quite the opposite. It is something that emanates and is created by things, by people, and the constellations that happen between them. Atmosphere is not conceived as something objective, as a quality that belongs to objects; and yet atmosphere is object-like because it articulates the spheres of its presence. Nor is atmosphere something wholly subjective, moods experienced by someone. And yet it is subjective, or belongs to the subjective

because it can be felt as a physical presence by the spectator and this sensation is, at the same time, a physical self-discovery of the subject in space.

(Ibid.: 33–4)

In our context, this description and definition of atmosphere seems particularly interesting in terms of two aspects. On the one hand, Böhme defines atmosphere as 'spheres of presence'. That is to say that objects and humans perceived as part of an atmosphere – as objects from which the atmosphere seems to emanate – demand the attention of the person perceiving in a very intense way. They cannot be ignored. They make their presence conspicuous. They impose their presence on the perception of others.

On the other hand, Böhme locates atmosphere neither in the objects which seem to radiate it nor in the subjects who sense it physically but rather in the space between and around them as well as both at the same time. That is to say, it is the atmosphere which binds performers and spectators together; atmosphere can be regarded as a kind of environment which results from and, at the same time, surrounds them, into which both are immersed. Thus, there seems to be a certain transformational potential inherent in atmosphere.

We learn that the atmosphere created in *Oedipus Rex* but also in the *Oresteia* was of a very special quality. The elements which contributed to atmosphere such as the sounds, voices, music, movements, rhythm, smells, light and colours – not only the spotlights but also the flickering flames of the open fire on the two altars as well as the torches held by a group of half-naked young men as they 'raced like savages through the orchestra up and down the steps to the palace'[11] – all have two things in common: first, they have a strong physical impact on those who perceive them and, second, they are all transitory and ephemeral.

These elements work on the senses and the nerves of the spectators. Sounds, voices or music, for instance, not only surround the perceiving subject they also, in a way, invade his body. In his body, the sounds begin to resonate and trigger similar vibrations. Particular sounds are even able to cause physical pain which can be clearly localized. The listener can only protect himself against sounds by blocking his ears. Usually he is exposed to them without defence. At the same time, the boundaries of the body are transgressed. When the sounds, voices or music turn the body of the listener/spectator into a space of resonance, when they resonate in his chest; cause physical pain; give him the shivers or butterflies in his gut, then the listener does not hear them as something that comes to his ear from the outside; rather, he senses them as a procedure within his body which sometimes arouses a kind of 'oceanic' feeling. Through the sounds, the atmosphere invades the spectator's body and opens it up to reception.[12]

Comparable, if not more powerful, is the impact of smells. They invade the whole space and affect everybody present. It is impossible to escape them. They intrude into everyone's body. As Georg Simmel stated:

> When we smell something, we draw this or that impression deeply into the centre of our being, assimilate it intimately, as it were, through the vital process of breathing, which is not possible for any other sense to do of an object – unless we eat it. That we smell the atmosphere of someone else is the most intimate perception of him; he permeates our insides in gas form.
>
> (Simmel 1923: 490)

The person who smells will be bodily affected by the subject or by the object which emanates the scent. There is no defence against it. The smell, thus, can be regarded as a component or ingredient of atmosphere which contributes to the possibility that atmosphere may extend across space, between actors and spectators, that it surrounds the spectator, even invades him in a decisive manner. The smell not only has the effect that the object from which it emanates seems present in a particularly intense way to the spectator, but also that the spectator feels his own physical presence in an extremely intense way. By using elements which emanate strong smells such as the torches, the fire on the altars, or the horses (in the *Oresteia*), Reinhardt exploited such possibilities to the full.

Lighting is another factor which contributes enormously to the creation of atmosphere. Although Reinhardt did not yet utilize a computerized lighting board – as Robert Wilson does nowadays – he pushed the technical possibilities of his time to the extreme and changed the colour, tone, shadow etc. of the spotlights – as well as their focus. With each lighting change, the atmosphere changed. The scale went from dreary, cold, depressive or eerie to cheerful, happy or joyous with all possibilities and nuances in between. Particularly powerful was the change from colours that are sensed as cold to those we perceive as warm. The warmth, in particular, was emphasized by the fire on the altars and the torches. Even if only those who sat close to the arena could literally sense the warmth of the fire, it also evoked the impression of warmth for others who could only see it. In this context, it has to be considered that we perceive light not only through our eyes but also receive it through the skin. It penetrates through the skin into the body. Any human organism responds sensitively to light. If the spectator is exposed to frequently changing light, as was the case here, his condition and overall feeling will also change accordingly. The experience will not necessarily be felt consciously, nor can it be controlled. His inclination to let himself be drawn into the atmosphere, however, is considerably increased.

All these elements were related to each other through rhythm. It is rhythm which unites the sounds, voices, music and movements of the bodies, objects and light. The reviews often mention 'the rhythmic effects'.[13] It was Georg Fuchs, who in his small book on *Dance* (1906) pointed to the possibilities of working on the bodies of the spectators through rhythm. Here, he emphatically defines the art of acting as

> the rhythmical movement of the human body in space, executed out of a creative urge to express an emotion through the means of the own body, with the aim of throwing off that inner urge with such a passion that one draws other people into the same or similar ecstasy.
>
> (Fuchs 1906: 13)

Even if rhythm is not used to induce ecstatic states, it usually works in some way on the person perceiving it. This is small wonder considering the fact that rhythm is a principle given of the human body. It is not only our heartbeat, blood circulation or breathing that follow their own rhythm; not only do we execute bodily movements such as walking, running, dancing, swimming, writing with a pencil and so on in a rhythmical way and make rhythmical sounds when speaking, singing, laughing or weeping. But even those movements that are created within our body without us being able to perceive them are carried out rhythmically. The human body is, in fact, rhythmically tuned.[14]

This is why we are particularly capable of perceiving rhythm and to resonate or vibrate with it. Performances which organize and structure their timing through rhythm – as Reinhardt's productions did – bring together different 'rhythmical systems': that of the performance and that of the spectators, the latter being different with each and every spectator. In terms of the course of the performance and its impact, particularly significant seems the question of how the rhythmic tuning takes place and whether and to what extent the performance succeeds in adjusting the spectators to its own rhythm – which, of course, changes itself, in tune with the resonance of the spectators who provide new impulses for the actors; whether and to what extent some rhythmically similarly tuned spectators are able to have an impact on other spectators or on the actors, and so forth. In any case, the performance is carried out as a mutual resonance between the rhythm of the actors and spectators and, in this sense, as a physical interaction between actors and spectators. It is rhythm which opens up the transformational potential and forms a community out of actors and spectators. And it was able to work particularly powerfully because the performance of *Oedipus*, which lasted for about one and a half hours, was not interrupted by an intermission.

All the elements listed and discussed here such as the different sounds, voices, music, smells, colours of light, rhythm, may also have a symbolic meaning. But it seems that in no case was there an unequivocal symbolic meaning common to all people present at the performance. Rather, those elements dominated whose meanings were somewhat vague such as the sounds of the fanfare, the fire on the altar or the torches. They could be associated with a number of different, even partly overlapping, meanings.[15] Thus, it was not so much symbolic meanings that could be accorded to the elements in question. It was their atmospheric effect which dominated over any kind of symbolic meaning that might have been attributed to them in terms of a particular tradition, ideology, religion, world view or political system. It is to be assumed that the associations which individual spectators connected to them differed enormously according to the social group, class or strata to which they belonged as well as their very personal beliefs.

Even voice was not only used for the sake of producing shared linguistic meanings. As one critic complains, Reinhardt did not work with voice,

> to create an intellectual effect, but rather to create acoustic waves which are a significant part of the modern register of atmosphere. The chorus thus, must produce all kinds of sounds imaginable: muttering, gasping, screaming or sobbing. And even when the chorus speaks, it is not the sense of the words which is important, but the sound.
>
> (Paul Goldmann, *Neue Freie Presse*, November 1910)

The special atmosphere was particularly created by the desemantization of language addressed by the critic, the shift of focus from the meaning of the spoken word to the particular sound and timbre of the voice that emphasized the physical presence of the voice as well as of the speaker. Even with regard to language it can be concluded that it was not common meanings which came to the fore but the atmospheric value of the individual voice as well as the harmony or disharmony of the different voices ringing out simultaneously. On the other hand, such a desemantization released a multitude of possible meanings which might be attributed to the spoken words by different spectators.

This had far-reaching consequences for the kind of community that came into being in the course of the performance of *Oedipus Rex* and the *Oresteia*. Since the sense of community did not arise through a common symbolism which explicitly referred to beliefs, ideologies etc. shared by all spectators – or, at least, by a majority of them – but to very special physical effects brought about by the presence of the masses in the space and by the frequently changing atmosphere, it cannot be regarded as a political, national, religious or ideological community. It came into being mainly, if not exclusively, through performative means developed and refined by Reinhardt in his theatre since the turn of the century. Therefore, I shall call it a theatrical community.[16] A theatrical community is not only a temporary community, as transitory and ephemeral as any performance. It exists, at best, throughout the whole course of the performance and dissolves, at its latest, at the very end. Moreover, it is a community which is not based on common beliefs and shared ideologies – not even on shared meanings; it can do without them. For it comes into being through performative means. As long as the performance lasts it is capable of establishing a bond between individuals who come from the most diverse biographical, social, ideological, religious, political backgrounds and remain individuals who have associations of their own and generate quite different meanings. The performance does not force them into a common confession; instead, it allows for shared experiences. Through such experiences, the self of the people who undergo them does not necessarily dissolve but it certainly cannot be conceived of as something stable, permanently fixed, or rigid. Rather it is thought of as becoming fluid, undergoing transformations while the experiences are lived out. (It seems that the community presented and represented on stage was conceived and displayed in this way. At no time did the individuals vanish or dissolve into the chorus; they remained individuals who, as such, became members of a community.

'The people push and shove each other, they crowd together, separate. They move as a unit and yet at the same time stand out from one another; each individual remains himself – one in red, one in green, one with a bare chest, and yet he is also one piece of the whole. He belongs to the "people". I have never seen such a thing happen in a scene before.'[17] Following this description, other critics emphasize that individual voices could clearly be distinguished, one whispering, while another mumbled and a third screamed the same sentence.)

The community that came into being during the performances of *Oedipus Rex* and the *Oresteia* was not able – nor did it aim – to establish some kind of collective identity among its members. Since it was primarily based on shared, short-lived experiences, emotions or bodily sensations, and dissolved the moment after it happened, it was a community in a liminal state – never able to acquire an identity of its own. In some respects, it may appear as a kind of utopian community. On the other hand, the question arises – which will emerge repeatedly in the course of the following chapters – as to whether this kind of community is the only conceivable kind in modern heterogeneous societies; whether, in the case of such societies, a community can only come into existence if the idea of a collective identity valid and binding for each and every member is given up. As the enormous success of *Oedipus Rex* on its tour through Europe indicates, this kind of community brought forth by the performance highlighted and, at the same time, satisfied certain needs felt by various different European countries. Thus, it was Reinhardt's performances of the Theatre of the Five Thousand which posed the question, phrased above, as a challenge to his contemporaries, as a kind of unknowing response to Durkheim and the Cambridge Ritualists.

(3) The dynamic and energetic bodies moving through the whole space

In many reviews, the performance of *Oedipus Rex* and the *Oresteia* were characterized, as one critic put it, 'as something in movement, something explosive, something whipped by the wind, like a tornado, becoming fire'.[18] This impression largely resulted from the dynamic and energetic bodies moving in and through space, dominating the performance. Most of the reviews suggest that there was a permanent commotion from the very beginning until the end:

Oedipus has barely found refuge in the palace when the spectacle breaks out. Torch-bearers hunt the arena [...] leap up the
steps, disappear into the Palace. At the same time, the muffled
sound of a drum, slowly getting louder, is heard. The Palace
doors open. Ten maidens burst onto the scene. They moan and
sob; they twist and turn as if wracked with cramps. Some race
down the steps (the speed with which they accompany this down
the steep steps is amazing, worthy of the circus in which they
perform) [...] And now on top of that, the five or six hundred
members of the chorus storm into the arena, running chaoti-
cally with wild gestures and bursting in with inarticulate
shouting.

(Paul Goldmann, *Neue Freie Presse*, November 1910)

Coincidentally, it was particularly these rapid, literally breathtak-
ing movements which some critics felt were unsuitable to a Greek
tragedy. Fiercely objecting to the 'naked runners who, holding
torches in their hands, race like savages through the orchestra up
and down the steps to the palace', the critic Siegfried Jacobsohn
complained that it was not historical. He came to the conclusion that
it was 'a sorry waste of energy to try and convey an approximation of
the ancient Greek theatre in a circus ring.'[19] After Reinhardt's
London production of *Oedipus Rex*, a similar discussion arose there.
Gilbert Murray, who had translated the play, referred to the above
scene in order to challenge the critique that the production was not
Greek:

Professor Reinhardt was frankly pre-Hellenic (as is the Oedipus
story itself), partly Cretan and Mycenaean, partly Oriental, partly
– to my great admiration – merely savage. The half-naked torch-
bearers with loin-cloths and long black hair made my heart leap
with joy. There was real early Greece about them, not the
Greece of the schoolroom or the conventional art-studio.

(cited in Styan 1982: 85)

Murray obviously saw the image of Greece come to life in the
performance as the Cambridge Ritualists had elaborated it.

But what was at stake here was not the question of how Greek or
un-Greek the performance was. The stance taken by another critic
seems more appropriate: 'Was it the spirit of modern times that
revealed itself in the wild, breath-stopping charge of the masses? Not
a hint of classical Hellenism. It was the wild passion of today.'[20]

However, the movement of the masses also served another purpose: they even set the spectators in motion. Alfred Klaar criticized 'the division of action into the space in front, between, beneath and behind us, which forced us to keep changing our viewpoint'; that 'tears the illusion apart'. Jacobsohn felt equally shocked:

> Didn't the man who built the Kammerspiele to bring us together notice how this circus achieves the opposite effect? Our poor eyes, tortured by spotlights, confronted with five entrances and exits for the actors, are forced to shift restlessly from one to the next. We have to try and distinguish the heads of the spectators from those of the extras who act in the midst of the audience.
>
> (Siegfried Jacobsohn, *Vossische Zeitung*, 14 October 1911)

What Klaar, Jacobsohn and other critics were complaining about was that they were forced out of the complete immobility of their bodies familiar to them from the box-set stage. One of the prerequisites for illusion to be created in theatre was to sit immobile in the dark with a clear focus on the lit stage. To forget one's own body, to lend one's own soul to one or other protagonist allowed empathy with the *dramatis personae*. But here – as before in *Electra* – no illusion came into being. Moreover, instead of demanding and furthering empathy, the performance not only worked on the senses and the nerves of the spectators but also set their bodies in motion. The permanently moving bodies of the performers triggered not only physiological and affective impulses in the spectators but also energetic and motor ones. The spectators had to turn around constantly, move their heads, and let their eyes wander from one point in space to another. Spectating literally became a physical activity, not only restricted to the eyes – and the ears – but involving the whole body, which could even be touched by the bodies of the performers who 'jostled against' it. On the one hand, this activity directed the attention of the spectator to his own body. He became very much aware of the physical impulses triggered by the process of looking on: the physiological, affective, energetic and motor impulses. He did not follow the actions of the performers in his imagination only, but also physically. In this sense, he became bodily involved and this established a bond between him and the performers as well as between him and the other spectators.

On the other hand, such physical activity helped to individualize the spectators. Since one cannot assume that they carried out all their movements simultaneously, their perceptions must have differed, sometimes only slightly, sometimes considerably. That is to say, the spectators did not all perceive the same things at the same time. While one spectator was turning around in order to see what was going on behind him, another might let his eyes wander over the whole auditorium in order to find where all the extras appeared from and a third focussed his attention on the actors in the arena. In the end, each and every spectator perceived something different and, in this sense, participated in a different performance. The spectator became part of a community but still remained an individual.

It was not only the 'masses' who were constantly moving, but also the protagonists, although in a different manner. They seemed to avoid any kind of monumental attitude or static pose so often associated with Greek tragedy; instead they were permanently in motion. Some critics felt this to be inappropriate because it distracted the attention of the spectators from the meaning of the words spoken and directed focus to the phenomenal body of the actor, thus providing 'hords of spectators who grew up at bull fights' with 'thrilling entertainment':

> When Orestes is about to kill his mother, it is more than sufficient to dash after her out of the palace door, hold her at the doorway and push her back into the palace when the exchange of dialogue is finished. Here, he chases her down the steps into the circus ring, fights with her there and finally drags her, painfully slowly, up the steps. It is terrible.
>
> (Jacobsohn 1912: 49)

Notwithstanding such a critique, even Siegfried Jacobsohn had to admit that in the *Oresteia* the acting of Alexander Moissi (Orestes) and Mary Dietrich (Cassandra) had the same extraordinary impact on the spectators as Paul Wegener (Oedipus) and Tilla Durieux (Jocasta) had in *Oedipus Rex*.

The idea suggests itself that such permanently moving dynamic and energetic bodies both incorporated and realized the new ideal of body culture developing at the turn of the century, the liberated body set in motion. This is certainly true to an extent. However, it is not the only remarkable thing achieved by the particular use of the body which the actors playing the protagonists or the chorus or other group formations such as the half-naked runners provoked. As we have already seen, they used their bodies in order to dominate and occupy the space. In doing so, they demanded the full attention of the spectators, forcing them to direct their attention to their bodies – not to the semiotic qualities of their bodies, i.e. not to their bodies as texts composed of signs telling a story or revealing a particular psychology which must be deciphered by the spectators. Rather, the attention of the spectator was drawn to the phenomenal bodies of the performers, attracted in particular by the energy that seemed to emanate from them, pour into the space and spread and circulate among the spectators. This energy, which the spectators sensed radiating from the bodies of the performers from the very beginning, certainly struck them as something which was by no means foreseen or expected, but which evaded their control. It was something that could not be grasped but which captivated them completely. It might have been sensed as a power emanating from the performer forcing the spectators to focus individual attention on him without, however, feeling overwhelmed by this power. Or, the spectators might have sensed it as a source of power in themselves. The energy emanating from the performers' bodies seemed to circulate in the space, infect the spectators and energize them. The energy accumulated and generated by the spectators in the course of the performance was released at the end by the standing ovations given to the performers by the spectators.

It seems that the energy radiating from the performers towards the spectators caused a sense that the performers were present in an unusual and unique way. This conferred the spectators with the ability to sense their own presence in an especially intense way.

This was possible because the performers' bodies which attracted the attention of the spectators did not appear to be mindless bodies. The energy which they generated was not received as a purely physical quality but as a mental quality, too. Both qualities resulted from physical as well as mental processes, which brought forth one another. At the very moment the spectator sensed the energy emanating from the performer and circulating in space among all those present, he sensed it as a mental as well as a physical force. He felt it as a transformational and, in this sense, vital force – as the vital force of the performer and, at the same time, as his own vital force. This is the reason why the bodies of the performers might have seemed transfigured to the spectators.[21]

This use of the body presupposes or entails a particular concept of the body, regardless of whether such a concept was actually formulated. It can be connected with Hellmuth Plessner's (1970) dialectics of being a body and having a body which constitutes humanness first elaborated by him in the 1920s. Since we *are* our body and *have* a body, there can be no division of body and mind.

From today's point of view it seems to be the concept of embodied mind. There is no division or even opposition between body and mind as Christian cultural tradition presupposes. There is no mind outside and beyond the body. It can only be understood if it is conceptualized as embodied. In this sense, human beings have to be understood as embodied minds.[22] In experiencing the presence of the dynamic and energetic bodies of the actors in *Oedipus* and the *Oresteia*, the spectators seem to have experienced the performers as well as themselves as embodied minds, i.e. as human beings in an emphatic sense of the word.

Reinhardt's productions of *Oedipus Rex* and the *Oresteia* succeeded in collapsing dichotomies between individual and community, between mind and body which were deeply rooted in Christian culture. As we have seen, in the performances of his Theatre of the Five Thousand both relationships were fundamentally redefined. This also implied the collapse of another opposition – that between elitist and popular culture. By using the most 'sacred' texts from the cultural tradition of the *élite* on the one hand and, on the other, by playing in a circus which emphasized the body, providing 'thrill' and 'entertainment', Reinhardt bridged the gap between elitist and popular culture. In fact, a new people's theatre was created in which members of all social groups, classes and strata met and formed a community together. This new people's theatre hailed and celebrated a future culture as a new performative culture which would be based on and incorporate the achievements of the former textual culture. It was conceived of as a culture in which there would no longer be any opposition between mind and body where human beings are understood as embodied minds, and as a culture which allows for communities without annulling the individual.

The basis and prerequisite of this utopian vision of a new culture seems to lie in the sacrifices performed on stage. It was the excess of violence on stage, previously unknown, which had a big impact on the spectators; the particular use of the bodies physically involved them and created a community between spectators and performers.

The overwhelming success of Reinhardt's tour through Europe with *Oedipus Rex* shows that this connection between archaic sacrificial rituals and the utopian vision of a new performative culture which would collapse the traditional dichotomies, strongly appealed to European audiences. However, there are good reasons to believe that such a connection was only successful as long as it referred to Greek culture. Theatre performances which highlighted sacrificial rituals of a 'primitive' culture without drawing upon Greek culture, did not create a community between actors and spectators; they generally provoked a scandal instead.

Probably the most famous of these scandals was caused by the first night of Igor Stravinsky's *Le Sacre du Printemps* – which was originally to have been entitled *The Sacrifice* – with choreography by Vaslav Nijinsky and dancers from Diaghilev's Russian Ballet. It took place on 29 May 1913 at the Théâtre des Champs-Elysées in Paris. It seems that there was scandal in the air from the very beginning. Gertrud Stein reported that there was such uproar in the auditorium that she could literally hear nothing of the music during the entire performance (Gosling 1980: 21). In contrast, the impresario Gabriel Astruc (1929: 88) stated that shortly after the performance began he managed to tame the audience with his words: 'Ecoutez d'abord! Vous sifflerez d'après!' ('Listen first! Hiss later!'). Carl van Vechten tells us about a young man who got up from the seat behind him in the middle of the performance in order to have a better view:

> The intense excitement under which he was labouring, thanks to the potent force of the music, betrayed itself presently when he began to beat rhythmically on the top of my head with his fists. My emotion was so great that I did not feel the blows for some time. They were perfectly synchronized with the beat of the music.
>
> (van Vechten 1915: 88)

Whatever the spectators related after the event, they seemed to agree in one respect: 'The event had the effect of an earthquake' (Eksteins 1990: 27).

In this performance,[23] a ritual was represented on stage which, in some respects, evoked the anthropological theory of the Spring Demon Ritual. The dancers represented different groups or members of an ancient Slavic community, celebrating the coming of spring. The feast ends with a virgin sacrifice: one of the young girls sacrifices herself 'in the great holy dance, the great sacrifice', as it is described in Stravinsky's libretto (cited in Stravinsky and Craft 1978: 75), a dance reminiscent of Electra's final nameless dance.

The music and the choreography were extremely innovative. Many spectators felt strongly repelled by music which they felt to be violent, dissonant and overflowing with ugly cacophonies. Debussy called the work 'an extraordinary, wild thing. One could say it is primitive music with all the mod cons.' One of the critics characterized the music as 'Hottentot music refined'; another judged it to be 'the most dissonant composition ever written. The cult of the false tone has never before been pushed to the extreme with such diligence, ambition, savagery' (cited in Eksteins 1990: 86).

Following the dissonance in the music, Nijinsky cut away all the highly developed techniques of classical ballet for which he was so famous as a dancer himself, and proceeded from one basic stance: the dancers' bodies faced the audience with bent knees, toes turned inwards, arms folded, turning their faces to the side, in profile. From this position they developed two modes of movement choreographed by Nijinsky: hopping or skipping awkwardly with both legs and walking, either fluidly, or stamping. Most of the movements were performed by all groups – for instance, the old men and the young girls – in synchrony. The dancers had to orientate themselves to the rhythm of the music which was particularly difficult since the rhythm changed with each bar.

The critics reacted to the choreography by accusing Nijinsky of being a 'maniacal beginner' or a 'ballet master without a concept, without even a spark of common human sense' (cited in ibid.: 30).

Although some spectators hailed the evening as the birth of modern theatre, the press almost unanimously tore Nijinsky to pieces. *Le Figaro*, 2 June, discussed the performance on the front page, 'I have no hesitation in placing in the front rank the question of the relationship of Paris with the Russian dancers, which has reached a point of tension where anything can happen'. The Russian barbarians, under the leadership of Nijinsky, 'a kind of Attila of dance', had transgressed all boundaries. 'It seems that they are not at all aware of the customs and practices of the country they are imposing on, and they seem ignorant of the fact that we often take energetic measures against absurd behaviour' (Capus cited in Eksteins 1990: 89–90).

The elements in the performance which repelled the critics were those which had to do with the new cultural model which they found strange and threatening, that is to say, barbaric and primitive. A similar conclusion can be drawn from an article by Maurice Dupont which appeared in the *Revue Bleue* one year later in July – i.e. literally on the eve of World War I. Here the performance is characterized as 'a Dionysian orgy dreamed of by Nietzsche and called forth by his prophetic wish to be the beacon of a world hurtling toward death' (ibid.: 91). Despite the allusion to a 'Dionysian orgy', the critics felt the performance had no relation to Greek, let alone French, culture. The 'Dionysian orgy' connected it to Nietzsche. And Nietzsche was not associated with Greek but with German culture. Thus, the performance was incapable of bringing forth a community of dancers and spectators – although it worked strongly on the senses and the nerves of the spectators and set their bodies in motion. Instead, it aroused aggression in the spectators and, in this respect, anticipated the outbreak of the war.

After the war was over, when people all over Europe were mourning for the hundreds of thousands of victims and were facing a society broken to pieces, Reinhardt hoped that it would still be possible to realize his new people's theatre. In 1919, the architect Hans Poelzig rebuilt the Circus Schumann into Reinhardt's Grosses Schauspielhaus. The new theatre was inaugurated by a performance of the *Oresteia*, this time with the addition of *The Eumenides*. On the occasion of its opening, the Deutsches Theater published a booklet in which playwrights, stage designers and dramaturges who co-operated with Reinhardt summarized the most important arguments in the debate on a new people's theatre which had been raging since the turn of the century. (Romain Rolland's influential book *Le théâtre du peuple* appeared in 1903.) Heinz Herald, Reinhardt's dramaturge, emphasized that in the arena, theatre will 'turn again from a matter of the few to a matter of the masses'; for an audience was to be assembled here, 'which derives from all classes', and would 'comprise the masses who, up to now, have been strangers to theatre' (Das Deutsche Theater 1920: 11). Carl Vollmoeller who adapted the *Oresteia* for Reinhardt's purposes, praised the arena theatre as

> Today's public meeting place [...] That which the depoliticizing of our nation by the imperial regime has hindered for fifty years is now possible today: to unite the theatrical space of thousands into a community of citizens who participate, who are swept along and who sweep others along with them.
>
> (cited in ibid.: 21)

Likewise the expressionist poet, Kurt Pinthus, celebrated the arena theatre as the only possible path not only towards a 'future people's theatre', but also towards 'the future of mankind'.

> For up to now, theatre has been left far behind other human developments because it maintained its representative buildings and those designed for entertainment from a long-since sunken social class. [...] The people's theatre has an enormous task to fulfil [...] Theatre has regained the meaning which the people have always accorded to it. Theatre is merging art, faith, and politics. It is theatre for all.
>
> (cited in ibid.: 54)

When Reinhardt restaged the *Oresteia* in 1919 at the opening of the Grosses Schauspielhaus, it was obvious that the new people's theatre enthusiastically celebrated and praised in the booklet *Das Grosse Schauspielhaus* could hardly be realized under the given political and social conditions. The awareness of this dilemma was expressed in a review by the critic Stefan Grossmann on the opening performance:

> The image of a community of thousands was wonderful and heartrending. Perhaps all the more heartrending for the intellectual German citizen because the spatial unity of the masses reawakened his yearning for an inner sense of belonging. Can we be one people? Here sits Herr Scheidemann, over there privy councillor Herr Roethe, there is Hauptmann's Goethe-like head, over there Dr. Cohn waves to a comrade. But Scheidemann looks past Roethe and Cohn passes Hauptmann with only a shrug of the shoulders. Even outside the work environment there is no feeling of unity. There is no nation on earth which so lacks a feeling of community and the war has consumed us even more [...] So we have the greatest people's theatre, but no people.
>
> (Stefan Grossmann, review of the 'Oresteia', *Vossische Zeitung*, 29/30 December 1919)[24]

In summer 1920, Reinhardt opened the first Salzburg Festival with a performance of *Everyman* (in Hofmannthal's version) in the square in front of Salzburg Cathedral. The same year he resigned from his directorship of the Berlin theatres. Through the Salzburg Festival he tried to continue and revive his concept of theatre as festival. However, the Salzburg Festival would later betray the cause, as after the first few years it decayed into a fashionable event for the upper classes.

Yet while Reinhardt's concept of a people's theatre seems to have failed after 1918, its main aesthetic devices did not. We will find the three devices which he elaborated in the performances of his Theatre for the Five Thousand applied again, albeit in a different manner, to the mass spectacles between the two wars: (1) in the way the masses occupied the space, (2) in the way a particular atmosphere functioned and (3) in the dynamic and energetic bodies moving through the space.

3 Re-inventing ritual
The Olympic Games

The obsession with ancient Greek culture widespread in nineteenth century Europe was nourished by texts and monuments even though some of these artefacts and monuments had disappeared from the earth and were yet to be rediscovered. In fact, it was the texts that led to the monuments. Heinrich Schliemann claimed, for instance, that it was Pausanius who guided him to the Mycenaean tombs, and Homer who directed him to Troy. The excavations, thus, appear to be a consequence of purely textual study. This was also the case with Olympia. At the end of the eighteenth century, texts which deal with the *agones olympikoi* were much discussed among advocates of a bourgeois physical education. Still earlier than this, Winckelmann had planned an archaeological expedition to Olympia. His untimely death in 1768 thwarted the project. In about 1800, British and French archaeologists started the first excavations in Olympia. In 1820, Lord Stanhope mapped its topography and in 1828/29 Albert Blouet excavated parts of the Temple of Zeus and transferred fragments of the Heracles metopes to the Louvre. In 1875, Ernst Curtius systematically began to unearth Olympia[1] and bring it into the awareness of a broader public. Between 1875 and 1881, the German government contributed to the popularization of Olympia by publishing annual reports on the progress of the excavations and, in particular, on the various finds by Curtius and his team. This meant that Curtius' own reports were eagerly awaited when they finally appeared between 1890 and 1897.

Following the prevalence of textual culture in the self-understanding of nineteenth century Europeans, the excavations highlighted and exposed the material culture of ancient Olympia. It was Baron *Pierre de Coubertin* (1863–1937) who dreamt of reviving its performative culture, of bringing the events – rituals and performances – of the *agones olympikoi* to life. Though not the first to advocate such an idea,[2] Coubertin is the most interesting in our context – not only because he fused ritual and theatre and succeeded in creating a new kind of cultural performance which survives until today, but also primarily, because he hoped this fusion would be a way out of the cultural and social crisis which was felt and addressed at the turn of the century by scholars, writers, artists, directors and many members of the educated middle classes. In a speech to the Athenian Club 'The Parnass' in 1894, Coubertin hailed the reinvention of the Olympic Games as an answer to the crisis:

> If we begin to study the history of our century we are struck by the moral disorder produced by the discoveries of industrial science. Life suffers upheaval; people continually feel the ground tremble under their feet. They have nothing to hold on to, because everything around them is shifting and changing. [. . .] I think this is the philosophic origin of the striking physical renaissance in the XIXth century.
>
> (de Coubertin 1966: 8)

As Coubertin's wording betrays, his attitude towards the crisis was much more conservative than Durkheim's. However, he was actually only emphasizing another aspect of the same problem.

Coubertin held the opinion that a new religion was necessary in order to overcome the crisis – a religion that required rituals and ceremonies. The religion he proposed was the 'religion of muscles', of sports. The reinvention of the Olympic Games, therefore, was intended to be a new religious service which would defeat the crisis. Coubertin regarded this form of religion as 'the first essential feature of ancient as well as modern Olympia' (de Coubertin 1986: 435).

In fact, ancient olympism was a constitutive part and element of religion. The Olympic Games, which were held from the tenth/ninth century BC[3] until AD 393 when the Christian emperor Theodosius prohibited all pagan sacrifices, formed an important part of the cult of Zeus. People went to Olympia in order to sacrifice and play sports – in this precise order and not the other way round. The sacred centre of Olympia was the altar of Zeus – a very special altar, in fact. It was a heap of ashes. The remains of the sacrifices were never removed, only covered by mud from the river Alpheus. Sacrificial animals, usually bulls, were slaughtered at the altar. It was a custom introduced by Prometheus, or so Hesiod claims, that the bones and fat of the animal intended for Zeus were deposited on the altar, while the meat used for the sacrificial meal among men was prepared for cooking. The cooking was done in a tripod cauldron standing over a fire.

The topography of the holy precinct was laid out in such a way that the race track, the stadium, led directly to the altar. As Philostratus reports, it was the honorary task of the winner of the race to ignite the fire on the altar as well as under the cauldron.[4] That is to say, the sports contest, which originally only consisted of this one race, that later formed its heart and kernel, took place at the moment of hiatus within the sacrificial act, namely, between slaughter and prayer on the one side, and the igniting of the fire for the gods and the sacrificial meal for the mortals, on the other.

The *heroon* of Pelops was located beside the temple of Zeus. The daytime sacrifice for Zeus was preceded by a sacrifice for Pelops at night. Here, it was a ram that served as a sacrificial animal. Those who participated in the sacrifice to Pelops were not allowed to enter the holy precinct of Zeus and, accordingly, were excluded from the sacrificial meal consumed here. Undoubtedly, the problem of 'eating' vs. 'not-eating' is implied here. It may be explained by referring to one of the many myths about Pelops. After Tantalus feasted at the gods' table – had eaten, so to speak, in Zeus' house – he invited them for a meal. He presented the dismembered body of his son Pelops as a dish to the gods. With the notable exception of Demeter who was mourning the loss of her daughter, the gods noticed at once where the meat came from. They punished Tantalus and restored Pelops to life – using a piece of ivory to replace the shoulder which Demeter had eaten.

The athletes had to arrive in Olympia several weeks before the opening of the Olympic Games. During this time they had to endure a particular fast which did not allow them to have sexual intercourse or eat meat – their diet was restricted to cheese and figs – and demanded compliance with special rules of behaviour. In conjunction with the myth of Pelops' dismemberment and rebirth, the implementation of such regulations suggests that the Olympic Games were performed as a rite of passage – as a ritual of initiation.[5]

What the relationship between the sacrifice and the *agon*, or between the cult of Zeus and the initiation rite might have been, is hard to explain. In his chapter on 'The Origin of the Olympic Games' in Jane E. Harrison's *Themis* (1962), Francis M. Cornford attempts to give an explanation. Here, he elaborates on the thesis of the Cambridge Ritualists that the Olympic Games originated in an *eniautos-daimon* ritual. This kind of ritual can be performed as a death and rebirth ritual as in the origin of theatre, or as a contest generating a winner, as in the Olympic Games. According to Cornford, the Games derived from a race of Kouretes. The winner in the race became the new daimon of the year, the god or spirit of the New Year. Considering the fact that the Olympic Games were held every four years, one has to bear in mind that the term *eniautos*, which Harrison introduced, not only means a solar or lunar year but also a longer period of two, four or even eight solar years. The daimon of the group of Kouretes as well as the luck of the new 'year' was incarnate in the victor of the race. While other Classics scholars interpreted the worship of Pelops at his *heroon* as evidence that the Olympic Games sprang from a cult of the dead, Cornford defined such worship with reference to the *eniautos-daimon* ritual. He claimed that the chariot race between Oenomaus and Pelops, reported by Pindar, was a contest between the old and the New Year. Thus, he suggested that the twelve rounds of the chariot race at Olympia may well have represented the course of the sun through the twelve signs. He explained the marriage between Pelops and Hippodameia, Oenomaus' daughter, in a similar way. The old year was defeated and dead and the victory of the New Year was celebrated by a sacred marriage between the sun and the moon. 'The union of the full moon and the full-grown Sun is one form – the astronomical – of that sacred marriage which in many parts of the ancient world was celebrated at mid-summer. This union, we suggest, is symbolised by the marriage of Pelops and Hippodameia' (Harrison 1962: 226). That is to say that Cornford held it to be a rite of passage or initiation ritual which was performed at the Olympic Games.

Whereas ancient olympism as part of a religion was rooted in the community and created through a shared religion, modern olympism was invented as a religion to re-establish a bond between modern individuals. Like Durkheim, Coubertin complained about the disintegration of modern society; about the loss of any feeling of solidarity, although with quite different emphasis. He deplored the fact that modern individuals – among whom he counted only men, not women – had liberated themselves from the obligations and rewards of traditional societies. In his view, this not only resulted in a loss of tradition, in degeneration and effeminacy, it also caused disorder, even chaos. He thought modern olympism would be capable of inducing religious feelings in the individual and, thus, promote social integration. It was something which would enable the individual to bring himself into harmony with the whole, to participate in a generally binding order.

Coubertin, himself a rationalist, did not believe that reason would allow such participation. In one of the 'Olympic letters' he wrote a critique of modern democracy:

> Do not imagine that a democracy can live healthily if its citizens have nothing to hold them together but legal texts and electoral summons. Formerly there were public solemnities in Church and the splendid pomp of the monarchy. How are you going to replace them? By unveiling statues and making speeches in frock-coats? Go on! There is only one cult which is capable of engendering a permanent kind of civic unity today, and that is the cult which will develop around youthful exercise [...].
>
> (Letter of 4 December 1918, cited in de Coubertin 1966: 56)

In his view it was not texts and monuments that established a bond between individuals, but performative means only – the rituals of the religion of sports.[6]

This is why Coubertin conceived the Olympic Games as a great festival. Obviously, the Games are characterized by the two paradoxes constitutive of festivals: the paradox of periodicity and liminality of time and the paradox of regularity and irregularity, of order and excess.[7] Recurring every four years, the Games follow cyclical, not linear time. The linearity of time, the concept of progress, is annulled. The Games are, in Harrison's sense, a *dromenon*, a thing re-done, something commemorative, in that they commemorate the ancient Olympic Games; they are a thing *pre*-done yet filled with anticipation because they foresee a universal community of athletes and spectators from different countries. The athletes and, to a certain extent, even the spectators have to follow particular rules, to observe a strict discipline. On the other hand, Coubertin never tires of claiming that the Games demand excess. He celebrates the Games as a 'cult of energy' (de Coubertin 1909; 1966: 21), as 'outbursts of energy' (1918; ibid.: 45), which honour 'the successive arrival of human generations' (1935; ibid.: 132), as a cult of 'youth, beauty and strength' (1910; ibid.: 34), as a glorification of 'the freedom of excess' (de Coubertin 1935; 1986: 436):

> Like athletics of antiquity, modern athletics are [...] a cult, an impassioned soaring which is capable of going from 'play to heroism'. Grasp this essential principle and you will begin to consider the sportsmen whose excesses you at present criticise and censure as an élite of energy-stimulators [...].
>
> (1929; de Coubertin 1966: 118–19)

These two paradoxes, found in all traditional festivals, are joined by another. It cannot be overlooked that sports, as Coubertin agrees, have a kind of double face – are paradoxical. On the one hand, it develops and trains features that are fundamental to 'the survival of the fittest' in industrial, capitalist societies – features such as competitiveness, self-assertion, strong will, endurance, performance. In this respect, sports contribute to shaping and affirming the autonomous bourgeois individual. On the other hand, sports allow the passions, emotions and desires of the body, which have to be repressed in modern working life, to be acted out, albeit within clear limitations of time and space as well as in a strictly regulated form. It is this ambivalence which made modern sports so attractive to modern societies. And it is this ambivalence which is celebrated in and by the Olympic Games.

In his *Memoirs olympiques* (1931) Coubertin reports that it was a visit to Wagner's Bayreuth Festival which inspired him to conceive an 'Olympic horizon' (de Coubertin 1931: 64), that it was Wagner's *Gesamtkunstwerk* (total work of art) which inspired the idea of the great festival of the Olympic Games. This does not come as a surprise. For as Coubertin conceived sports as a religion, so Wagner accorded elements of religion to the arts. Both agreed not only in their fundamental critique of modern commoditization. They contrasted the profane, seemingly omnipresent, market with a sacred festival, a temple to the arts and sports. They also believed that their new religion would bring about salvation from the diseases of modern times. According to Wagner's understanding of historical process, the dissolution of the Greek *polis* resulted in a confrontation between the individual and community as well as in a fragmentation of man whose wholeness disintegrated into a physical, emotional and reasoning being. Wagner believed that the *Gesamtkunstwerk* would reconcile the individual with the community and redeem man from fragmentation.

In Greek paganism, Coubertin (de Coubertin 1929; 1966: 110) also saw a 'cult of the human being, of the human body, mind and flesh, feeling and will, instinct and conscience' i.e. a cult of the 'wholeness' of man. As a Cartesian, he claimed a fundamental opposition between body and mind, *res extensa* and *res cogitans*: 'Sometimes flesh, feeling and instinct have the upper hand, and sometimes mind, will and conscience, for these are the two despots who strive for primacy within us, and whose conflict often rends us cruelly. We have to attain a balance' (ibid.). Coubertin believed that by keeping the two opposing forces in balance, sports would restore man to his full human nature and establish a bond between individuals. It seems that it was the excess of energy in particular which was assumed to trigger both processes.

Coubertin conceived the Olympic Games as a festival and, at the same time, as a very particular fusion of ritual and theatre. The ritual was to be performed as a *Gesamtkunstwerk*, as he understood it.[8] He was very much concerned about what he called the 'eurhythmic' of the Games, which had been so perfect and impressive in Bayreuth. In 1906, he complained:

> The crowd of today is inexperienced in linking together artistic pleasures of different orders. It is used to taking such pleasures piecemeal, one at a time, from special fields. The ugliness and vulgarity of settings do not offend it. Beautiful music thrills it, but the fact that it sounds amid noble architecture leaves it indifferent. And nothing in it seems to rise in revolt against these wretchedly banal decorations, these ridiculous processions, these detestable cacophonies and all this frippery which compose what nowadays is called a festival – a festival where one guest is always missing – taste.
>
> (de Coubertin 1906; 1966: 17)

In order to guarantee that the festival of the Olympic Games should be structured by 'eurhythmy', so admired in Bayreuth and that it should be realized as a *Gesamtkunstwerk*, Coubertin planned to open a competition in architecture, sculpture, painting, music and literature in 1906. He proposed that modern Olympia should be held every four years at a different site and that it should be created by all the arts together. Thus, he considered the 'architecture' for the design of the festive space; 'dramatic art', in particular 'open-air performances'; 'choreography' of 'processions, parades, coordinated movements of groups – rhythmical dances'; 'decoration' such as 'poles, garlands, scarves, flowers' and by night 'sports in the flickering flames of torches', 'music', 'orchestra and choir in open air', 'rhythm', 'fanfares'; 'painting' and 'photography', 'sculptures' and 'medals' (ibid.: 17–18). As we can gather from this list, the performative aspect should dominate, for this would allow the participants to undergo physical and emotional experiences, to sense a particular 'atmosphere' (de Coubertin 1906; 1986: 26), a common lived experience. It seems that, in this respect, the festival of the Olympic Games as envisaged by Coubertin and the festival of Reinhardt's Theatre of the Five Thousand had much in common, despite one notable difference. While Reinhardt invented new, and in part, stunning scenic devices, Coubertin as we shall see, turned to the storehouse of European festival culture from which to choose elements that had already proven their effectiveness in history.

Coubertin used these elements in order to design and stage the ceremonies of the Olympic Games as a rite of passage. He explains the rite in phrases echoing Frazer's year-spirit and the Cambridge Ritualists, *eniautos-daimon*. He calls the Olympic Games 'the quadrennial festival of the human springtide' that honours 'the successive arrival of human generations'.

> But neither the child nor the beardless youth is the human springtime [. . .] The human springtime is expressed in the young adult [. . .] which is ready to enter into full movement. It is he in whose honour the Olympic Games must be celebrated and their rhythm organised and maintained, for upon him depend the near future and the harmonious linking of the future with the past [. . .] It follows from what I have said that the true Olympic hero is in my view the adult male individual.
>
> (de Coubertin 1935; 1966: 132–3)[9]

Since it is not the initiation of boys into the community of men that is performed here, the question arises as to what specific transformations were brought about by participating in the Olympic Games – both as athlete and spectator.

As has already been stated, three phases of a rite of passage can clearly be distinguished and identified in the Olympic Games. The opening ceremonies cause a separation from everyday life, initiating the period of public liminality. The contests and the victory ceremonies form the threshold or transformation phase. And the closing ceremonies work as rites of closure and re-incorporation into the normal, everyday order. All these ceremonies were designed in detail by Coubertin himself, or in later years, were expressly approved by him. Thus, the development of the ceremonies until his death can be regarded as following Coubertin's idea of the Olympic Games. But he could neither foresee nor control how they actually worked or what kind of response they really triggered. It may well be that he hoped for a popularization of a new bodily ideal, the ideal athletic body, as realized in Greek statues of the classic period.

At the first Olympic Games, which took place in 1896 in Athens in the ancient stadium rebuilt from ruins, the opening ceremony consisted of a procession of athletes into the stadium in national formations, carrying national flags. It was a transgression from a non-festive space into a festive space – an adaptation of traditional processions from a profane area to the heart of a sacred site. The official opening of the Games was made by the Greek King, followed by the firing of a salute – normally used for the announcement of the birth of royal children and other festive occasions – a flight of doves and a chorus. All these elements can be read as symbols; however, not as symbols that convey unequivocal meaning to all members of European cultures – and only members from European countries were assembled here. As symbols, they remained rather vague. Instead of transmitting a clear meaning, they were able to allude to situations in which they once featured and to induce a particular, familiar mood. Thus, the procession of the athletes was reminiscent of processions on Christian holidays; the firing of the salute might have triggered memories of or associations with some other festive and solemn event that was announced by or began with such a practice. The chorus seem to have sounded very much like a church choir or at least was reminiscent of one, evoking the particular edifying mood usually brought forth. The flight of the doves could be related to the dove as a symbol of the Holy Spirit or of peace, or with regard to carrier pigeons, as a symbol of international communication and understanding. In any case, the flight of such a multitude of birds, flapping their wings and flying up towards the sky, had a strong emotional effect.

After the procession of athletes in Antwerp in 1920, the Olympic flag, designed in 1914 to symbolize the interrelationships between the five continents, was carried into the stadium and lifted above all the national flags to the sounds of Olympic fanfares and the Olympic anthem. In this way, the flag symbolized the subordination of nations under the Olympic idea. Without doubt, it was the fanfares and the music of the Olympic anthem attached to the flag which contributed to its being accorded a particular emotional value. In the same year, 1920, the Olympic oath was added. Coubertin conceived it as a kind of cleansing rite that was supposed to cleanse and distinguish the athletes from the corrupt world of economy and finance and to bind them to an *esprit du sport*. The swearing of an oath is a very particular performative act whose self-binding consequences usually confer an aura of sacredness, a kind of halo, evoking quasi-religious feelings.

In Amsterdam 1928, after the doves were released, the Olympic flame was ignited on a tower erected for this very purpose for the first time in the history of modern Olympics. It was to serve as a symbol of the rebirth of the Olympic spirit. As explained above with regard to the sacrificial flames and the torches in Reinhardt's *Oedipus Rex*, fire is a highly polyvalent symbol. Moreover, because of its particular sensuous qualities, the flickering of the flames and its warmth, it works directly on the senses of those who perceive it and envelops them with its special atmosphere.

In Los Angeles, in 1932, a pageant of scenes from the history of the United States was performed, and thus served the process of nation-building for the American athletes and spectators.[10] In a general way, it marked a move from the solemn atmosphere of the opening ceremony to the more festive, joyful mood of the Games to follow.

Berlin 1936 – the last Olympic Games to take place under the 'patronage' of Coubertin[11] – was the first time the Olympic flame was lit in ancient Olympia in the sacred precinct by young women (choreographed by Leni Riefenstahl) and brought into the stadium by runners in a kind of relay race. In places where the torch was handed over, a festival was celebrated. The last runner ignited the Olympic flame in a so-called sacrificial bowl, a tripod bowl, reminiscent of the cauldron in which the sacrificial meal was prepared in ancient Olympia. On the one hand, the torch relay was intended to symbolize a bond between ancient Olympia and Berlin as a modern Olympia. On the other, it was meant to point to the particular relationship between Germany and Olympia established by Curtius and his excavations. And finally – if not foremost – it should proclaim Nazi Germany as the genuine heir of and successor to ancient Greece. This idea is also suggested by the opening of Leni Riefenstahl's film on the Olympic Games of 1936 *Fest der Völker; Fest der Schönheit* (Festival of the Nations, Festival of Beauty). Whether the athletes and spectators and, in particular, those from abroad, did in fact accord these meanings to the torch relay is somewhat doubtful. When the last runner brought the torch into the stadium and ignited the Olympic flame in the 'sacrificial bowl' placed at the so-called Marathon-gate,[12] it seems to have been experienced as a great moment, not just symbolizing but actually establishing a bodily, living bond between ancient and modern Olympia. It caused an upsurge of emotion – similar to that experienced during the Olympic Games in Sydney in 2000.

Instead of the pageant introduced in Los Angeles, a *Festspiel*, or festive play entitled *Olympic Youth* was performed featuring thousands of girls and boys, young women and men. First, it highlighted the carefree and happy life of children by focusing on romantic aspects such as boys assembled around a campfire, playing guitar and singing. It then presented two opposing groups of warriors, the leaders of which met in an *agon*, a so-called weapon dance, danced by Harald Kreutzberg and the former Kurt Joos disciple Werner Stammer, which ended with the death of both *agon* leaders. Finally, a lament for the dead, choreographed by Mary Wigmann, was performed.[13] In accordance with Coubertin's wishes, the lament was followed by the last movement of Beethoven's ninth Symphony, including Schiller's 'Ode an die Freude' (Song to Joy): 'Seid umschlungen, Millionen ...' ('With one embrace, I greet you, millions ...'). Thousands of torches and a sea of fire were ignited on the upper rails of the stadium to the sounds of the symphony and before the background of the night sky, flak spotlights formed a kind of cathedral of light, undoubtedly giving many a participant 'holy' shudders and, thus, arousing quasi-religious feelings in the masses present.

Most of the studies on the opening ceremony of the Olympic Games focus on their symbolic potential and offer detailed and enlightening interpretations of the various symbols used. The emotional impact of the opening ceremony, so often witnessed and reported, thus, appears to be a result of the specific symbolism used. In contrast, I shall argue that it was instead aroused by the particular atmosphere brought about by the interplay of different elements. Accordingly, my emphasis is on the atmospheric value of the elements concerned – to which, nevertheless, their vague symbolism also contributed. Whatever elements were chosen at the first Olympic Games in Athens and added later through the years, they either originated in or alluded to a religious context. They brought about and reinforced an atmosphere of solemnity, dignity and ceremony, the atmosphere of something 'sacred'. As we have seen in Reinhardt's Theatre of the Five Thousand, it is the atmosphere which, through music, sounds, smell, rhythm, envelops all those present, even invades their bodies. It proves to be something highly contagious, to use Herrmann's term. An atmosphere which is able to induce quasi-religious feelings in some of the participants will infect others and thus spread throughout the space, so that in the end nearly all those present are seized by the same emotion.

These shared quasi-religious feelings induced by the opening ceremony brought about a particular communal experience. They transformed the athletes and the spectators from different countries, cities or places into members of a quasi-religious community, a kind of Olympic congregation. In Reinhardt's Theatre of the Five

Thousand the audience was heterogeneous in terms of the social group, class, strata, to which the individuals belonged. But here, the participants were even more heterogeneous: athletes and spectators came from different nations and cultures, albeit mostly Western. It was the particular atmosphere brought about by the opening cere- mony and surrounding all participants; the quasi-religious feelings it induced which united them and transformed them into members of an international Olympic community. However, it was a community that respected the different national origins of its members as indi- cated by the national flags. Thus, the opening ceremony established a bond between the individuals participating. The Olympic community, formed by individuals of different nations and cultures was, in fact, a temporary community. Despite the fact that it was renewed by each and every competitive event and award ceremony, its existence could not survive the end of the Games. However, it demonstrated that such a community is possible, in principle. MacAloon's colourful and lively description of the atmosphere in the Athens stadium when the Greek winner of the Marathon race, Spiridon Loues, arrived amid enthusiastic cries of the masses chant- ing the historical words announcing the Greek victory at Marathon 'Nenikekamen': 'We have won' gives an impressive idea of the over- whelming impact that such an Olympic community can have on its individual members.[14] By suggesting the idea of a worldwide community, the Olympic Games realized and conveyed a utopian view of the future that, pre-World War I, was thought capable of actually bringing about such a community.[15]

The community brought forth by the opening ceremony of the Olympic Games was even more utopian than that which emerged through performances of Reinhardt's new people's theatre. This was not only because the masses involved were much more hetero- geneous, but foremost, because it demanded and even provided a kind of collective identity. The athletes affirmed and committed themselves to such an identity by swearing the Olympic oath. The spectators accepted it by respecting the *esprit du sport*, i.e. by display- ing 'fairness' towards the athletes, assessing individual performance regardless of their origins. Even in this respect, it was a quasi- religious community, bound together by a minimum of shared values. Whether the values constitutive of the collective Olympic identity also formed an integral part of the individual identity of ath- letes or even spectators after the Olympic community dissolved is hard to decide. Considering that the *esprit du sport* is opposed to the rules of the 'market', of capitalist everyday life, it is probably to be assumed that they did not survive the existence of an Olympic community which dissolved after the closing ceremony. The transformation that took place during the liminal phase, thus, proved to be reversible – as was the case with Reinhardt's performances.

The competition and the award ceremonies featured the individual bodies of the athletes. It was their prowess which was displayed. In the competition, emphasis was laid on their dynamic and energetic bodies. Bearing in mind that Coubertin celebrated the Olympic Games as a 'cult of energy', 'outbursts of energy' and as glorification of the 'freedom of excess', the Olympic Games can be regarded as an excess of energy. In terms of the dynamic and energetic bodies of the performers in Reinhardt's new people's theatre, I have defined energy as a physical as well as mental quality, as a contagious force emanating from the phenomenal body and spreading out in space, circulating among all those present, affecting and energizing those who sense it. The athletes in the contest not only generated energy and spread it into the space. According to Coubertin, it seems that they overflowed with energy, even 'wasted' it. Some critics of Reinhardt's performances complained that the phenomenal body of the actors sometimes outshone their semiotic body, that the circulation of energy let the phenomenal body come to the fore and pushed the semiotic body, the fictitious character, into the background. In the competition, it was only the phenomenal bodies of the athletes that counted. There was no expressivity that might contravene performativity. Thus, it seems highly probable that the energy emanating from the athletes was sensed by the spectators and had an immediate impact on them; that they were infected by this energy, that they became energized themselves. MacAloon's description of the first Olympic Games in 1896 as well as international reporters and commentators on the Games in 1936 – or even Leni Riefenstahl's film, although it seems to be a rather problematic witness – do, in fact, suggest and confirm this.

With regard to Reinhardt's performances, I have argued that the circulation and exchange of energy allowed the spectators to sense the actors and themselves as being present and alive in an unusually intense way; that in experiencing the presence and liveliness of the dynamic and energetic bodies of the actors, the spectators experienced the performers and themselves as embodied minds. In terms of the Olympic Games, I shall argue accordingly: the excess of energy displayed by the athletes made the athletes appear to the spectators as embodied minds and, at the same time, aroused in them a sense of themselves as embodied minds.

In my view, this new body concept underlying the display of dynamic and energetic bodies is to be regarded as one of the greatest achievements of the period between the turn of the century and World War I. It was not yet articulated discursively. However, by theorizing it, people took recourse to the traditional dichotomy between body and mind, between man's sensuous and spiritual nature. So, when talking about the liberation of the body from the constraints put upon it by the process of civilization, this process was still conceived of and described in terms of the old Western dichotomy. Since it was the mind which subjugated the body, the body had to be freed from this yoke, to be removed from the mind's control and be granted equal rights. Thus, a reconciliation of body and mind, of *res extensa* and *res cogitans* could be brought about. However, what articulated itself in the cultural practices of the *Lebensreform* movement, of the physical culturists, in Reinhardt's performances as well as in the Olympic Games through performative means only, was the idea that the body is the existential basis of culture and self, that, accordingly, human beings must no longer be conceived as a battlefield between body and mind, but as embodied minds. Therefore, I do not regard the display of dynamic and energetic bodies in Reinhardt's performances and in the Olympic Games as a utopian anticipation of a final reconciliation of body and mind that will take place some time in the future. In my view, a new anthropology was emerging and articulating itself through performative means; an anthropology that would do away with the old Western dichotomies and reach out for a fundamentally new understanding of humanity. Here, it articulated itself tentatively – however convincingly – in aesthetic and cultural practices and not yet in texts. Its discursive articulation was still to follow. It was, above all, Hellmuth Plessner in the 1920s and somewhat later Maurice Merleau-Ponty who dedicated their work to the elaboration of this anthropology.

In the competition, the emphasis was on the individual athlete and his performance. So, in the award ceremony it was first and foremost his unique achievement that was honoured. The athlete not only gave his all to satisfy his own ambitions but also, if not foremost, for the sake and honour of his nation. As McAloon's report of the first marathon race suggests the runner sacrificed himself for his nation; he almost died in the competition in order to be reborn and win victory for his nation. He was awarded the medal and adorned with olive fronds.[16] From now on, this athlete had to be regarded as the most powerful and fittest individual in the world. As such, the athlete was almost canonized by the ritual of the award ceremony. It was not only the victorious individual who was honoured but also his nation by raising the flag and playing the national anthem. Since, thus, it was not only the winner who was honoured but also his nation, the athlete was expressly addressed as a 'son' of his nation, someone who was indebted to it for his victory while, at the same time, the nation profited from his individual achievement. The victory was an offering given by the winner to his nation. The transformation that took place in this ceremony not only referred to the individual athlete who belonged to a particular nation, however. It also addressed his generic identity, his being part of mankind. The winner, in fact, gained a new social status, namely that of a victor at the Olympic Games and this granted him a particular aura. From now on, he was incorporated in the international community of the victors at the Olympic Games, in the community of the very 'best', not only of his own nation but worldwide. It was a kind of ascension to Mount Olympus – being accepted by the gods as their equal. As in a rite of passage, the transformation brought about in the liminal phase was irreversible and socially accepted, functioning as a kind of initiation.

The competition and the award ceremonies demonstratively presented and shaped the community brought forth by the opening ceremony as a community that respects and acknowledges the needs, achievements and rights of individual members. Here, there was no conflict between individual and community – quite the contrary. In a way, the athlete sacrifices himself for the sake and honour of his national community. On the other hand, the international community formed and experienced itself as one that is willing and able, even eager, to honour individual outstanding performances; which does not allow any tension to arise between itself and its individual members, whether they are individual men or individual nations. For it proved itself to be a community which not only included different individuals but also different nations. The competition was performed as a contest between individuals and nations, it is true. But the award ceremony demonstrated that the international Olympic community was proud to honour the 'best' individuals and their nations. Even in this respect, the Olympic community appeared utopian, as a temporary anticipation of the future hoped-for modern societies.

The closing ceremony was performed as a rite of closure and reincorporation. It annulled the festive order and reintegrated the normal order by reversing, in a way, the opening ceremony. The athletes processed into the stadium in national formation,[17] this time without their flags. The flags and country banners were carried into the stadium in alphabetical order by young people from the host country. The flags of Greece, the host country and the prospective next host country were lifted and their respective national anthems played (from 1924). The President of the International Olympic Committee spoke the closing formula, the Olympic flame was extinguished (from 1928) and the Olympic flag was lowered and carried out of the stadium (from 1920) to the sounds of the Olympic hymn. Finally, a salute was fired, and the exit of the athletes out of the stadium was accompanied by choral singing to finish the Olympic Games. However, the scenes which, according to MacAloon, took place at the end of the first Olympic Games seem to have been representative for later Games to follow. Many spectators did not leave the stadium, instead, they assembled here, occupying the space of the athletes and performing rites of their own, thus protracting the incorporation phase and delaying the end.

The Olympic Games can be regarded as a paradigm of a new performative culture that was expected to lead out of the crisis which was so strongly felt between the turn of the century and World War I. They proved capable of forming a community out of individuals coming from most diverse biographical, social, ethnic, gender (regarding the spectators), national and cultural backgrounds. Moreover, it was a community that did not repress its individual members but honoured those who gave outstanding performance without any regard for their origin. It was a quasi-religious community in that it was based on a minimum of shared values provided by the *ésprit du sport*. Here, the 'religion of muscles', of sports, had shown that it was, in fact, able to establish a bond between individuals from all over the (Western) world. Still, it was a temporary community only.

Moreover, by displaying dynamic and energetic bodies that had an immediate impact on those who perceived them, the Olympic Games annulled the dichotomy between mind and body so characteristic of Western culture and, instead, introduced a new anthropology. They defined the human being as embodied mind, albeit through performative means only.

In this way, the Olympic Games bridged the gap between elitist 'textual' and popular 'performative' culture. Through performative means, they brought forth and celebrated a new *elite* which proceeded and profited from as well as nourished the old *elite* enthusiasm for ancient Greek culture.

Although Coubertin claimed that the Olympic Games were reinvented as an answer to a crisis, as a solution to the problems and cure for the disease of the times, it cannot be overlooked that they were only able to work as a successful model because they were designed as a festival which only took place every four years. They were not meant to bring about a new social order to replace the old order of industrial capitalist society. Rather, they were able to reconcile it by creating another world, a *heterotopos*, which although it proclaimed different values was still able to incorporate those valid and dominant in everyday order such as competitiveness, self-assertion, strong will, endurance, performance and to celebrate them as such, i.e. independent of their origin in the capitalist order. That is to say, in contrast to modern societies they allowed for a community that did justice to its individual members by demanding fairness, and provided a sense of belonging to a generally binding and accepted order. However, they featured exactly those values on which modern societies are based and which, in the everyday order, cause loss of solidarity and disintegration. Because the festival is liminal time and festive space is liminal space, the festival of the Games opened up the possibility of temporarily reconciling such contradictions. It seems that it was this ambivalence that made the Olympic Games so successful.

All the models of a new performative culture discussed here so far – i.e. the reconceptualizations of theatre and ritual, Reinhardt's new people's theatre, the Olympic Games – were not 'influenced' by each other although they were all heading, more or less, in the same direction. We can neither assume that Reinhardt read the Cambridge Ritualists or took notice of the Olympic Games. Nor do we have any evidence that Coubertin was familiar with Durkheim's writings or that the Cambridge Ritualists attended the first Olympic Games in Athens in 1896. So it seems that they elaborated their models independently of each other, though as an answer to the same crisis they all felt, but formulated differently. Nonetheless, as we have seen, they have much in common with regard to the relationships between text and performance, individual and community, mind and body, elitist and 'primitive' culture. Moreover, they did not understand the model of a new performative culture which they advocated, hailed and displayed, as a fundamental counter-model to the existing order of industrial capitalist society which made them suffer, but rather as a remedy for its negative consequences, which they felt so deeply – such as loss of tradition and solidarity, disintegration, fragmentation, 'degeneration'. The models they developed were utopian in the sense that they presupposed the possibility of reshaping modern society in a way that its negative consequences were abolished without changing the fundamental principles of industrialism and capitalism. Reinhardt's new people's theatre was the most realistic model in that it admitted its necessarily temporary existence and did not attempt to bring forth any kind of permanent collective identity. Coubertin's Olympic Games were the most successful because they allowed the participants to renounce the world of the market, i.e. of capitalism, and at the same time to celebrate the values and virtues on which it is founded. It is most likely that this ambivalent structure is the reason for their long life and the source of their apparently never-ending, permanently growing attraction, particularly among the 'new' modern societies, even in times of globalization.

Part II

Mass spectacles between the Wars – in search of a collective identity

Introduction

When the War broke out in summer 1914, the majority of European nations welcomed it with overflowing enthusiasm. There was widespread belief that it would purge Europe, which was willing to make sacrifices for such a holy cause, and bring about a new 'spring'.[1] Enthusiasm did not last long, however, and by the end of the war, disillusionment, despair, misery, suffering and horror prevailed. Thus, the idea suggests itself that the very concept of sacrifice that had been so cherished in the theories of religious and classics scholars, amongst sociologists and anthropologists since the turn of the century, was now completely discredited. There was not the slightest probability that a sacrifice could bring about a utopian community. Nonetheless, some models elaborated before the outbreak of World War I were picked up again after it ended, although in a significantly changed way. This is particularly true of the concept of sacrifice which again played a prominent role. To a large extent, this is due to the necessity of coming to grips with the horrible fact that thousands and thousands of people – the masses – were victims of the war, and later revolution. Each nation insisted on the belief that it had sacrificed itself for the sake of a holy cause; that the dead should be commemorated as heroes and not be forgotten as part of an anonymous crowd. New kinds of memorial cult dedicated to the memory of national fallen heroes sprang up, keeping alive and praising their sacrifice.

The war had abolished traditional cultural and political orders – radically so in Russia, devastatingly in Germany and Austria and to a certain extent even in the Western democracies. As a consequence, politically motivated violence escalated in many countries such as Russia, Germany and Italy that had to be channelled quickly in order to avoid the risk of even greater destruction. Violence was the most visible and disastrous symptom of a widely felt identity crisis to be overcome. This suggests the idea to expand the range of application of the term liminality. Not only rituals and theatre performances are to be regarded as liminal phases, but also longer periods of crisis in a society like famine, war, revolution. In order to cope with the crisis particular rituals are needed. World War I can be seen as the first long-lasting liminal time of the twentieth century. Others were to follow. The 'rituals' that were created in order to overcome such crises between the two wars, were political mass spectacles.

It has often been suggested that mass spectacles were invented by totalitarian states in order to manipulate the masses.[2] However, I shall propose instead that the mass spectacle originated in a deep yearning for communal experience widespread in European culture at the turn of the century which stimulated the exploration of different kinds of fusion between theatre and ritual. One of these forms was modern pageantry and it can be regarded as the beginning of the modern mass spectacle.

Pageants were conceived and intended as a bulwark against what was felt to be the evil consequences of industrialization such as loss of solidarity, disintegration of society and disorder. A 'properly conducted pageant' should be 'designed to kill' the 'modernising spirit', as the initiator of the pageant movement, Louis Napoleon Parker (cited in Withington 1963: 195) suggested. In a way, the pageant movement was also searching for origins, i.e. going far back into history in order to construct a utopian vision of the future.

Parker (1928: 278), a playwright, composer and director explained what the pageant was not: 'It is not a street procession. It is not a gala. It is not a wayzegoose. It is not a fete. It is not a bean-feast. It is not done on trolleys. It is not tableaux vivants.' As his first pageant in 1905, *The Pageant of Sherbourne* commemorating the 1200th anniversary of the town demonstrates, pageants were played in open fields, near monuments. They included large casts of amateur actors and a number of local artists (writers, composers, musicians, builders, painters and so on). In terms of structure, the pageants resembled chronicle plays. However, the hero of the play was not a saint or some other individual, but a provincial town. The pageant consisted of a series of historical episodes connected by prologues and epilogues, narrative and dramatic choruses, musical interludes and long parades. Typically, it would start from the Roman period in the town and continue up to the Civil War, reaching its climax and quasi-apotheosis with the resistance of the besieged townsfolk against the Cromwellian usurpers. Parker even made a generic prescription that no episode should be shown which went beyond the mid-seventeenth century. In this way, the modern age, with its class divisions, political struggles and debates were excluded. Accordingly, Parker (ibid.: 285–6) claimed the social aims of pageantry to be a 'festival of brotherhood in which all distinctions of whatever kind were sunk in common effort', that it 're-awakened civic pride' and 'increased self-respect'.

In his autobiography, Parker confessed that he was deeply indebted to Wagner[3] for inspiration in creating the new genre. He also drew on William Morris' Arts and Crafts movement that had generated fresh interest in authentic village culture, as well as on his experiences at German folk festivals.

There are two principal characteristic features of the pageant. The first is its 'communitarian ethos' (Esty 2002: 248). The pageant was popular because it enabled, even demanded, that a huge number of people participate. The whole community was involved either in the preparations of the pageant and/or as actors or spectators. That is to say that thousands and thousands of people participated – in some towns it was noticeably more than in Reinhardt's Theatre of the Five Thousand. It was claimed that the pageant movement had created a theatre of the people, by the people, for the people, and therefore had 'enlarged enormously the sum-total of the world's artists' (The Earl of Darnely 1932: 34). In any case, the pageants did in fact allow for a communal experience.

The second feature was the pageant movement's claim to authenticity. As Parker wrote:

> Scenes in a Pageant convey a thrill no stage can provide when they are represented on the very ground where they took place in real life; especially when they are played, as often happens, by descendants of the historical protagonists, speaking a verbatim reproduction of the actual words used by them.
>
> (Parker 1928: 280)

The authenticity of the locale seemed to generate and guarantee the continuity of history. 'The typical pageant managed to represent hundreds of years of English history by suggesting that all the important things had stayed the same, by dissolving linear time into the seductive continuity of national tradition' (Esty 2002: 249).

The utopian vision contained in a pageant was manifold, if contradictory. From its very inception, the pageant blended progressivism and anti-modernism, traditional civic and religious ritual and the promise of artistic innovation. On the one hand, a kind of participatory democracy was proclaimed to which anybody could contribute, in which all are equal. On the other, the pageant provided a reassurance that even in times of upheaval and change, history will never cease to be a continuum and that by its very course, it confirms the community's identity rooted in and guaranteed by its history. The pageant both declared everybody taking part in it to be an artist, able to bring about artistic innovation, as well as allowing for a communal experience at the same time, and this tempted the people to believe in the possibility of using the pageant to overcome the diseases brought about by industrialization.

When the pageant movement was introduced to the United States, on the occasion of the commemoration of the 225th anniversary of Philadelphia in 1908, this contradiction was still characteristic of the genre, although in the so-called Progressive Era, progressivism outweighed anti-modernism. Now the pageant was grounded foremost in 'the belief that history could be made into a dramatic public ritual through which the residents of a town, by acting out the right version of their past, could bring about some kind of future social and political transformation'(Glassberg 1990: 4). That is to say that emphasis was laid on the transformation brought about by participating in a pageant.

Percy MacKaye (1912: 15), one of the most distinctive promoters of the pageant movement, explained such a transformation as 'the conscious awakening of a people to self-government'. On the same grounds, Glassberg (1990: 283) calls historical pageantry 'a public ritual of communal self-discovery' which, in the end, 'would lead to the integration of the town's various peoples and point to the reforms necessary for their continued future progress'.

The American historical pageant was a particular amalgam of earlier forms of presenting history in public processions, *tableaux vivants* and costumed re-enactments, and new features such as modern dance, the re-enactment of scenes from social, domestic and political life and an elaborate grand finale resembling fairground holiday festivals. Its content was 'the theme of community development, the importance of townspeople keeping pace with modernity while retaining a particular version of their traditions, the rite-of-passage format signifying the town in graceful transition' (ibid.: 285). Supporters of the pageantry movement assumed that the immediate sensation of expressive playful social interaction would be able to establish an emotional bond between the participants, to break down social and cultural barriers between local residents and, in particular, to integrate the immigrants. In this way, the immigrants would also become familiar with the history of the town and the nation, so that a renewed sense of citizenship would arise among all the citizens and lead to a lasting sense of civic commitment. Thus, pageants contributed to forming a coherent public out of a society that Percy MacKaye (cited Glassberg 1990: 284) characterized in 1914 as a 'formless void', i.e. a hotchpotch of different social classes, interests and immigrant groups, by creating a coherent history out of a succession of recent social and technological changes. However, the conflicts that accompanied those changes, especially resistance to the expansion of industrial capitalism, were excluded from the story of inevitable progress told by the pageants – just as black people or organized labour remained outside the boundaries of the public to which the pageants gave shape.

However, some excluded groups appropriated the new genre and assimilated it to their own purpose. In 1913, *The Paterson Strike Pageant* took place in the arena of Madison Square Garden, New York. Although performed only once, on 7 June, it became one of the landmark public statements against capitalist oppression, and called for major reforms in the political and economic system. The pageant was organized and directed by John Reed; Robert Edmond Jones designed the set and programme cover. Over 1,000 people participated as performers and more than 15,000 as spectators.

The pageant presented a re-enactment of the strike of workers from silk factories in Paterson, New Jersey, that had begun in February, organized by the IWW (Industrial Workers of the World). The mill owners had hired police and private detectives; by June two workers had been killed by random gunfire and nearly 1,500 strikers and sympathizers had been arrested.[4]

The pageant started with a march along Fifth Avenue to Madison Square Gardens. In the hall, a huge platform was erected at one side; a 200 foot back-drop picturing the dismal front of a Paterson silk mill, with lights blazing through the 'windows' hung over it and an entrance was created where 30 men could pass through abreast. The auditorium was decorated with IWW banners featuring the colour red. A roadway stretched right across the auditorium, from the stage out to the entrance to the Gardens. It was intended that audience participation would be triggered by performers marching along this roadway through the middle of the auditorium. And in fact, the audience did join in the strikers' singing, cheering the Wobbly speakers, and booing the police.

The first episode shown was the outbreak of the strike. 'Down from the stage and the entire length of the main aisle the workers marched, cheered all the way by the sympathetic audience of 15,000 working men and their families.'[5] The second episode showed a line of quiet, determined pickets patrolling the entrance to the deserted mill, including some slapstick scenes. The third episode was a re-enactment of the funeral of the rebel Vincenzo Modestino. (His mother and his three children sat in a box, all dressed in black.) The coffin was carried by strikers through the auditorium. The fourth episode consisted of singing songs which had grown out of the strike in various languages – English, German and Italian. Also included were the 'Marseillaise' and the 'Internationale'. There were Italian and German choral groups. The fifth episode represented May Day 1913 in Paterson as well as the day when the children were sent away from their homes to foster parents in New York to guarantee their safety. It began with a May Day parade through the audience and up to the stage. The final episode was a strike meeting with speeches by the strike leaders. After a passionate debate, the strikers voted for an eight-hour working day and announced the programme, 'No court can declare the law thus made, unconstitutional'.

The reviews were mostly favourable, stressing that the mass of strikers had been most effective and vigorous because they had escaped all staginess since they had refused to be theatrically 'produced'.[6] *The Independent* related the pageant to Elizabethan plays and brought up the question of genre. 'It was not a pageant of the past; but of the present – a new thing in our drama', but still it was a pageant. In accordance with this, the critic commented, 'It is an unequalled device for clutching the emotion of an audience – this parade of the actors through the center of the crowd'. He cited the dramatic liturgy of the Roman Church, the processional in the Episcopal, and even the familiar wedding march. In New York theatres it had barely been seen before – one year earlier when Max Reinhardt's *Sumurun*[7] toured there, and in one or two other cases, but 'never with more effect than in this performance, where actors and audience were of one class and one hope'.[8] *The New York Times*, however, recognized the intention to spark a revolution:

Under the direction of a destructive organization opposed in spirit and antagonistic in action to all the forces which have upbuilded this republic, a series of pictures in action were shown with the design of stimulating mad passion against law and order and promulgating a gospel of discontent [. . .] IWW leaders have at heart no more sympathy with laborers than they have with

Judges and Government officers [...] The motive was to inspire hatred, to induce violence.

(*The New York Times*, 9 June 1913)

In a way, *The Paterson Strike Pageant* foreshadowed the political mass spectacles springing up in different European countries after the war. It exposed and dealt with exactly the same conflicts the historical pageants were eager to hide and to exclude in order to sustain their view on history that the new society would grow out of the past organically.

While historical pageants of the 1910s seemed to be able to reconcile contradictory elements – in this respect quite similar to the Olympic Games, i.e. to foster modern social organization *and* traditional community feeling, popular culture *and* high art, attachment to locale *and* loyalty to nation, this was no longer the case after the war. Historical pageantry was soon overtaken by the newest trends in popular culture that had developed during the war, and it was left behind by trends in elite culture. In the years between the wars, political mass spectacles and folk symbolism split apart.[9] Pageants commemorating local history continued to flourish – or flourished anew – after the war. In the 1920s, they blossomed even in the Deep South and in the West. But, as Glassberg explains, the pageant movement that propagated historical pageantry as a vehicle for the social, aesthetic and moral regeneration of a town did not survive the war. As early as 1917, the optimism which had been the driving force in the Progressive Era was gone.[10]

The pageant movement shares some striking constitutive features with the Olympic Games. Both strived for a reconciliation of contradictory phenomena in order to cope with the crisis brought about by industrialization and modernization. Both succeeded in creating a communal experience that united all the participants emotionally. Finally, both demanded the shaping and acceptance of a common collective identity based on a set of shared values. Whereas the Olympic Games are still very much alive, the pageant movement did not survive World War I. For while the Olympic Games insisted on a reconciliation of opposites and a collective identity for the duration of the Games only, i.e. for a limited time-span every four years (although Coubertin hoped for even longer lasting effects), the pageant was more ambitious. The aim was to reconcile differences in a permanent way and to bring about a stable collective identity to be acted out and confirmed repeatedly by lasting civic commitments. Needless to say, they failed to do so.

After World War I, new forms of mass spectacle sprung up in various Western cultures that were supposed to accomplish what the historical pageants had missed – to shape and establish a lasting collective identity. Part II of my study analyses three – very different – such attempts: the Soviet mass spectacles during the Civil War, i.e. between 1917 and 1920; the Nazi *Thingspiel* during the first years of the Third Reich, namely between 1933 and 1936, i.e. from the seizure of Nazi power until the Berlin Olympic Games; and finally, the American Zionist Pageants between 1933 and 1946 that were conceived and performed as an answer to Hitler's persecution of the Jews. In each case, I shall argue that the time-span under investigation can be regarded, in certain respects (yet to be explained), as liminal time and that this condition served as the decisive prerequisite for embarking on such an enterprise.

4 Times of revolution – times of festival

The Soviet mass spectacles 1917–20

The October Revolution in 1917 marked the decisive beginning of the Bolshevik revolution though not yet its accomplishment. The Revolution did not end until the Civil War was over, i.e. not before mid-November 1920.[1] In a way, it was a mass spectacle, *The Storming of the Winter Palace* performed in Petrograd on 7 November 1920 in commemoration of the October Revolution[2] that announced and celebrated the final Bolshevik victory. The revolution was over. Everyday life had to begin anew.

Revolutionary times are liminal times – times in which society undergoes substantial changes and decisive transformations. The old order is abolished; a new one not yet established. A multitude of possibilities seem to emerge; contradictions can coexist in peace; anything might happen. Petrograd, the centre of the mass spectacle, was in a permanent state of emergency. People were starving, reduced to poverty, dying. The civil war consumed all available resources and little was left for the people. However, as a transformed, renamed city, Petrograd was also the place of sumptuous mass festivals. On the new holidays introduced by the Bolshevik calendar,[3] additional food was distributed and grandiose mass spectacles were organized which attracted thousands upon thousands of people. In 1920, for instance, on May Day the spectacle *Mystery of Liberated Labour* was performed between the portals and on the stairs of the former Stock Exchange, directed by Yury Annenkov and Alexander Kugel. More than 35,000 spectators were present. On 20 June, the transformation of Rock Island into Vacation Island was celebrated on the island by a performance of *Russia's Blockade* directed by Sergei Radlov; 150 performers and 10,000 spectators took part. On 19 July, *Towards a World Commune* was performed at the Third Internationale, again at the Stock Exchange, directed by a team consisting of Sergei Radlov, Vladimir Soloviev and Adrian Piotrovsky, headed by Konstantin Mardzhanov. And the series finally ended on 7 November, with *The Storming of the Winter Palace* in the square in front of the Winter Palace, again directed by a team of directors, this time consisting of Nikolai Petrov, Annenkov and Kugel, led by Nikolai Evreinov and featuring 8,000 performers. The performance was attended by more than 100,000 spectators. As can be gathered from this list, the directors were the elite of Russian avant-garde theatre. Almost all resources they demanded for the spectacles were put at their disposal despite the fact that this was a time of terrible starvation and poverty.

This apparent contradiction can hardly be explained by the widespread suggestion that the intention was to manipulate the masses. This would presuppose that all involved in the making of the spectacles shared a similar ideology which they wanted to instil into the spectators. This, however, was not the case.

All these assumptions ignore the vagaries of symbolic communication, the subjectivity injected into the process by the audience, and the chaos and confusion of Civil War Russia. Propaganda was a dialogue, with the audience as the silent interlocutor. It was a living interaction in which audience and maker were in constant communication. [. . .] If the revolutionary festivals did ultimately serve to strengthen Bolshevik power – which is not at all clear – they did so because artists displayed their magic according to their own rules. Politicians did not make the festivals.

(van Geldern 1993: 10–13)

The coexistence of contradictions, thus, was not due to any kind of manipulation which, as van Geldern rightly argues, was somewhat unlikely. It was the liminality of revolutionary times and, in particular, of festival time with its paradoxes that allowed for such coexistence. If any kind of collective identity was to take shape in, or to grow out of, the threshold phase represented by the spectacles, it was by no means a prescribed or predetermined identity, but rather an identity that would emerge through the process of participation, i.e. it was an identity that no one could figure out or fix beforehand. It could not be foreseen or planned.

The efficacy of the mass spectacles in shaping and bringing forth such a collective identity is often doubted. One of the main arguments concerns the relationship between the intellectuals on the creative side, and the common people who served as performers and spectators. It is argued that the intellectuals produced 'utopian abstractions' to which the people did not really have access so that, ultimately, the mass spectacles remained without consequence.[4]

At first glance such an argument may appear sound – particularly in consideration of the new concepts and ideas of theatre developed by the theatre avant-garde before the war. More was drawn from Western models than from Russian popular culture. Ancient Greek theatre, medieval mysteries, commedia dell'arte, Spanish theatre from the Golden Age and Wagner's *Gesamtkunstwerk* served as models from which a new concept of theatre would derive that would overcome the cultural crisis, deemed so virulent at the turn of the century.[5] Irrespective of the many differences among them, the avant-garde agreed in their assumption that the forestage, which separated actors and spectators, had to be removed; that both parties had to be 'reunited'. One of the 'hottest' issues in this debate concerned the relationship between theatre and religion. Evreinov argued that the instinct for theatre was pre-religious. In order to make his point, he coined the term 'theatricality', which he defined as a 'pre-aesthetic instinct' which underlies all cultural activity, i.e. religion, art, customs, law etc. (Evreinov 1923). Therefore he argued that religion originates in theatre and not the other way round:

> In order to believe in gods, man had first to acquire the gift of conceiving these gods, of personifying them as a dramatist personifies ideas, feelings and passions. Were it not for the gift of transfiguration, of imaginative creation of things and beings that cannot be seen on this earth, man would have no religion.
>
> (Evreinov 1927: 30)

Therefore he defined theatre as a game played by actors and spectators alike as Herrmann did, rather than as a ritual. In 'Ancient Theatre' he explored medieval mystery plays in the season 1907/08, and the Spanish Golden Age theatre (1911/12). A commedia dell'arte cycle was planned for the season 1914/15. In these performances, he highlighted and celebrated the paradox between ceremony and coarse buffoonery, so characteristic of traditional festive spirit.

The symbolist Vyacheslav Ivanov, who after the revolution would work at Narkompros' (Commissariat of Education) theatre section (TEO), took quite another stance regarding the relationship between theatre and religion. He saw the origin of theatre or, more precisely, Greek tragic theatre in the ecstatic rites of the demotic cult of Dionysus, following Nietzsche's *Birth of the Tragedy*. He conceived a future theatre as a new choric theatre, in which actors and spectators would be united in one mystic community: 'The spectator must become a doer, a participant in the drama. The crowd of spectators must merge into a choral body, like the mystic commune of the ancient "orgies" and "mysteries"' (Ivanov 1909: 206).[6] Therefore, theatre had to merge with ritual, to turn back into ritual 'again'. The community should be represented as well as brought forth in a performance. The chorus, which Nietzsche had addressed as the origin of tragic theatre, accordingly, had to take over the role of the protagonist, as was, in fact, later the case in Proletkult productions after the Revolution. It had to serve two functions:

> the minor chorus, tied directly to the action [...] and a chorus symbolizing the entire community, which can be increased at will by new participants – a chorus, hence, that is manifold and inserts itself into the action only at moments of the highest ascent and full liberation of Dionysian energies.
>
> (Ibid.: 212–13)

Inclusion in the action was intended to establish a bond between the actors and the spectators so that the theatrical event turned into a 'real', social event.

Ivanov was not the only theorist who believed in a new cultic people's theatre. The Bolshevik Anatoli Lunacharsky was also deeply impressed and influenced by Nietzsche[7] as well as by Richard Wagner. In 1910, when the Russian translation of Romain Rolland's book *Théâtre du peuple* (1903), which refers directly to Wagner, appeared, it was strongly advocated by Lunacharsky who also wrote the foreword. So, it is small wonder that among the first titles to be printed by Narkompros' newly established publishing house in Petrograd in 1918 was Wagner's pamphlet *Art and Revolution*, first translated into Russian as early as 1906. The foreword was written by the People's Commissar, Lunacharsky. Like the Communist Manifesto of 'our brilliant teachers' Marx and Engels, this brochure by 'the no less brilliant Richard Wagner' was, he explained, a product of the German Revolution of 1848. Its topicality, however, was undiminished, and Lunacharsky (1918: 3) recommended it 'for the edification of both artists and the victorious workers' democracy'.

In this context, it seems quite striking that in spring 1918, Reinhardt's *Oedipus* was re-staged in the Chinizelli Circus, where it had been performed on Reinhardt's guest tour in 1911. The re-staging was initiated by Yuri Yurev, the leading actor of the Aleksandrinsky

Theatre. The original sets of the 1911 performance were still intact, so that an 'authentic' space was secured. Yurev asked Aleksander Granovsky,[8] a Reinhardt disciple who had just returned from Berlin, to direct the revival. Yurev played the part of Oedipus and Granovsky directed the chorus, so fundamental to the 'original' production, and the mass scenes. The revival proved to be as huge a success as the original, attracting in its week-long run spectators of all social classes.

Looking back at the main sources of inspiration on which the avant-gardists drew, they seem to be very far removed from Russian popular culture. However, it cannot be concluded there was no common ground between the intellectuals and the peasants, soldiers and labourers that would enable a collective identity to emerge in the course of spectacles directed by the avant-garde as a major contribution to and element of a Bolshevik festival. It is often forgotten that the people, though illiterate, were quite able to occupy a space in an ordered formation, to immerse themselves in an atmosphere created by a particular use of light, sound, smell or images and to respond to it by establishing an emotional bond between all those present in the space, and thus, to bring forth a community – not as a 'utopian abstraction', but as a lived experience – composed of highly heterogeneous individuals. It was, in fact, religion that accomplished such a 'miracle'. People acquired this capacity by participating in the rituals of the orthodox liturgy. Here, they were on common ground with the *élite*.

Thus, it may not come as a surprise that the early revolutionary festivals often aroused experiences and triggered forms of behaviour and demands on the participants similar to those created by a great Orthodox holiday as some witness accounts show:

> There was a radiant joy on all their [i.e.: the soldiers] faces. They frequently halted as the people embraced and kissed one another in jubilation. Everybody said: 'Here it is at last, triumphant Easter has arrived.' They were all smartly dressed, as if for a big holiday. As in the capital, the Easter tradition of celebration became confused with the revolutionary festival.
>
> (Figes and Kolonitskii 1999: 43–4)[9]

What is emphasized here is the moment of ultimate transformation as the moment of redemption brought about by the revolution as well as by the revolutionary festival.

Whether innocently or on purpose, the mass spectacles were

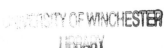

modelled on patterns provided by Christian mythology. As in the medieval mystery plays – which Evreinov brought to life again – the history of the World was narrated as a teleological process from its creation to the redemption of mankind brought about by Christ's sacrificial death and resurrection. Most spectacles followed a similar story line. They narrated the history of oppression from its earliest manifestations through time until the outbreak and victory of the October Revolution as a constant battle between Evil and Good, between the forces of Darkness and of Light which finally ends with the triumphant victory of Good over Evil, of the forces of Light defeating those of Darkness for ever. Emperors and kings were featured as oppressors, as were bankers and factory owners. They acted as the evil incarnate, as the forces of Darkness trying to oppress the forces of Light, the masses of slaves, workers and peasants. The story as battle was punctuated by repeated temporary 'victories' by the oppressed, as when Spartacus led the Roman slaves to revolt, when the French Revolution was victorious or when Stenka Razin stirred the Cossack rebellions. For each temporary victory, sacrifices had to be made. Every revolt, rebellion, revolution contributed a good score for the forces of Light and anticipated their final glorious triumph as achieved by the October Revolution.

This was actually a mythical story, retold in different versions but all following the same pattern. It consisted of a sequence of episodes each of which could be replaced by others without running the risk of destroying or even damaging the pattern. It was to be performed in the open air, preferably on 'sacred' sites such as the square in front of the Winter Palace, where the Storming actually took place. Whenever an episode of the recent history of revolution was presented, performers were chosen from among those people who actually took part in the event. And it was mandatory to use only 'real' objects in the performance.[10]

This short list of characteristics of the mass spectacle suggests an obvious resemblance to the pageants. In a way, it seems to mirror Parker's claim to authenticity,[11] although here, such a claim played quite another role. A fundamental difference, however, can be stated regarding the underlying concept of history. In the mass spectacles, it was a teleological concept. History was conceived as a teleological process which aimed to redeem the oppressed masses and this was finally accomplished by the Revolution. The Revolution brought history to an end. Similarly, the orthodox Easter liturgy celebrates Christ's resurrection as the awaited and hoped for end to history which started with the Fall and Adam and Eve's banishment from Paradise. The mass spectacles celebrated the Revolution as the long awaited and hoped for end to the seemingly infinite battle between Light and Darkness which determines history and seems to benefit the oppressors. It hailed the final and irreversible victory of Light.[12]

It can be assumed that, as in the case of the historical pageants, the concept of history underlying the mass spectacles would be decisive in shaping a collective identity.

The first mass spectacle which is usually regarded as the prototype of the new genre was *The Overthrow of the Autocracy*. It was performed on 16 March 1919, i.e. on the anniversary of the Tsar's abdication celebrating the victory of the February Revolution (later overturned by the Bolsheviks). It was the first performance by the newly founded Red Army Studio, directed by Nikolai Vinogradov-Mamont. Vinogradov, a former improvisation teacher at the Mobile-Popular Theatre[13] and a disciple of Meyerhold, believed – like Ivanov – that theatre was a universal art. He formulated his programme for a new theatre in 'Seven Points':

1 The theatre is a temple.
2 Universality.
3 Monumentality.
4 Creativity of the masses.
5 An orchestra of the arts.
6 The joy of labour.
7 Transfiguration of the world.

(Vinogradov-Mamont 1972: 13)

He founded the Red Army Studio in order to realize his programme. As we shall see, the soldier-performers and the spectators realized it in a very particular way.

The production took four weeks to prepare, allowing for thirty rehearsals. It was performed in the Volodarsky Hall of the Rozhdestvensky House of the People in Petrograd. While all the mass spectacles to follow were open-air performances, the first took place indoors. The Hall was meant to allow for approximately 600 spectators only. Two platforms were erected on opposite sides of the Hall, one covered with red cloth – the 'Platform of the Revolution' – the other with green – the 'Platform of the Reaction'. A broad aisle (measuring approximately 4.3 by 74.5 metres) cut through the middle of the Hall connecting the two platforms. While 'individual' scenes took place on the platforms, the aisle was used for battle, revolution and other mass scenes. The spectators were placed at both sides of the aisle so that they were facing each other. When the spectators entered the Hall, the performers had already taken their places: One group playing the Tsarist guards was assembled at the 'Platform of the Reaction'; another – a group of workers – huddled together at the 'Platform of the Revolution'; a third – also in working dress – stood along the walls and at the door; a fourth, consisting of six elderly skilled workers, had taken their seats among the spectators. The audience, thus, was encircled by the soldier-performers of the Red Army Studio.[14]

The performance began with a battle alarm produced by drums and accordions followed by a prologue spoken by Vinogradov who appeared on the 'Platform of Revolution' holding a bayonet and a fragment of a bullet in his hands:

> We are the Red Army and we fight at the Front. We've got a few days free between the battles. We've decided to give a performance on a political theme. Who are the actors? We are the actors. Do we have a play? – No! We've written one ourselves. Where is the theatre? – Yes, here, where fighters get together, where they sit and sing, this is our theatre. The set? Seven fir trees which we cut down and have fixed on a stand; that is our forest! And instead of the theatre bell, I shall strike the case of this great artillery gun. I shall strike it with my bayonet. First bell. Second bell. Third! The Red Army's version of 'The Overthrow of the Autocracy' shall begin.
>
> (Ibid.: 61)

Seven episodes followed: 9 January 1905, so-called bloody Sunday, when the revolt was brutally put down; arrest of an underground fighter, interrupted by a 'military interlude' featuring slap-stick scenes, singing choirs, accordion and dances; the seizure of the arsenal by workers; the Volhynian regiment and its fraternization with Petrograd workers; the erection of barricades on the streets; the revolution at the Northern front; the Tsar's abdication from the throne.[15] The sequence of scenes as well as the story line was fixed. Within this framework, the performers were encouraged and free to improvise. Quite a few of them had taken part in Bloody Sunday and in the February Revolution. Thus, the actions in which they had been involved were re-enacted, their own experiences acted out, in the performance.

The play had a collective hero – the oppressed masses who liberated themselves. Those who acted as the masses wore everyday dress and no make-up. Unlike everyday life, however, the soldier-performers were clean-shaven and their hair cut, thus, paying homage to the 'holiness' of theatre. On the other hand, the actors playing the Tsar and his entourage wore costumes and make-up. Within the context of Russian orthodox culture, donning a mask was understood to be a sign pointing to all kinds of intended deception from disguise to the perversion of political power as in the case of usurpers. Therefore, a mask indicated Evil and the underworld; it stigmatized the person who donned it as being someone influenced by the Devil (Uspenskii 1994: 84–7 and 105–6). Thus, from the very beginning there was not the slightest doubt that the masked individuals were Evil incarnate and that the groups of workers and soldiers were suffering and fighting for the victory of Good.

In the performance, a community was represented as well as brought forth; sometimes, as we shall see, by the same act. The community represented was shown to be self-organizing and self-organized. This impression was suggested not only by the lack of a leader, but also through the synchronized movements of the groups in and through the space. Whether in a battle scene or funeral procession, revolutionary action or the process of fraternization, the performers presented coordinated gestures and movements, changing the underlying rhythmic pattern from scene to scene. The community which they represented might have come into being in and through common suffering. However, it was renewed by common action in the fight for liberation from oppression. It was confirmed by the blood they shed – or sacrificed – in the fight for the common cause – by shared mourning of their dead as well as shared revolutionary actions. In the course of the action, a new collective identity emerged for the community. It was no longer the identity of the oppressed, of suffering, of victims, but the identity of those who had the courage, determination, strength and energy to overcome their oppressors and to liberate themselves. Since the performance took place as a re-enactment of events that had actually happened, of events in which the performers had been involved in more or less the same way as they showed in the performance, it is to be assumed that the new collective identity they acquired as they took part in revolutionary actions was reflected in the performance, acted out and, thus, consciously adopted and expressly confirmed in the presence of the spectators. In this respect, the re-enactment worked as a kind of incorporation ritual for the performers.

On the other hand, from the very beginning, the performance

strove to initiate the audience into the community represented. This was principally accomplished by applying the three devices which Reinhardt had already developed in *Oedipus Rex*: (1) occupation of the space, (2) working of an atmosphere, (3) movements of dynamic and energetic bodies in space. However, here, occupation of space and movements of dynamic and energetic bodies in and through the space were indissolubly intertwined.

The spatial arrangement described above made it possible for the performers to encircle the spectators and allowed them to act in the middle of them, almost as part of the audience. This resulted in the impression that the action proceeded from the auditorium, from the spectators. The performers occupied the whole space, running up and down the aisle and to each wall, imposing their dynamic and energetic bodies on the spectators.

> The soldiers rose up and began the attack. After three years of battle at the front they ran, stumbled, fell and got up again – not as if they were running across some parquet floor but rather over earth ploughed deep into ruts and thrown up by artillery shots [. . .].
>
> (Vinogradov-Mamont 1972: 55)

Even after the final scene, the abdication of the Tsar, the performers again 'stormed' the spectators: 'The doors [. . .] flew open. They stormed in from the edges at both sides. A bayonet-spiked formation, appearing from above, from the left, from the right, from behind, from below. Majestic call to arms of the bayonets and red flags. March into the auditorium' (ibid.: 72).

Not only had the 'storming' performers drawn the spectators into the action. The seating arrangement also contributed to this effect. Since the spectators sat facing each other, separated by the aisle, they always observed other spectators as they watched the performers and their dynamic and energetic bodies in the aisle. In this way, the gaze of the spectators embraced the audience sitting opposite merged with the action in the aisle.

While the spectators' eyes were challenged by rapid mass movements, their ears were bombarded by different kinds of sounds attacking their bodies, allowing them to feel as if they were actually taking part in a battle. The performers shot empty cartridges that are suitable for short distances and sound like 'real' rounds. Together with the smell emanating from the guns this evoked and disseminated 'a genuine combat atmosphere' (ibid.: 55). Thus, the particular atmosphere blurred the boundary between reality and play. One contribution particularly added to this: an unfortunate accident. Although the cartridges were empty, one soldier was severely wounded in the eyes. However, after being bandaged he continued his performance. The combat atmosphere alternated with various atmospheres evoked by the choir who sang well-known popular songs.

The interplay of the three devices resulted in lively audience participation. The spectators responded again and again with frenetic applause, shouting, 'hurrah'. In the funeral procession, when the soldiers carried their dead comrades around the Hall, the spectators spontaneously rose from their seats and united and joined the soldiers in a choral rendition of the hymn 'As a martyr, you fell'. 'Several young men and women joined the soldiers and followed the procession of fallen heroes' (ibid.: 59). After the performance, hundreds of spectators shed tears of emotion and enthusiasm. They surrounded the somewhat dazed performers, embraced and raised cheers to them. At the second performance a small riot broke out among the audience even at the first scene, Bloody Sunday, the moment the White Guards attacked demonstrators in front of the Winter Palace. 'The working youth among the spectators were on the verge of attacking the Tsarist soldiers Guard' (ibid.: 63). When the Volhynian regiment fraternized with the revolutionaries for the first time, a frenetic applause shook the Hall. And when the commanders were overwhelmed, enthusiastic laughter was heard. In the following scene, the seizure of the arsenal, the spectators joined the chorus of performers in their shouts of 'hurrah', while those playing the policemen ran away in panic. When the dead were carried out, the same response was triggered as in the first performance.

> Majestic chords of mourning. The procession walked slowly three times around the Hall. The women were sobbing. The young workers joined the soldiers. Vsevolod Meyerhold lifted up a rifle belonging to one of the fallen heroes, threw it over his shoulder and marched off with the Red Army in formation.
>
> (Ibid.: 68)

In another scene, a soldier suddenly addressed the famous singer Fiodor Shaliapin sitting in the audience and asked him to affirm the soldiers' dream of a better future they had just evoked by singing a song. Shaliapin got to his feet and belted out a popular song, 'Little Club' ('Dubinushka'), which tells the story of a club which is handed down from generation to generation serving different purposes until in the end it changes into a weapon against oppressors and exploiters.

After the 'storming' of the Hall at the end

> there was no finale. The freedom fighters climbed down from the stage into the auditorium with their red flags. In a wave of enthusiasm the masses, composed of workers and red army soldiers, surged towards them. It was not actors who were embraced, but people who felt the same in the same holy battle for the great goal, the revolution.
>
> (Ibid.: 72–3)

At first glance, the audience participation seems reminiscent of that in *The Paterson Strike Pageant*. This is small wonder. For in both cases, the performers re-enacted their own actions and experiences and this was partly shared by the spectators who came from the same social class. However, the differences which do exist must not be overlooked. What were triggered here were quasi-religious feelings. At the centre of the performance was a sacrifice, the actual and symbolic blood – shed for the sake of a cause common to performers and spectators alike. It was this sacrifice that renewed the bond between them that had already been established by their previous common suffering. The spectators became part of the community of performers at the latest at the moment they rose together at the sight of the 'dead' being carried out and as they joined in singing the hymn, 'As a martyr you fell'. In doing so, the spectators expressly confirmed that the blood of the dead was shed for them too and that they were ready and willing to accept and observe the obligations resulting from this fact. It was a quasi-liturgical process which began here, modelled on the orthodox liturgy. In church, the singing of hymns works as kind of anticipatory 'dismissal benediction', preparing for the 'final redemption' of the 'apotheosis' at the end of the service (Beck 1926: 80–1). In the performance, something quite analogous happened. When the spectators sang together with the performers it was in anticipation of their final initiation into the community of performers represented by the performers. This final initiation was accomplished by the 'storming' of the Hall and the following integration of spectators and performers brought about as they joined in, the exchange of embraces, the cheers. From this performance onwards, the press – which was allegedly 'atheistic' – used the term 'apotheosis' to designate the exuberance of the integration of performers and spectators, which commonly formed the finale of mass spectacles from now on.

In this 'finale', performers and spectators acted out a new collective identity that emerged out of their participation in the performance, i.e. in a self-organizing and self-organized community of which the spectators had become part by spontaneously joining in the singing and the procession of the performers. It was the identity of self-liberators – of those who liberated themselves from the age-old curse of oppression, of those who 'redeemed' themselves. This newly acquired collective identity was certified by a sacrifice – by the blood that was shed in the fight for liberation.

The parallels between the finale of the mass spectacles and the Easter liturgy are, in fact, striking. The liturgy confirms the collective identity of the congregation as one of redeemed souls whose redemption was brought about by the Saviour's sacrifice – the shedding of his blood for the remission of sins – and resurrection. However, while in the Church it was Christ who saved souls, in the performance it was the proletarian masses who saved themselves. Despite this important difference, the quasi-religious feelings triggered by the performance were most likely due to the obvious parallels. In this sense, the performance functioned as a rite of passage in the course of which the participants died in their former identity as suffering victims and were reborn into a new identity as redeemed self-liberators. And it was not so effective because new symbols such as the red flag had been introduced, but rather because it took recourse to a familiar ritual pattern which had a strong appeal to the emotions and habitual behaviour of the people and, thus, enabled them to bring forth new meanings themselves.

In a way, the community that came into being in the course of the performance, the community of actors and spectators, fulfilled the dream of a new kind of community, dreamt by so many before the war. On the one hand, it came into existence on the basis and as a consequence of a sacrifice, as Smith, Frazer, Harrison, Durkheim and others had stated with regard to 'primitive' societies, and also, in a quasi-religious context. On the other hand, it was a rather utopian community. As a self-organizing and self-organized community, the tensions between the individual and the community as a whole were considerably reduced. For each of its members participated in the process of self-organization. Not one individual or group of individuals alone would determine the course of the performance. Rather, each and every person who participated co-determined, so to speak, the further course of action and, at the same time, let themselves be determined by it. Thus, the community as well as the performance was brought about by this particular kind of interaction as realized in the process of self-organization.

This is a process in which phenomena emerge which were neither intended nor could be foreseen.[16] Self-organization yields the new, the unpredictable, and the unplanned. And this seems to have been the case with regard to the community coming into being in the process of the performance *The Overthrow*. The underlying ritual patterns in and through its course acquired a new meaning that now referred to revolutionary acts of self-liberation. It seems that even the relationship between mind and body was redefined in the process of self-organization. Before the revolution, peasants and workers had been regarded as mindless bodies determined to carry out only those activities which an external mind has ordered – the Tsar was the sole master of any semiosis and government. In *The Overthrow* all participants acted as embodied minds who, by organizing themselves, brought forth new meanings. Whatever meaning emerged during the performance, it was brought forth not so much as the expression of a pre-given meaning, but as something new, unexpected and unpredictable.

Thus, the community that came into being transformed all its members. It let those mindless bodies who were but tools in the hands of others and who only acted for the sake of another's intentions, 'die' and gave them new birth as embodied minds which are neither autonomous subjects nor completely externally determined, but subjects who co-determine common actions and who, at the same time, are willing and ready to let themselves be determined by them. This was a community of a new quality.

As *The Overthrow of the Autocracy* shows, a performance is not a suitable means of manipulation. What emerges out of the impact which the production has on the audience and from the audience responses which it triggers is, in principle, neither predictable nor controllable. This is obvious when active audience participation is engaged, as in this case. But it also holds true when the audience reaction is restricted to behaviour which can be perceived – sensed, seen, heard – without, however, directly interfering in the stage action, as is the case in each display of strong emotion – weeping, shuddering, trembling, laughing, restlessness, leaving the room – or any other kind of behaviour which indicates a particular attitude such as coughing, talking, shuffling the feet and so on. Such responses also have an impact on the performers as well as on other spectators – they prove to be no less contagious. That is to say that spectators, in this sense, are always active participants. They are not only influenced by the performance but also have influence on its further course. This means that both performers and spectators alike determine the course of the performance and are determined by it, although to different degrees and to a different extent. Accordingly, the spectators cannot be regarded as innocent victims being manipulated by those who planned and prepared the performance. By taking part in a performance they even accept a certain responsibility. As long as they remain in the performance space they are also responsible for the course it takes. Thus, that which emerges from a performance is not only determined by what the performers do, but also by the spectators' responses to it. That is to say that a performance can never be completely planned and controlled by individual subjects, or be completely at their disposal. In this sense, one could argue that the performance is brought forth by and made forceful due to a self-referential and ever-changing autopoietic feedback-loop. What emerges in the course of a performance, therefore, is unpredictable and cannot be foreseen.[17] The range of active audience participation can be reduced, however. This was the case in later mass spectacles that tried to deny the spectators admittance to the performance space by using rope barriers which, however, the spectators usually broke through in the finale. But ultimately, this only prevented active intervention, rather than all sorts of other responses which equally have an impact on the performers and other spectators. Manipulation by means of a performance seems extremely difficult to handle. What I have elaborated on the performance so far with regard to *The Overthrow* holds true for performance in general and, in particular, for all mass spectacles between the wars.

The Overthrow of the Autocracy was exceptionally successful. Various sources claim that it was repeated 250 times on different occasions and in different spaces.[18]

> The piece was performed daily. A tradition was established: before a military unit was sent to the front, a rally and a performance of *The Overthrow of the Autocracy* took place at the railway station. We marched to the performance in formation, shouldered our arms and sang.
>
> (Vinogradov-Mamont 1972: 80)

The new collective identity shaped and created by *The Overthrow* seems to have been eagerly and enthusiastically welcomed – even with a kind of religious zeal. In the following mass spectacles, it was re-enacted over and over again and, thus, repeatedly confirmed.

The mass spectacles to follow took place in the open air. This changed the significance of the device of occupying space considerably. For now, it meant occupying public spaces which had been 'off limits' before the Revolution. Previously, any kind of gathering, even of small groups, let alone demonstrations, had been strictly prohibited. Now, revolutionary actions conquered the public spaces for the proletarian masses – the peasants and the workers. In a way, each festival re-enacted this victory when the performers and spectators took possession of the public space, occupying it as thoroughly as possible. Occupying the public space suggested having gained power, being one's own ruler.

This holds true, in particular, with respect to the square in front of the Winter Palace, the Palace Square, renamed Uricky Square. Before 'Bloody Sunday' in 1905, it had been a taboo place, where political demonstrations were inconceivable. On 'Bloody Sunday' it was this very site where peaceful mass demonstrators carrying procession icons and portraits of the Tsar, headed by the Priest Gapon, were brutally put down; where the blood of many hundred people was shed. The very stones and soil of this site were soaked in the blood of murdered demonstrators. Therefore, the Square was regarded as a 'sacred space', a space, where the proletarian masses had sacrificed their blood for the common cause of a better future. On the other hand, the Winter Palace was held to be 'the same old ancestral seat, a nest of secrets and crimes, a cradle of ancient curses, like the unchanging Palace facade on the Greek stage' (Piotrovsky 1919: 2). And this Palace was ultimately transformed 'into a building hallowed by history' (Piotrovsky 1926: 78) by the 'storming' which took place on 7 November 1917 (25 October according to the old calendar) – which did not overthrow the autocracy but overturned the February Revolution, i.e. Kerensky and the Mensheviks.

Performing *The Storming of the Winter Palace* in this very space, on the anniversary of the original event – i.e. in periodical as well as liminal time – re-enacting it, seems to provide almost ideal conditions for allowing theatre and ritual to merge into spectacle. What happened here was, in fact, the creation of a myth of origin, the myth of the revolution[19] – to be taken up and further elaborated later, most prominently by Sergei Eisenstein in his film *Ten Days That Shook the World*. However, the performance included strikingly less ritualistic features than *The Overthrow* and other mass spectacles such as *The Mystery of Liberated Labour* or even *Toward a World Commune*.

The performance did follow the mythic scheme, however. It began at 10.00 p.m. in darkness – the lights of the Winter Palace were switched off – and it ended an hour and a quarter later with a fireworks display of red stars in the night sky and bursts of light. The searchlights of the battleship 'Aurora', which was anchored on the river Neva behind the Palace as it had been three years before, backlit the building, so that it seemed to become transparent, melting in light. Then, together with the searchlights in the Square, they shifted to a spot on top of the Palace where a huge red banner was lifted, now flooded with light, and in the windows of the Palace, red lights flashed on. With the success of the Revolution, Light had definitely defeated Darkness, and each and every participant was physically experiencing it.

In some respects the spatial arrangement in the vast Palace Square was reminiscent of that in *The Overthrow*. Two platforms were erected in front of the facade of the General Staff Headquarters that shut off the square at one side, and opposite the Winter Palace: one white, one red stage. Both of these stages were divided by platforms of varying levels. The red stage included buildings of red brick, factories, a large square and a memorial obelisk. The stages were connected by a bridge which mirrored the Headquarter's arch behind it. It was on the bridge that the inhabitants of the two worlds met and fought their battles. The orchestra, consisting of 500 musicians and directed by Hugo Varlich, was placed behind the bridge, under the arch of the General Staff.

The spectators stood in the middle of the square in two blocks, separated by a broad corridor leading from the entrance of the General Staff to the Winter Palace, and cordoned off for them. In addition, a special spectators' stand was built by the facade of the Archive on the left side of the square (seen from the Palace). It was reserved for some 'very important people' who had an overview of the whole square. In the middle of the square, marked by the Alexander Column, a platform was put up adjacent to the column; here stood the director who used field radio, light signals and motorcycle carriers to orchestrate the unfolding of the performance. Military units, trucks and automobiles were parked in the streets leading to the square waiting to be used – their combat order signalled to them by the director. In this respect, the performance resembled a military manoeuvre.

> Around 10 o'clock, there was the muffled boom of a cannon and the bridge command, which was set up around the Alexander

Column, gave the signal to begin. The arched bridge lit up and eight fanfares rang in peals of penetrating sound. As the sound faded, they disappeared into the darkness again. The silence that followed was broken by Litoff's powerful Robespierre, played by the Petrograd military symphony orchestra. And the performance began.

(Shubsky 1920: 4)

At this moment, 150 searchlights, mounted on the roofs of the surrounding buildings, were switched on, illuminating the performers on the White side who opened the action.

The main figures on the white stage were Kerensky, the provisional government, high officials and important financiers of the old regime, the women's battalion, land owners, bankers and merchants, fighters from the front, cripples and invalids, enthusiastic men and women ready to compromise [...]. The first light that fell on them showed their victory in caricature. Kerensky appeared before the waiting crowd accompanied by the 'Marseillaise' rearranged as a polonaise. The actor playing him mimicked the movements of the ex-Premier and, standing in his khakis, caught the attention of the crowd.

(Ibid.)

From the darkened Red stage, inarticulate murmuring was heard; while on the White stage, the continuation of war was decided. Now the searchlight switched to the Red stage, exposing workers, women, children, cripples staggering exhausted out of factories. Mutilated soldiers dragged themselves onto the bridge because new troops were needed.

The events on the Red stage seemed more 'impersonal'. The masses were at first grey, solid, disorganized, which nonetheless grew increasingly more active, better organized and more powerful. Urged on by the 'Militia' they were transformed into the Red Guard which took shape with flaming red banners.

(Ibid.)

In this way, the action switched back and forth between the White and the Red stages until the people from the Red stage marched onto the bridge into battle with the White performers. As a consequence of the Red victory, the bank of the secretaries of state col-

lapsed; two cars hurried to the steps of the White stage, and the secretaries and Kerensky who came down by a *salto mortale* disappeared
into them, their cars dashing down the corridor and into the gate of
the Winter Palace. From now on, the Winter Palace became the
main 'stage'.

There were 2,685 performers on the White stage, including 125
ballet dancers, 100 circus artists and 1,750 extras. Six hundred of
these wore make-up – those who played politicians, bankers, factory
or landowners and so on and their entourage. Kerensky and his
secretaries were played by professional actors and circus artists.
The style performed on this stage was farcical and slapstick. In
terms of the action taking place here, this guaranteed close audience
attention.

The Red stage was peopled by even more performers. Among
them was a large number who had taken part in the 'real' storming
of the Winter Palace three years ago. These performers wore everyday clothes and no make-up. They acted in a kind of heroic style. As
they began to coordinate and synchronize their movements and gestures, they gradually began to organize themselves. Here, not one
individual performer stood out above the others, drawing the attention of the spectators to his individual performance – as was the case
of the professional actors on the White stage. This was a direct result
of Evreinov's directorial orders:

> The age of the walk-on role is over. You are possibly more
> important than those actors from the old school. You are part of
> the collective actor. Out of the form and breadth of what you
> have experienced, out of what you have suffered, a new effect of
> a new plot has arisen.
>
> (cited O.A. 1920: 2)

The libretto emphasizes that the production would not feature
'drilled artists', but 'a collective actor, a virtuoso in his art' (O.A.
1968: 272). There is even mention of a 'mythical actor-giant' who is
'bearer of new, monumental theatre forms. Supported by the
rhythm of mass movement, he does not follow any calculable reckoning any more; its quantity is already melted into a new quality and
pours out like any individual actor as the source of new expressive
forms' (Shubsky 1920: 5). Piotrovsky (1926: 16–17) took quite
another stance. He criticized the fact that the chorus disintegrated
into 'a crowd of extras'.

The opposition between the two stages and the acting style in

each case recalls the opposition between coarse buffoonery and ceremony which Evreinov developed in his performances of the medieval
mystery plays before the war. In these plays, one scene features
prominently. It is Christ's descent into Hell to liberate the tortured
souls. While the devils (played in medieval times by professional
actors, the *ioculatores*) employed coarse buffoonery, Christ and the
poor tortured souls who yearned for the Saviour to come, were characterized by a rather ceremonial style. Christ's descent into Hell was
also a very popular subject in orthodox iconography. It is possible
that for many spectators, the scenes in the first part recalled Christ's
descent into Hell which precedes the resurrection. The performers
on the White stage, especially those who wore make-up, could be
identified with the devils; the labourers, soldiers, women and children on the Red stage resembled the tortured souls. And just as in
the mysteries where the crowd cried out for Jesus to liberate them,
the people in the Square called for Lenin: 'Timidly, the "Internationale" sounded and shouts of "Lenin! Lenin!" rose up from the
crowd above the music, at first singly and then from a hundred
voices' (Evreinov 1920: 279). A man wearing a coat and a cap
appeared on a higher platform. All eyes turned towards him as if
under a spell. He summoned the workers to the armed revolution.

This, indeed, marks a big difference. While in Christian mythology, Christ throws open the doors of Hell and liberates the souls,
here, Lenin calls upon the masses to liberate themselves, without
serving directly as their leader or sacrificing himself. Still, the first
part recalls in some way Christ's descent into Hell, which is to say,
Easter. Otherwise, there were no suggestions of Easter or the Easter
liturgy until the 'apotheosis' at the very end of the performance.
Audience participation was considerably reduced. It was realized as
laughter aimed at Kerensky and his people; as commentaries on
their later, well-deserved fate; as joining in the shouts of 'hurrah'
given by the soldiers and workers when Kerensky escapes in woman's
clothes from the Winter Palace after the proletarians have won the
battle. There was no common singing. The 'Internationale' was
mostly played by the orchestra alone. Only once, at the appearance
of Lenin, did a mighty chorus sing it. However, there are no documents suggesting that the audience joined in the singing. That is not
to say that there was no interaction between the two parties.

> In the trail of the growing revolutionary impetus, the spirits of
> the dense mass of workers and soldiers continuing to flood in
> also rose, as well as among the audience [...] there were cer-

tainly moments when the people venting their emotions sent electric waves of thrill and excitement and ultimately merged into two pupils and a gaping mouth fixed with attention.

(Shubsky 1920: 4)

And when the attack on the Winter Palace began, 'the spectators were electrified; the people were about to break down the barriers at any moment and storm forwards with the cars and the hordes of soldiers to break the hateful Kerensky crowd and their composure' (ibid.). This moment did not occur, however, before the end of the performance when Kerensky had escaped and the 'Aurora' which had bombarded the Winter Palace in 1917 fired its canons; i.e. not before the storming was over. The spectators joined the performers for the celebration of the revolution. Now the searchlights from the Aurora and from the Palace Square focused on the red flag on top of the Palace and there was a fireworks display; the performance, at least, ended with a common action: 'a common choir and a festive procession, joined by the audience' (Gregor and Fülöp-Miller 1928: 104). In the apotheosis, performers and spectators were finally united celebrating the victory of the revolution as their redemption.[20]

Concerning the community that was represented as well as brought forth by the performance, there were some differences in comparison to *The Overthrow* that should not be overlooked. While in *The Overthrow*, the community represented appeared as a self-organizing and self-organized community that could do without any leader, here, the masses on the Red stage were crying out for Lenin as for the Saviour. He appeared on a heightened platform – so to speak above their heads – and called upon them for a revolution. Although he did not lead the masses into battle himself, his appearance – almost conjured up by the calls of the masses – contributed remarkably to the ongoing process of their organization. In the end, it was they who liberated themselves. But the impression was suggested that for this process, the Saviour-like figure of Lenin was needed.

The second difference concerned the unfolding of the performance. It did not appear as a process of self-organization of those involved. And this not only resulted from the lack of improvisation and audience participation but, foremost, from the mighty presence of the director who could not be ignored. It was obvious that the unfolding of the performance needed a surveyor who organized and controlled its course. It was apparently the director on his heightened platform, who directed the searchlights over the space, switching back and forth, who commanded the canon fire and the fireworks display, who ordered the military units, the trucks and the cars to appear. Thus, the performance unfolded less as a process of self-organization than as a military manoeuvre that needs the surveillance and controlling gaze of a commander.

Finally, the actor–spectator relationship was redefined. At first glance, it might seem that the spatial arrangement in terms of the spectators simply developed the arrangement in *The Overthrow*. For on the one hand, the spectators stood right in the middle of the space and were surrounded by various actions; on the other, the action took place right in the middle of them, i.e. along the corridor, where the soldiers and workers marched to the Winter Palace, trucks and cars passed by in different directions, and fighting took place. Thus, it seemed that the spectators were ideally positioned to participate in the action, to join in. But, alas, the audience was cordoned off. Moreover, as spectators they were exposed to the gaze of other spectators who were seated on the heightened stand at the Archive. The privileged spectators who assembled here had a perfect overview of the whole space and all the events. For them, performers and spectators – even the director – together made up the spectacle that unfolded before their eyes. All these people performed before their distanced and surveying gaze. This changed the particular quality of the performance in a decisive manner:

> The masses [. . .] of people, the demonstration of its power, and the joy of the crowd is a confirmation of these days and an apotheosis. It is legitimate as long as no one watches it from a window, or from a special platform, otherwise it becomes a parade, a ballet in chains or brass band. And that is the reason why it is not a masked ball and not theatre.
>
> (Shklovsky 1923: 61)

There can be no doubt that Evreinov had, in fact, intended *The Storming of the Winter Palace* to be theatre, to be a first and exemplary model of the theatre of the future for which he struggled. This is why he reduced some ritualistic elements – as, for instance, common singing – and employed those that were reminiscent of Christian mythology and perhaps even of the Orthodox Easter liturgy, as expressly theatrical elements. Exposing the director in his proper function and also playing with the deeply theatrical relationship between seeing and being seen, he most likely intended to emphasize the theatricality of the spectacle. However, even Evreinov could not escape the impact of the 'sacred space', where the performance took place. It was the centre of power – of the power overthrown by the revolution, i.e. of a past and bygone power. And yet, it had also become the centre of the new power established by the revolution. And thus, what happened in the performance was not the transformation of participatory rituals into theatre but, instead, of participatory rituals into rituals of surveillance.

The Storming of the Winter Palace announced a new era that would develop cultural practices which highlighted a supervising authority:

> The most important element which 'short circuits' the whole action is the platform where the demonstrators march past. Whilst before the revolution and in the first years after it, the demonstrations imitated the [...] 'syntax' of a church procession which did not demand the witness and evaluating subject for its structure, now this subject actually appeared. 'The receiving organisation' becomes a necessary attribute of the ritual. [...] Whilst before the 'sacral encounter' with the existential took place in the soul of each and every demonstrator and did not need any outward manifestation (in this sense, all participants were equal), now this ideal procedure became 'material', it demanded a very clear expressive form.
>
> (Glebkin 1998: 100–1)

Such a change deeply affected the collective identity. In the liminal time of revolution and of festival it had developed as the identity of a self-organizing and self-organized collective of self-liberators, bringing forth new meanings. The collective realized itself as a community in which there was no opposition between the individual and the whole community. The collective was understood as a community that was regarded as the prerequisite for equal rights for all individuals, which did not allow for either an autonomous subject or totally external determination. *The Storming of the Winter Palace* marks the end of an era which made such a collective identity possible. In applying completely new artistic means, it allowed the spectators to bring forth new meanings. But, at the same time, it introduced a supervising authority on three different levels which openly contradicted the idea of self-organization. The spectators in the square understood this; not by deciphering particular symbols, but through their own bodily experience. They felt separated from the action, from the possibility of participating, by being cordoned off; and they sensed that they were being watched when they looked up to the stand in their turn. However, they did succeed in evading the control of the director and finally, actively participating in the performance when they broke through the ropes and joined the performers at the end for the final apotheosis. In this way, they once more – and for the last time? – displayed and confirmed a collective identity brought about by revolution and festival.

When the Civil War finished, the Revolution had finally come to an end. The great festival was over. Liminal time was replaced once more by the linearity of historical time. Everyday life had to begin anew. But, as it turned out, the collective identity as it was developed, adopted and repeatedly confirmed in the liminal time of revolution and festival, could not be incorporated in the everyday life that now began. Instead of the principle of self-organization on which it was founded, the principle of 'self-transfer' or even 'self-surrender' was reinstated. According to Lotman, this was the most important principle which regulated the interaction between individual and community in Russian orthodox culture:

> By expanding religious feeling to embrace the state, the psychology of this kind demanded to a certain extent the transfer of the whole semiosis to the Tsar, who became a symbolic figure who became, in a sense, a living icon. The fate of the other members of society became a zero-valued semiotic behaviour; a purely practical activity was all that was required. [. . .] The subordinates simply fulfilled a practical duty of service which ended in concrete results. A concern for the social or symbolic side of their life and their occupation was felt to be 'laziness', 'scheming' or even 'betrayal'.
>
> (Lotman 1992: 351)

The role of the all-supervising authority governing and controlling all processes of meaning production was now taken over by Lenin and, after his death, by Stalin.

Following the model of 'self-transfer' the individual has to give himself completely for the sake of the community embodied in the leader. In this sense, as early as 1922, Nikolai Bukharin characterized the Leninist cadre party as a 'revolutionary order', a kind of religious community:

> All Party Workers submitted themselves entirely to the Party: Party-patriotism, the absolute devotion to the execution of Party

instructions, the bitter struggle against enemy groups which could form anywhere – in factories, in offices, in street discussions and in clubs, and even in prison, turned the Party into a unique revolutionary order.

(Bukharin 1971: 320)

The individuals were to form the 'body' of the community which had but one 'mind' – the leader.

This new/old relationship between individual and community generated a new genre of 'mass spectacles' – the show trials. They reached their climax in the 1930s, in particular with the Moscow Show Trials. Prominent Party members and loyal, even devoted fellows of Lenin for many years, such as Sinoviev, Kameniev, Bukharin were charged with high treason, espionage, planning of terrorist acts against Stalin, as well as with various acts of sabotage on industrial plants. The trials served to affirm the authority of an all-knowing Party which is never wrong, embodied by Stalin. Thus, the defendants were expected to sacrifice themselves for the sake and welfare of the community, i.e. the Party, by publicly confessing those crimes for which they were charged; crimes which they never committed, invented by 'the mind' of the Party. They did not confess because they hoped to escape a death sentence. They knew very well that public confession would seal their fate. That is to say, they did not renounce the possibility of not confessing something they had neither devised nor committed, of publicly negating it, because they hoped to survive. In confessing publicly that they had, in fact, devised such plans, they repeated the act of self-surrender. They sacrificed themselves for the sake of the Party, a totalitarian state,[21] distorting in this way the self-sacrifice of the self-liberators and transforming it back into the old cultural practice of self-surrender. Hereby, they confirmed a collective identity as one shaped and brought about by a totalitarian state – an identity that was far removed from the collective identity which the mass spectacles of the revolution had created and celebrated.

5 Producing the *Volk* community – the *Thingspiel* movement 1933–36

In 1933, when the Nazis seized power, there was an upsurge of enthusiasm, hope and expectations not only among National Socialists and in Nationalist circles but also among nationally minded people. Euphoria spread to the extent that it even seduced an intellectual such as the poet Gottfried Benn to announce in a speech, held in May 1933, that the moment had arrived when history was about to mutate and breed its own people – words he deeply regretted by the end of 1934.[1] There were a number of people who regarded the months following the change of power as a time of eagerly awaited national revolution, as the beginning of liminal time. Among them were many playwrights who were keen to stage plays written during the last years of the Weimar Republic. The theatres were flooded with plays dealing with national themes, subjects and ideologies.

One of these plays was Richard Euringer's *Deutsche Passion 1933* (*German Passion 1933*). It had been written as a radio play in 1932 and was first broadcast in April 1933. It became one of the most popular plays of its time. By 1934, 30,000 copies of it had already been sold – rather unusual for a play. Moreover, it was awarded the National Book Prize 1934 and the Stefan George Prize. It premiered in the theatre on 28 July 1934 at the Heidelberg *Reichsfestspiele* held in the courtyard of the Palace. *German Passion 1933* was regarded as the prototype of a new theatrical genre to be called *Thingspiel*; it was the first play to be given the generic title 'Thingspiel' or Thing play.

The play opens in the world of the dead – on the battlefields of World War I strewn with dead soldiers. The Evil Spirit appears and runs them down:

Night. – Night. – Blood red night.
Silence. Finally. It is finished.
The last to stir,
I snapped his bones. Now he is quiet.
The war is over.
(cynically, mocking)
Peace has come.
(Fanfares)

(Euringer 1936: 5; translated
by Jo Riley)

But even now the dead soldiers cannot rest in peace. The lamentations of the chorus of children, the chorus of unemployed and the mothers stir and wake them up. The chorus of children complains that they are starving:

Children: (starved, poor) (scattered)
Desperate. – Desperate. – Desperate. –
Hunger. And no bread.
Oven, without heat.
(falling)
And no Fatherland.

(Ibid.: 8)

The chorus of unemployed complains that their fate is even more desperate than that of the dead:

The Unemployed:
(in the silent quiet) . . .
(out of the no man's land of the living)
We suffer a more desperate fate.
Six long years I have had no job.
Six long years I have not lifted a finger.
Six long years I've been growing crazy.
Standing in front of the mirror, I spit on my own face:
What part of mankind are you? What kind of man are you?
Are you dead or alive? . . .
(louder)
Ten million Germans too many!
You should be eradicated, root and branch!

(Ibid.: 10–12)

And the mother deplores the general state of the country:

> Germany is horrifying! Cover your face!
> Don't look at the tricks and shame!
> The people dishonoured. The women
> Fallen. Who wouldn't feel disgusted?
>   (Ibid.: 14)

One of the dead, an 'unknown warrior', deeply horrified by what he has heard, rises and decides to return to his people in order to bring about a transformation.

> The Crowd (scream):
> He rises from the dead!!!
> The Mother: A crown of thorns made of barbed wire!
> The Soldier: (Voice of the unknown warrior)
> I shall bear the suffering of the Passion!
>   (Ibid.: 14)

Wherever the unknown warrior goes, he meets only desperate people; among them a proletarian, a person crippled by the war, an old hag and a young girl. He learns how dreadfully they all live and tries to find out how to change their lives. The Evil Spirit tries to provoke counter-agitation. He tempts the people to excesses of all kinds, to mindless pleasures and pure consumption:

> Films these days are full of filth,
> the underworld reveals itself openly: [. . .]
> The dance hall becomes a brothel,
> Gaudy advertisements tempt the obscene,
> Need a woman? We'll deliver.
> Europe shall be a whorehouse.
> Survived three days! You're still young!
> Live tomorrow as flower dung.
> Hang on to men who seek action!
> Join in with men who seek fun!
> Despair in the suburbs!
> What is 'the people'! What is 'honour'! We are the state! [. . .]
> You shall know how far a man
> Can run in the race by his elbow.
> It's not enough for the masses.
>   (Ibid.: 21–2)

Despite the efforts of the Evil Spirit to provoke the unknown warrior and set the crowds on him, the soldier succeeds in delivering a speech to all social classes, groups and strata in which he challenges them to renounce greed and vindictiveness and unite in shared labour:

> Man the engines! You have the choice!
> Decide once and for all.
>
> (Ibid.: 28)

The people discuss his speech and one after the other they are slowly convinced that they should join together in 'one labour, one will, one world' (ibid.: 35). The play ends in the world of the dead.

> Unknown Warrior as Benevolent Spirit:
> (heroically, manfully, powerfully, calm)
> It is finished
> (He raises the sword) [...] (With the steel blade raised to the heavens, heroically, as a hymn)
> Do you hear the heavens, swathed in star showers,
> Hell that hears it, protects its ears.
> The spirit screams in tongues from stones,
> the people rise up from the grave. (mighty, preaching)
> The blood which flowed has
> not been swallowed by Satan's gorge!
> From disgust and horror – springs – both
> The Holy Reich!
>
> (Ibid.: 39–40)

The chorus of people takes up his words and repeats them, thus ending the play.

Euringer's *German Passion 1933* drew heavily on well known models such as expressionist poetry and plays, the choric plays of the social democrats performed at festivals of the workers' movement, and also – obviously – on Christian mythology. Each of these elements had proven its effectiveness. However, it was not the combination of them which alone accounts for the enormous impact the play had on audiences and other playwrights. Rather, it was another well known pattern underlying the play – Frazer's ritual pattern of death and rebirth. Although it did not apply to a god, at stake here, was the death and the rebirth of a nation – of the German people. As the play suggests, the nation was felt to die not only on the battlefields of

World War I but also, if not foremost, at the signing of the Versailles Treaty. During the Weimar Republic, it descended into a Hell of egoism, decadence, libertinage, obscenity, and a brutal clash of interests arose between classes and individuals; the nation would be reborn as soon as the people became willing to renounce such vices and unite their forces in common work.

The rebirth of the nation in the play did not happen as a miracle, nor was it awarded as a gift by a Saviour-like figure. Certainly, the unknown warrior – a representative of the masses, a kind of allegory of the people – followed Christ's example by wearing a crown of thorns – made of barbed wire – and by taking upon himself the Passion of returning to the world of the living, to his people. But it was not his Passion, his sacrifice that 'redeemed' the people. It was not he who formed a community from the masses of unemployed, proletarian, war cripples, mothers, starving children, scribes and artists etc. It was the people themselves who, as a consequence of his speech, decided to join forces. The community that comes into being at the end of the play is intended as a self-organizing and self-organized community, a community that can exist without a leader – a community that includes the living and the dead. The Evil Spirit is defeated, the Benevolent Spirit, the unknown warrior, can return to the world of the dead. The nation is reborn when the people are united in a *Volksgemeinschaft*.

The ritual pattern of death and rebirth of the nation seems to have had an enormous appeal to nationally minded people. Many plays written and performed in 1933/34 followed the same pattern. Undoubtedly, in combination with Christian mythology, it was able to trigger quasi-religious feelings, to be directed towards the nation, towards the fatherland. On the other hand, the seizure of power by the Nazis interpreted in such a ritual pattern seemed to be the beginning of a liminal period that was expected to bring about great changes, significant transformations – to accomplish the rebirth of the nation by accomplishing a cultural revolution. The later so-called *Thingspiel* movement certainly originated in such expectations and was nourished by it. It was a revolution of the theatre – which Georg Fuchs had already demanded and announced at the beginning of the century – that was hoped would bring about a cultural revolution that would result in the rebirth of the nation.

At the same time, the *Thingspiel* movement proceeded from less ambitious, less far flown ideas. Some of its roots lay in different open-air theatre and amateur movements that – like the pageant movement – sprang up at the turn of the century and were widespread and popular in the 1920s. They were advocated and propagated by most diverse groups: by the Youth and *Lebensreform* movement, by the social democrats, by the catholic and the protestant churches and also by nationalist circles. In 1926, Wilhelm Karl Gerst, a representative of the catholic *Bühnenvolksbund* (Volk League of Stages) founded the *Reichsausschuß deutscher Heimatspiele* (Reich Committee of German Homeland Plays), in order to bring together and to coordinate the different movements. In 1931/32 he founded another organization, the *Reichsausschuß für deutsche Volksspiele* (Reich Committee for German Volk Plays) that was to serve the same purpose more efficiently. And, finally, by the end of 1932 he founded the *Reichsbund zur Förderung der Freilichtspiele* (Reich League for the Promotion of Open-Air Theatre), together with representatives from the *Volksbühnenverein* (Volk Stage Association) and the *Genossenschaft Deutscher Bühnenangehöriger* (Co-operative of German Stage Workers). The statutes of the Association list its aims as follows: 'The Association aims to support and encourage the German open air theatre movement and amateur theatre in the sense of art appreciation and/or education with particular reference to the interests of the population who are less fortunate' (cited in Stommer 1985: 24). In 1932, Egon Schmid, another pioneer of the nature theatre movement who had already founded more than twenty such theatres by 1933, organized a 'Conference of German Playwrights' in Weißenburg in Bavaria, in order to initiate a wider variety of plays suited to open-air theatres in particular.

In Summer 1933, the *Reichsbund der deutschen Freilicht- und Volks-schauspiele* was founded in order to replace Gerst's *Reichsbund.* Members such as the expressionist writers Ernst Toller and Kasimir Edschmid were no longer included. Otto Laubinger, head of the Theatre Department in Joseph Goebbels' Ministry for Volk Enlightenment and Propaganda became President of the new 'Reich League'. This organization now monopolized all the open-air theatre and amateur groups listed above that had come into being quite independently of National Socialism, and transformed their innovative impulses into instruments of National Socialist cultural politics.

The term '*Thingspiel*' quickly came to replace the earlier prevailing terms 'people's theatre' or 'popular theatre'. '*Thingspiel*' was a term suggested by Carl Niessen, a theatre scholar at Cologne University. The word 'Thing' is old Germanic. It refers to a place where Germanic tribes would gather – probably under sacred oaks – to hold political meetings and tribunals. Political meetings, rallies and so on were sometimes given the name *Thing* after the Napoleonic wars in order to express and propagate the will to create national unification on the basis of a particular historical identity. In a way, the introduction of the term in 1933 continued this tradition, although now the ideas connected to this term were rather vague. The *Thingspiel* was understood to be a 'people's (*völkische*) liturgy' and a 'cultic site of the eternal German word' (Wilhelm von Schramm), as the 'monumental pulpit whence National Socialism will be preached' (Walter Tiessler), as 'a socialist, divine service for the people' (Günther L. Barthel), as the 'contemplation of oneself and the sacred idea of National Socialism' and 'artistic pilgrimage' (Wolf Braumüller), as 'a State celebration of holy days' and as 'tribunal' and 'cult of the dead' (Richard Euringer, all cited in Eichberg *et al.* 1977: 31). In any case, it was meant to combine the people's theatre as a mass spectacle with political rallies. Accordingly, it was conceived as *the* national theatre that would be in a position to represent the *Volk* Community on stage and bring it forth as a cultic and festive community.

In a speech to German theatre directors on 8 May 1933, Goebbels developed and explained this idea of a new people's theatre: 'The National Socialists will reunite people and stage. We will create a theatre of fifty thousand and hundred thousand; we will draw even the last *Volk* comrade into the magic of dramatic art and enthuse them again and again for the great substance of our national lives' (cited in Stommer 1985: 31). It is no coincidence that the expression 'Theatre of the Fifty Thousand and Hundred Thousand' recalls the term Max Reinhardt coined for his new people's theatre: the 'Theatre of the Five Thousand'. Just as Reinhardt referred to the ancient Greek theatre when he staged *Oedipus Rex* and the *Oresteia* in an arena at the Munich *Volksfestspiele*, so the sites for the *Thingspiel* plays in some respects followed the same model. At so-called sacred sites – as for instance the Loreley on the Rhine – *Thing* arenas were to be erected and built into the landscape. They were intended to hold if not 50,000 or 100,000, then at least 20,000 spectators. In August 1933, the Academic Association of Architects held a conference to develop and discuss plans for the construction of such sites. The arena stage was divided into different kinds of steps and levels and broad aisles intersected the auditorium so that the *Thing* site could also be used for military displays and rallies. Ludwig Moshammer, architect of several *Thing* sites described the architecture and the possible effects of such sites in the journal *Die Bauwelt* (1935):

On the one hand, the site for the Thing plays has a ranked auditorium criss-crossed with broad aisles running from side to side and from top to bottom. On the other hand, it has a performance area layered like a terrace, with different areas – front, middle, upstage and side – linked to each other by steps. These performance terraces reflect the pattern of aisles in the auditorium and together with it create an architectonic whole, in which there is no more separation. The performers and chorus can pour out onto the performance areas from amongst the spectators and the play can be carried by the performer right into the audience so that the spiritual tension of the spectator rises towards a feeling of total communion with the play and full participation.

(cited in Eicher *et al.* 2000: 37)

The multi-levelled *Thing* sites emphasized the vertical axis, thus proving them to be 'sacred' sites. Since they abolished any kind of separation between performers and spectators, they seemed to be able to create festive communities of actors and spectators. It was intended that about 400 *Thing* sites should be erected across Germany. The first sites underwent construction as early as 1933.

Alongside the planning for the construction of the *Thing* sites, the performance of 'preparatory plays' was scheduled for 1933. Even during the Conference of the Architects, it was decided to found the *Rheinische Spielgemeinschaft für nationale Festgestaltung* (The Rhine Performing Arts Association for National Festivals). The association should prepare the first model performance and itself serve as a model for the foundation of later *Spielgemeinschaften.* Each *Spielgemeinschaft* consisted of professional actors as well as amateurs (for the choruses).

The first and, to my knowledge, only preparatory play that was performed in 1933, was the performance of *Das Spiel von Job dem Deutschen* (The Play of Job the German). The play was written by Kurt Eggers, the music composed by Werner Egk. Hans Niedecken-Gebhard, a disciple of Rudolf von Laban, directed the production. He was famous for his mass spectacles and his productions of Händel operas. The choruses were directed by Franz Goebels. Eugen Kloepfer, a well-known actor from Berlin and member of the National Socialist Party, played the part of Job. Almost all actors who took over leading parts did not come from the Rhine Performing Arts Association but from Berlin theatres, which emphasizes the importance accorded to the enterprise. The performance took place in the huge Exhibition Hall in Cologne and 500 actors/performers and 4,200 spectators participated in the premiere on 16 November 1933. Between 16 and 22 November, seven performances took place, all of them sold out. In sum total, 50,000 spectators took part in the performances and this was regarded as evidence that a genuine people's theatre had been created.

The Play of Job the German follows the same ritual pattern as Euringer's *German Passion 1933.* Starting with a bet made between God and the Devil over Job's soul – alluding to the beginning of Goethe's *Faust* – it tells the story of the biblical figure of Job who loses everything except his faith in God and, in the end, is generously rewarded. In the play, Job the German suffers the War, the loss of his seven sons, experiences poverty and temptation (in the Weimar Republic) without losing his faith in God and, in the end, is richly rewarded:

> *The Lord of lords:*
> I shall give the joys of the earth
> To you and your line.
> Your people from now on shall be
> The people of my revelation.
>   (Eggers 1933: 62; translated
>   by Jo Riley)

Job the German suffers his Passion and death, before he is reborn to a newer and even greater glory.

Although the ritual pattern seems to have had an effect on the audience and although especially the ending followed National Socialist ideology, the play was harshly criticized after the first performance by all those interested in the *Thingspiel* movement. Critique of the drama centred particularly on the language of the play, the lack of dramatic tension, and its tendency to be banal. The play was never officially awarded the generic title *Thingspiel.* It may be that this was not – or not only – due to obvious deficiencies in the play but also, if not foremost, to the fact that it turned a biblical story from the Old Testament into an allegory on the fate of the German nation. Thus, it was not in line with, even openly contradicted, the style of anti-Semitism preached by National Socialists.

Even those who criticized the play praised the performance highly. Alongside the excellent performance by the actors, in particular Eugen Kloepfer, it was Werner Egk's music that attracted the attention of the critics. It seems that it was uniquely able to function as a rhythmic link synchronizing the performers' action with the chorus, the dancers and dance groups as well as the movement chorus. It also served the function of structuring the performance. Thus, the overall impression was positive, although it was conceded that the group arrangements and organization of marches on and off by no means exceeded the devices developed and introduced by Reinhardt. However, the Reich Dramaturge, Rainer Schlösser, suggested that 'the extremely strong impression made by the first attempt seemed to guarantee that performances of this kind would be more attractive than any theoretical discussion no matter how well-meaning'.[2] The impression is created that Schlösser and other critics underestimated or consciously ignored the part played by ritual patterning and the religious atmosphere to which the biblical story contributed, which allowed for quasi-religious feelings that formed an important ingredient of the strong impact Schlösser mentions. Following Schlösser's statement, one could conclude that it was exclusively those devices known since the days of Reinhardt's new people's theatre that caused the strong impact: use of space, creation of a particular atmosphere – which in this case was also religious if not primarily so because of the story – and the rhythmical movement of dynamic and energetic bodies in and through the space – devices which the *Thingspiel* movement unashamedly stole from Reinhardt.

These were, in fact, the same devices as those that dominated the celebration of official holidays of the National Socialist state: Labour Day (1 May, which was already celebrated by the workers' movement), the anniversary of the storming of Annaberg (22 May), the summer solstice (24 June; also a pre-existing important holiday in the workers' movement), the *Reichsparteitag* (1 September), Harvest Thanksgiving (1 October), and the *Reichstrauertag der Partei* (Reich Party Memorial Day, 9 November). As soon as the *Thing* sites were finished, they would be the sites of celebration on these holidays. For the *Thing* sites were conceived as 'heart of the whole festive national politic and artistic life of the individual cities', where art and life were supposed to merge under the 'primacy of politics' (Schlösser 1935: 61).

Goebbels underlined how important it was for the National Socialist state to celebrate its holidays:

> The festivals, too, which this government celebrates with the people, have a deeper meaning. These are not festivals organised by the government at the expense of the people. Quite the contrary, they are festivals in which government and people

become one unity in order to demonstrate to the world that people and government no longer stand in opposition to each other, but that people and government have become one. This was also the idea of the great festivals which we celebrated, together in the past few months. [. . .] Our national self-confidence was resurrected in Potsdam. The idea of a social Volk Community was born of 1.5 million people at the Tempelhofer Feld on 1 May and the recovery of German honour rose above the Tannenberg Monument and united Germany raised its immortal head above the Nuremberg days.

(Goebbels 1933: 2)

Strikingly, the rhetoric of death and rebirth of the nation permeates the whole statement. It seems as if each of the festivals mentioned commemorated and celebrated the death and rebirth of the German people no matter what the official dedication of the particular holiday was. In fact this was the case, as the example of the Harvest Thanksgiving of the same year demonstrates. In Berlin, the festival was celebrated in the Grunewald stadium. Its climax was undoubtedly the speeches by Hitler and Goebbels, framed and punctuated by marching formations and flags. The celebration ended with the performance of Gustav Goes' play *Brot und Eisen* (*Bread and Iron*), written for performance in a stadium, i.e. as a mass spectacle. Under the title *Aufbricht Deutschland!* (*Germany Arise!*) the play was premiered on 13 May 1933 at the Potsdam Stadium. Up to 1935, there were more than 30 productions of the play, even at the newly erected *Thing* sites. Although the play was never given the generic title, *Thingspiel*, it follows exactly the same pattern as *German Passion 1933* and *The Play of Job the German*; the ritualistic pattern of death and rebirth of the German nation, beginning with World War I and ending with marching 'Storm Troopers of Young Germany' (SA, SS, League of Frontline Soldiers, Women's Union, League of Youths) (Goes 1933: 25). In many respects, the performance was exemplary of the new choral mass-spectacle, of the *Thingspiel*. It comprised masses of performers (2,000 in Berlin, 17,000 in Potsdam) and spectators (60,000). Its main devices were occupation of the space, creation of an atmosphere and the movement of dynamic and energetic bodies in and through space. As in the Russian mass spectacles, all three devices were so closely intertwined that it makes no sense to try and separate them. It was these devices that mainly contributed to the particular atmosphere. The dynamic movement of the masses as they occupied and filled the space, music and light were the most important atmospheric factors. Rhythm not only bound together movements of the bodies, light and music, but also worked upon the bodies of the spectators, allowing for very particular experiences to be made in the course of the performance. To further these aims, experiments were made with microphones and loudspeakers that were meant to reinforce the rhythm of the music and the spoken word. At the end, the performance showed how a community comes into being out of the self-organizing and self-organized movements of the 'Storm Troopers of Young Germany'. Moreover, it also succeeded in bringing forth a community of performers and spectators by allowing for and inducing very particular experiences. It was mainly the working of light and music, combined with the underlying ritual pattern that triggered quasi-religious feelings and established an emotional bond between all those present.

In this respect, the performance did not differ much from the Russian mass spectacles or from mass spectacles performed at social democratic festivals in the 1920s. In Leipzig, from 1920, the festivals of the Workers Union always included mass spectacles: *Spartacus*, in 1920; *Poor Konrad*, in 1921, a play on the Peasants' War; *Pictures from the French Revolution* by Ernst Toller in 1922; *War and Peace* by Toller in 1923 and *Awakening* by Toller and Adolf Winds in 1924. They were performed in cycling arenas, in Exhibition Halls and Fair Grounds, stadiums, amusement parks and so on. At the performance of *War and Peace*, one critic from the *Leipziger Volkszeitung* wrote:

> A large community needs, in order to be confident of itself, repeated demonstrations, communal celebrations, demonstrations of joyful events, of mourning, of commitment, of readiness to attack and defend things which have meaning to each and every member of the community. It is the task of art to clothe these moments of intense community spirit in moving expression [...] The mass-spectacle with speaking chorus is a significant beginning [...] perhaps it is already more than just the beginning.
>
> (*Leipziger Volkszeitung*, 14 August 1923)

Clearly, the festivals of the social democrats proceeded from the assumption that the participants already formed a community because of their common class interests and intentions. It was the purpose of the festival and, in particular of the mass spectacles, to confirm the sense of community, to renew the emotional bond between its members. This demanded a new kind of festival culture. It was regarded as part of a 'socialist development of emotion', that was opposed to the 'over-estimation of formal knowledge', so dominant in bourgeois culture:

> *Weltanschauung* grows out of instinct. Emotion is better than knowledge. It was feelings such as hate, revolt, and so on, which inspired most workers towards the socialist movement [. . .] Even will is first formed by an emotion. It is vital to awaken the will and strengthen and transform it into action.
>
> (Franken 1930: 39)

In 1932, the new proletarian festive culture initiated and propagated by the Social Democrats reached its climax with a series of new mass spectacles. Among them was the Festspiel *Wir!* (*Us!*) by Hendrik de Man. It was performed as part of the May Day celebrations in Frankfurt upon Main. The author expressly declared it to be a *Lehrstück* and, at the same time, a 'cult play'. Here, the new *Gefühlskultur* (culture of emotions) was supposed to integrate 'religious mass feelings' (de Man 1932: 3–5). Thus, the aims of the mass spectacle were best served by choruses (speaking, singing, moving), spotlight effects, music, dance and mass movement – that is to say by devices initiated by Reinhardt.

And the Reich Dramaturge Rainer Schlösser recommended exactly these devices for the development of the *Thingspiel* movement. However, there were significant differences between the festive performance of the socialist workers movement and the *Thingspiel* movement. While in the performances of the Social Democrats the participants shared unifying ideas, interests and social situations and in this sense formed a community that was confirmed by the event, it was the task of the *Thingspiel* plays to create and form a community out of members of different social classes and strata, a community of different interests and intentions which did not yet exist. Moreover, the socialist performances did not so much focus on the ritual motif of death/rebirth. Rather, they followed a structure of antagonist conflicts resulting from the class struggle. Whereas on the performative level, a number of affinities can be observed, on the semiotic and symbolic level the differences stand out clearly.

Schlösser returned to devices on the performative level. In a speech, 'On the People's Theatre of the Future', held in 1934 at the first conference of Otto Laubinger's 'Reich League' in Berlin, he listed them as follows:

> First, the oratorio, that is, a programme of choruses and individual speeches; second mimed allegory, *tableaux vivants*, consecration of flags, festive acts; third, processions and parades, festive processions, assemblies, and fourth, dance-ballet, free dance, gymnastics, sports events.
>
> (Schlösser 1935: 53)

Thus far, one could take this as a list of the elements of a pageant. As a 'connecting link' between these elements, Schlösser highlighted music. It was assumed that it could fulfil this function best through rhythm. Accordingly, rhythm became a leading artistic category. Thus, in Heidelberg 1935, when the *Thing* site Heiligenberge was inaugurated by a polyphonic, melodious male choir, this was sharply criticized by the spokesman of the *Thingspiel* movement:

> With shocking clarity, this has demonstrated that tremolo tenors letting off steam and psalmodizing cantatas will never, ever suit the National Socialist search for form. Their fundamental attitude is petit bourgeois and often somewhat reactionary, particularly when espousing patriotism. It comes close to defaming the whole National Socialist idea. The songs of the people nowadays are the marches and war songs of the street, the revolutionary fanfares of unity, not those of a liberal-individualist alehouse of vocal plurality.
>
> (Braumüller 1935a: 219)

Thus, it was sharply accentuated music that was regarded as suitable expression of the 'movement' – as, for instance, Carl Orff's music for the play *Olympic Youth*, performed as part of the opening ceremony of the Olympic Games in Berlin. This kind of music seemed particularly able to unite performers and spectators into a community and to confirm the feeling of community.

Despite the use of rhythmic music and chorus, there was still some concern that 'the musical and gestural effects' and even the most perfect 'choreography of dance' would be insufficient to unite performers and spectators into a community. Moreover, it would be unable to provoke the spectators into action. This seems to have been one concern the spokesman of the *Thingspiel* movement, who declared that he even wanted to activate the spectators physically, shared with Erwin Piscator, who strived to realize just this, particularly in his famous political revue *Trotz alledem!* (*Inspite of Everything!*). This was originally prepared as an open-air performance for the festival of the summer solstice in 1925, organized by the Workers Cultural Trust, and finally performed in Reinhardt's *Großes Schauspielhaus*. In order to also achieve this aim, Schlösser recommended both a 'preference for choral declamation and mass acting', and the idea of overpowering the spectators with action: 'action and more action [...] feats and more feats', which only the 'tale of the plot' could guarantee. It was only thought possible to activate the spectators when rhythmic movement, speech and music were combined with action. The passivity of the audience in the bourgeois theatre, repeatedly lamented by the avant-garde from Reinhardt to Meyerhold and Piscator, had to be overcome by devices that worked on the spectators' senses, overwhelming them and, thus, spurring them into action. As we have seen, many such devices had been invented by Reinhardt and, in the 1920s, by Piscator.

Thus it is small wonder that Goebbels very much wanted to win both stage directors for the *Thingspiel* movement. Reinhardt left Germany after his last Berlin production, Hugo von Hofmannsthal's *Salzburger Großes Welttheater*, which premiered on 1 March 1933 at the *Deutsches Theater*. The actor Werner Krauss was sent after him to offer him honorary Aryan status and to talk him into coming back. Reinhardt declined the offer, however. In 1935, Goebbels asked Edward Gordon Craig, on his departure for Moscow, to try and persuade Piscator to return to Germany and realize his idea of a political theatre within the framework of the *Thingspiel* movement.[3] Thus, it seems that at least Goebbels and, probably, others were aware of the continuity that linked the *Thingspiel* movement to Reinhardt's new people's theatre on the one side, and to Piscator's political theatre on the other, although publicly he claimed a total break.

Like Reinhardt and Piscator, Schlösser was convinced that he needed not only special scenic devices but also, if not foremost, a particular space if he was to activate spectators and create a community of performers and spectators. He defined the architecture of the *Thing* sites as 'the expression of the Volk Community' and its task was to enable its participants to share in 'the experience of a living community'.

In place of one-dimensional perception during a performance on a box-set stage with apron, there will be multidimensional perception. The great National Socialist meetings have triggered this movement; they have given the first example of the experience of a living community out of which the new cult spectacle can develop.

(Schlösser 1935: 37)

Only within the framework of this new space can the 'spectator be transformed into co-actor and the actor become one of the people (*Volksgenosse*)' (ibid.: 61).

Thus, it can be concluded that apart from the *Thing* sites yet to be erected, most of the elements recommended by Schlösser had been in use for quite a while already: not only in the performances of *Bread and Iron* and *The Play of Job the German*, but also in the mass spectacles by the Social Democrats in the 1920s.

In 1934, the first *Thing* sites were finished. On May Day, the *Thing* site in Brandberge near Halle was opened with a special ceremony, a so-called 'festive *Thing*' (Laubinger 1934: 26) and the *Thing* site in Heringsdorf opened with a cultic play. The opening of the *Thing* site in Stolzenau followed on 10 May, inaugurated by a performance of Goes' *Germany Arise!*. The 'real' inauguration of the *Thing* site Brandberge took place a month later. On 5 June 1934, Kurt Heynicke's Thingspiel *Neurode. Ein Spiel von deutscher Arbeit* (*Neurode. A Drama on German Labour*) was performed by the *Mitteldeutsche Spielgemeinschaft*. This play was clearly different from the preceding plays that adopted the ritualistic pattern of the death/fragmentation and rebirth of the German nation. Instead, it presented the transformation of individuals into members of a community, a *Volk* Community.

In the foreword to the published version, the author claims that the action of the play refers to a historical event:

> In Neurode in Silesia, long before 1933, National Socialist Labour ideology and Volk Community already existed. Disregarding their personal needs, some miners, workers, and employees joined together voluntarily to maintain a mine that had long begun to crumble – in order to save an important industrial building as part of their heritage. A large proportion of the population supported the enterprise by founding a working community.
>
> (Heynicke 1935: 5; translated by Jo Riley)

The performance opened with choruses and performers marching through the auditorium towards the playing field, singing:

One: Stand at the ready!
All: Stand at the ready!
One: Take up positions!
All: Take up position, workers!
One: Close the ranks!
All: Close the ranks!
Across all Germany.
Where one sows the young seed,
Another mows the ripened corn,
Another drives the wheel and piston,
Another hammers, another writes –
The man of heavy brow, the man of great fists
Arise when the oath resounds so clear:
Even if the path is stony,
And we must climb the mountain,
We are forever one,
All Germany marches as one!

(Ibid.: 9)

Thus, from the beginning, the song conjures up the *Volk* Community as a classless community that comes into being through common labour. When the performers reached the 'stage', the play on the impending closure of the mine unfolded. The consortium of mine owners insists on closing down the mine since it is no longer profitable. The mineworkers, in their turn, insist on their right to work. Supported by the director of the mine and the mayor, they decide to found a working community in order to secure the mainte-nance of the mine; to which everyone, regardless of social class sub-scribes a sum of money: 'all – bureaucrats, bourgeoisie, workers' (ibid.: 44).

Consortium Syndicate:
I don't understand. All I see is that something unexpected is happening. Then someone says the word: Faith! And it becomes a mighty power! Then someone mentions the word home – and everyone makes sacrifices, freely and with joy. I don't under-stand! The world has changed!
(Exits)

First Leader of the Chorus:
The world has changed.
Great things have happened here.

A community has come about,
A new understanding
has taken hold of people.

Chorus: ·
Strength will never be consumed by nothingness,
As long as community embraces us.
People, you are faith itself.
People, you are victory itself.

(Ibid.: 47)

The performance ended after three hours with 1,000 performers marching up, holding flags and singing the song from the beginning and, finally, the audience joined in with the Horst Wessel Song.

The community represented here was, in fact, a classless community, conjured up by the opening and closing song. It came into being as a self-organizing and self-organized community. Certainly, there were two individuals who stood out in some way. One was Radke, the return emigrate mineworker, who arrived the very day his brother was killed by an accident in the mine. Insisting on the workers' right to work, it is he who provokes the common decision to found the working community. The other individual was the Stranger, the representative and deputy of 'new Germany' who contributes precisely the sum needed by the workers, citizens etc., to acquire the mine for themselves at auction. However, neither individual acts as leader of the community. As a member of the community, Radke triggers the process of self-organization and the Stranger contributes to it by including himself into this self-organizing and self-organized community. The community that had come into being here stands for Germany, for the whole *Volk* Community. Thus, the *Volk* Community as it was conceived here can be regarded as a classless community that comes into existence because of the sacrifice each and everybody is willing to make for the common cause. It is the recovery of the homeland, the rebirth of the nation which demands and is worthy of such sacrifices. The community that comes into being on this basis is a community that organizes itself. On the one hand, it was presented as an ideal community with which to identify. The assembled audience – also composed of members of all social groups, classes and strata – was called upon to do so. On the other, it was expected that the performance would bring forth a community of performers and spectators as an ideal community by allowing for and triggering the living experience of such a community. Whether this actually happened is doubtful. The reviews which praised the general tendency of the play nonetheless criticized the lack of dynamic and demanded that the 'Tempo [...] must be increased [...] the people must be moved faster' (Deutsche Bühnenkorrespondenz 1934 cited in Stommer 1985: 73), and complained that the choruses did not move in the space after they had taken up their positions on the play area – which marked an important difference not only from Reinhardt's choruses but also from those in the Social Democrats' performances. Thus one can conclude that the occupation of space was static, not dynamic, and that the bodies of individual performers moving in and through the space were neither dynamic nor energetic, so that any energy that did circulate in the space was not transferred to the spectators and could not energize them. Thus, a living experience of a community or the experience of a living community could not emerge. An ideal classless community was shown on stage, it is true. However, a corresponding community of performers and spectators could hardly come into being.

This problem also arose in other performances of *Thingspiel* plays in 1934. At the premiere of *German Passion 1933* in the courtyard of the Heidelberg Palace, this deficiency was still attributed to the lack of an appropriate space, a *Thing* site:

> This new element that the name Thingspiel carries [...] is so powerful and so real, so earthbound, that it demands a special place for its realisation more than ever before. This new place can only be the Thing site [...] If this work is presented in a different place [...] we are shaken by the powerful effect of the 'piece' without being moved by the gripping sense of community spirit among all who participate.
>
> (G. Röhrdanz 1934, 'Deutsche Passion 1933',
> in *Der Führer* 207, 30 July 1934)

However, when the play was performed on the *Thing* site Brandberge in August 1934, the living experience of a community of performers and actors still seems not to have come into being. 'A tentative search for new forms of community spirit, which the proposed architectural frame, despite a design of true maturity and artistic inspiration, can only fill temporarily' (Liskowsky 1934: 1–2). Despite the critique of the immobility of the choruses in *Neurode*, here again they were arranged 'as a solid, intractable wall' (Dürre

1933/34: 282), so that they were unable to mobilize any energy in the spectators.

Regardless of whether a community of actors and spectators came into being in and through the performances, the concept of community underlying *Neurode, German Passion 1933* and other *Thingspiel* plays is rather ambiguous – in particular when comparing it with the concept of *Volk* Community officially heralded by the National Socialists. Since World War I, parties of various political and ideological backgrounds used the term *Volk* Community. It was the Nazis who introduced a particular nuance to it.

In the *Thingspiel* plays, as we have seen, a community was re/presented by a performance that is self-organizing and self-organized. In this respect it can be equated to the community re/presented in the Russian mass spectacles. The community comes into being because the people make sacrifices and join forces in common labour. This marks an important difference. For in the Russian mass spectacles the sacrifices made by the people were offered for their self-liberation. Another significant difference refers to the criteria of in- and exclusion. In the Russian mass spectacles the community that was re/presented – as well as brought forth between performers and spectators – was the community of the former oppressed, now liberated, workers and peasants. This is what created and guaranteed their new collective identity. In the *Thingspiel* plays, on the contrary, the community was conceived as comprising people from all social classes, groups and strata belonging to one nation and, in this sense, as a 'classless' community – moreover, as a community comprising not only the living but also the dead. In Reinhardt's new people's theatre, the spectators had come from all social classes, groups and strata; and a community came into being out of performers and spectators in the course of the performance in the sense of a 'classless' community. It was conceived as temporary, ephemeral, unable to bring forth any kind of collective identity. In the *Thingspiel* plays, on the contrary, this community was supposed to bring forth and confirm the collective identity as a national identity defined by the desire for unity and sacrifice for the sake of common labour, for the fatherland. But whereas the early *Thingspiel* plays seemed to proceed from a vague, rather inclusive concept of *Volk* Community (although in the second act of *German Passion 1933*, when the unknown warrior returns to his people he is confronted with polemics against 'visionaries and scribes/criminals and democrats/Jews and pacifists/Marxists and crimson Christians' [in German: 'Himbeerchristen'] (Euringer

1936: 17)), later plays such as Kurt Heynicke's *Der Weg ins Reich* (*Road to the Reich*, 1935) in this respect, and in accordance with the official Nazi concept, openly excluded non-Germans (Jews, Roma, Sinti) and 'un-Germans' (communists, homosexuals, libertines etc.). This seems to indicate that by this time, the liminal period had already come to an end. However, the working of the autopoietic feedback loop, explained in the last chapter, made performances of even this play seem unpredictable to a certain extent. The audience response could not be completely planned, controlled or even foreseen. The direction of the feedback loop, therefore, was somewhat contingent and unpredictable. This is why it was so difficult to exploit the performance of the *Thingsspiel* plays for manipulative purposes.

The concept of community underlying the early *Thingspiel* plays was in any case not quite in line with the National Socialist concept of *Volk* Community. This meant the unity of all people in a social order that would allegedly be free of class conflicts on a national and racial basis. The concept of *Volk* Community was realized in the Third Reich by and in a social order that was to overcome the class conflicts caused by capitalism. In place of the democratic principle of equality and majority, a *Führer* Principle was installed. The social rank of an individual should no longer be determined by work status, education, fortune, by ownership of property, or means of production, but by accepting natural inequality amongst men which leads to a natural division into a *'Führer'* and the *'Gefolgschaft'* (followers), the leader and the led. The relationship between them was regarded as being defined by consanguinity and moral responsibility – which meant that the followers owed loyalty to the *Führer* and found comradeship with each other as his followers. Moreover, from the very beginning, the concept radically excluded all non-Germans and un-Germans, in particular Jews and political enemies.

It cannot be overlooked that the concept of community underlying the *Thingspiel* plays deviated from the official concept of *Volk* Community in one striking respect. The *Thingspiel* plays presupposed the community was self-organizing and self-organized, as a community that can do without a leader. The *Führer* principle was ignored. Moreover, the early *Thingspiel* plays even missed clear criteria for exclusion from the *Volk* Community. This might be one of the reasons for the rather short life of the *Thingspiel* movement, as will be explained later.

In 1934, however, the *Thingspiel* movement was at its peak. By the end of the year, the *Thing* sites at Halle, Heringsdorf, Holzminden, Jülich, Schmiedeberg and Stolzenau were already in use and approximately twenty others were under construction. Six or seven *Spiel-gemeinschaften* were producing for the finished *Thing* sites; they performed at the ritual first cutting of the sod for a new *Thing* site as well as at temporary sites. The list of officially accepted *Thingspiel* plays was not long – by August 1934 it only included eight plays, of which four were not even performed in 1934; however, other plays were performed. In 1935, nine *Thing* sites were finished and inaugurated and another six dramas were added to the list of officially acclaimed *Thingspiel* plays. Thus, it seemed that the *Thingspiel* movement was well on its way.

In 1935, a particular highlight was anticipated: the completion and inauguration of the *Thing* site Heiligenberge near Heidelberg. The inauguration took place on 22 June at a celebration of the summer solstice. And Kurt Heynicke's play *Der Weg ins Reich* (*Road to the Reich*) was performed at the Heidelberg *Reichsfestspiele* of the same year on the *Thing* site. In some respects, the play followed the model set by *Neurode*, i.e. it presented the transformation of different kinds of individuals into members of a *Volk* Community, but this time clearly excluding others. Lothar Müthel directed the performance and Werner Pleister was in charge of sound control. Professional actors even performed in the choruses. Although everything was done to secure success, the performance – as indeed the solstice celebration – was unable to meet the high expectations associated with it. One critic, however, conceded that the performance came close to such expectations:

> The form of the *Thingspiel* is still quite problematic. These events must find a link between the national political life of the Volk and art; they must make the work of art carry the concept, must clothe National Socialist ideology in an artistic form. Only from this can the collective nature of the experience grow which binds actor and spectator into one community. With 'The Road to the Reich', Kurt Heynicke has come exceptionally close to this ideal form and has developed far beyond his 'Neurode'.
>
> (*Münchner neueste Nachrichten*, 22 July 1935)

It seems that this critic very much approved the coming into being of an exclusive community on stage.

Even Wolf Braumüller, a *Thingspiel* expert from the Rosenberg fraction which fundamentally opposed the *Thingspiel* movement as too Christian, too Catholic, admitted:

For the first time since the National Socialist revolution, a truly pioneering attempt and venture towards the future shape of the *Thingspiel* has happened at the *Thing* site at Heiligenberg. A declaration of belief in a certain Weltanschauung has been attempted, carried out and found success, i.e. has made a lasting impression.

(Braumüller 1935b: 2)

Though planned as the climax to the *Thingspiel* movement, however, it actually seems to have been the beginning of its end. Goebbels complained afterwards that there were no playwrights, 'who possess sufficient visionary powers to pour the emotion of our time into a dramatic form' (Goebbels 1935: 11). Thus, the lack of 'good' plays was blamed for the disappointment. But as at least some of the mass spectacles of the social democratic festivals in the 1920s and the Russian mass spectacles show, a 'good' play is not necessarily needed to create an effective performance which can unite actors and spectators into a community and establish or confirm their collective identity (even the proletarian mass-spectacles in the 1920s had not all been really successful).[4] It was the firm National Socialist belief in the power of the word that led them to distrust performative means not guided and controlled by the word. Since, as the critic of the *Münchner neueste Nachrichten* put it with regard to Heynicke's play, a 'work of art' was assumed to 'carry the concept' and the National Socialists believed this could only be accomplished by the power of the word in theatrical form,[5] therefore words were regarded as the most important element of the performance. Words were supposed to attribute an unequivocal meaning to the performative means through which the community was represented and created.

In September 1935, Goebbels' Ministry decreed the liquidation of the *Spielgemeinschaften*. Otto Laubinger had fiercely protested against such a step, but being severely ill, he could easily be overruled. He died at the end of October. A few days before his death on 23 October, further use of the term *Thing* was significantly restricted by the Ministry of Propaganda:

The Ministry of Reich Propaganda has been given orders from on high that from this moment, any such terms as *Thing*, or *Thing* site may no longer be brought into conjunction with the Party, Party political events or state enterprises. Nor may National Socialist ideology be tainted by connection with such terms as 'cult'. The various *Thing* sites such as Heidelberg, Stedingsehre and so on will be forthwith described as 'open air theatres' until such time as a new linguistic rule has been found.

(Bundesarchiv Koblenz Zsg 101/6: 153–4; cited in Kloss 1981: 75)

In 1936, the *Thing* sites were used for rallies, celebration of the summer solstice, consecration of flags and the like. Apart from a performance of Euringer's *German Passion 1933* in January on the anniversary of the seizure of power – and, of course, the performance of Eberhard Wolfgang Möller's *Frankenburger Würfelspiel* (*The Frankenburg Dice Game*) on the Dietrich-Eckart Stage in Berlin at the Olympic Games – there were no performances of *Thingspiel* plays in the year 1936. Nonetheless, some new *Thing* sites were completed.

In May 1936, Goebbels decreed a prohibition of the *Sprechchor* (speaking chorus), i.e. the main artistic means of the *Thingspiel* plays. From the beginning of the *Thingspiel* movement, the chorus had been regarded as the embodiment of the *Volk* Community; its task was to bring forth and confirm the sense of community. This happened, as we have seen, on an egalitarian basis through the self-organization of the community. Now it was stated:

It is unnatural that an important philosophy of life, a major concept, can be thought through in a chorus. Only one inspired individual, can have such thoughts; thus one individual must voice them [...] This structure shapes the organisation of our new State, our constitution. Well written drama and festival events must therefore necessarily follow the same structure.

(Bauer 1935/36: 244–8)

While the chorus embodied the *Volk* Community as a self-organized community to which each and any member contributes as an embodied mind, the *Führer* Principle meant that the *Führer* alone was the mind and his followers formed the body that executed the intentions of the mind. The *Führer* was conceived as the mind of the *Volk* Community and his followers its body.

However, it was not only the National Socialist government that caused the *Thingspiel* movement to end. It was also the waning enthusiasm of those who had hoped to bring about a cultural revolution through a revolution in theatre – a cultural revolution that would accomplish a rebirth of the nation. That is to say that both parties, those who launched the *Thingspiel* movement as a means of cultural revolution as well as those who usurped and monopolized it for their cultural politics, were no longer sufficiently supportive of it, if at all.

What were the reasons for such a development?

Let us begin with the initiators. Within the National Socialist Party, it was particularly sections of the Hitler Youth and the SA who demanded a 'completion of the National Socialist revolution' and who wanted to build up a genuinely 'Fascist culture'. They regarded the *Thingspiel* movement as an adequate means to realize their goals. A decisive blow was landed against these revolutionary inclined forces, in particular the SA, after the alleged *Röhmputsch* in June 1934. It signalled quite clearly that such tendencies would no longer be tolerated. There would be no such thing as the awaited cultural revolution. The liminal times of national revolution, which had nourished these hopes, were definitely over.

This was also understood in nationally minded circles in the course of the year 1934 – as a letter from Gottfried Benn on 24 November 1934 to F.W. Oelze demonstrates[6] – and at the latest by the end of 1935. In September 1935, the Nuremberg Laws were passed. They decreed that Jews could no longer obtain citizenship in the Reich, nor any province or town, nor were they allowed to marry 'Aryans'. That is to say that Jews were to be excluded legally from the *Volk* Community. More than anything else, such laws made it clear that the liminal times which people believed followed the seizure of power by the Nazis, were over – if they had existed at all. For already in April 1933, the 'Aryan Paragraph' which excluded 'non-Aryans' from the civil service – whether as professors, judges, teachers, police officers, tram drivers or anything else – had been issued. There was no liminal time when everything is in transformation, everything seems possible. It was not festivals, celebrations, or *Thingspiel* performances that were able to bring about a community, to establish a new order. They only pretended to allow for that. In fact, it was the new laws being passed by the National Socialist government from the very beginning that defined who belonged to the *Volk* Community and established its new order. When people understood that the liminal times were over directly after the *Röhmputsch* in 1934 or maybe even later in 1935, when the Nuremberg Laws were decreed, or even worse, that there never had been liminal times, their enthusiasm for the *Thingspiel* movement, which was a typical offspring of revolutionary liminal times, waned.

The National Socialist government had quite different reasons to withdraw its support from the *Thingspiel* movement. Since an official explanation was never given and the *Thingspiel* movement was never openly suppressed but rather allowed to whither by withholding permission for the performance of *Thingspiel* plays on the *Thing* sites, we can only guess what the actual reasons might have been. To this end, it seems promising to compare the performance of *Thingspiel* plays to other National Socialist cultural performances which were taking place on a regular basis – as, for instance, the celebration of the summer solstice 24 June, the *Reichsparteitag* on 1 October, the Reich Party Memorial Day on 9 November – in order to find out why the *Thingspiel* movement was no longer in the Government's favour.

The Reich Party Memorial Day (*Reichstrauertag der Partei*) was held from 1933 to 1939 on a very large scale, though during the war years on a smaller one. It was a festival that celebrated and re-enacted the heroic myth of the founding of the Third Reich. In 1923, on 9 November – the anniversary of the proclamation of the Weimar Republic in 1918 – National Socialist agitators marched through the centre of Munich in order to propagate and spark off a Putsch. The police finally succeeded in putting them down at the Feldherrnhalle – at the cost of some bloodshed: sixteen rebels were killed.

On the eve of Memorial Day, Hitler held a commemorative speech that was broadcast all over the Reich. In it, he explained the meaning of the anniversary. He expressly interpreted the blood that was shed as 'The baptism water of the Third Reich' (in Hitler's commemorative speech on 8 November 1934, cited in Domarus 1965: 458).[7] The celebration was meant to re-enact the Passion and the death of the 'movement' in 1923 as well as its rebirth in and as the Third Reich. The allusions to Christian mythology should not to be ignored. The *Völkische Beobachter* even went so far as to call the celebration a divine service.

Thus, before the celebrations for Memorial Day had even began, its overall meaning was secured – this was the framework and context in which to perceive, interpret, understand and experience the single actions, the performative means of this ritual of commemorating the dead.

The celebrations started with a National Socialist procession that re-enacted the march of 1923. Carrying the 'blood banner' of 1923, the procession moved in silence through the same streets taken by the agitators. The streets were decorated in a way that suggested that this was the *via dolorosa* of the National Socialist movement. Columns were erected on both sides of the streets, symbolizing all the dead heroes of the Party throughout the battle. As the *Völkische Beobachter* from 9 November 1935 explained: 'Here they appear again before us in heroic transfiguration and create a silent guard of honour'. In this way, the procession was shown to be the 'offering of the movement' (*Völkischer Beobachter*, 19 November 1933).[8] The columns were of brownish red colour, bearing the inscription 'Roll Call!' in golden letters, and underneath the names of the dead. A censer with a 'sacrificial flame' was placed on top. From above, the *via dolorosa* was marked off as a sacred space by huge flags displaying the swastika. When the avant-garde of the procession, i.e. the carriers of the 'blood banner' and, at its head, the *Führer*, reached each pair of columns, the names of the 'martyrs' of the Party resounded from a loudspeaker. Drum rolls and drumbeats accompanying the calling of the names accentuated the rhythm of the procession. At a solemn speed, the Horst Wessel Song was heard emanating from the loudspeakers, accompanied by the *Marsch der Alten Kämpfer* (Old Campaigners' March) and reminded the participants that the dead, even if invisible, were joining the march of their surviving comrades.

The procession came to a halt in front of the Feldherrnhalle, at the sacred site where the martyrs of the movement had shed their blood, at the 'altar', as the steps of the Feldherrnhalle were also called. Here, sixteen shots were fired. Hitler alone went into the Feldherrnhalle, where the coffins of the martyrs were put on a bier. He laid a wreath as an offering and stood in 'silent dialogue' with the heroes. Meanwhile, the melody of 'Gute Kameraden' (Good Comrades) rang out.

After commemorating and honouring the dead in this way, the 'sacrificial procession' was transformed into a 'triumphant procession'. It went through the Siegestor and through a 'forest of flags' to the newly erected temples to the victims of the Putsch. Now, the procession was accompanied by the national anthem resounding out from the loudspeakers. This 'triumphant procession' re-enacted the victorious march through the Brandenburg Gate in Berlin on 30 January 1933, i.e. the day the Nazis seized power. When the triumphant procession left the Feldherrnhalle some high-ranking officers of the *Wehrmacht* also joined in, thus re-enacting the reconciliation between former opponents of 1923. The 'culprits' and 'traitors' of 1923 now participated in the honouring of 'their' victims. As Hitler explained in his speech:

> Ten years have gone by and it is the greatest joy for me today, that the hope from those days has now been fulfilled, that we stand here together. The representatives of the Army, and

members of our Volk have become united, and this unity shall never be broken again in Germany. In this, our first blood sacrifice receives justification; it was not shed in vain. For, we marched together towards something which has finally become reality today.

(cited in Domarus 1965: 328)

The end of the procession was the Königsplatz, where the ritual performed at the Feldherrnhalle was repeated. The celebration continued with a particular initiation rite in which members of the Hitler Youth were admitted to the Party or the SA, symbolically stepping into the shoes of the dead heroes.[9] It ended with the guard of honour marching in front of the temples erected for the dead, who in their turn, acted as guards themselves: 'They are not dead to us, and these temples are not vaults, but they are two guard houses and they shall guard Germany here, guard our Volk' (quoted from the propaganda movie 'Eternal Guard' from 1936, cited in Behrenbeck 1998: 51). The celebration was broadcast and recorded for the Weekly News to be shown in cinemas so that, in principle, the whole nation was able to participate in it.

At first glance, the affinities between the commemorative ritual and *Thingspiel* plays such as *German Passion 1933*, *The Play of Job the German*, or *Germany Arise!* etc. seem striking. The ritual pattern of death and rebirth is obvious; the allusions to, even borrowings from Christian mythology and Catholic liturgy cannot be overlooked – they are so blatant. The ritual was, in fact, understood as a religious act by its organizers and this is proven in the following utterance from a publication intended for members of the Party only:

The Memorial CELEBRATIONS on 9 November [...] took place in the context of a sacred ritual firmly anchored in German religious feeling [...] It expressed the ancient German IDEA OF ETERNAL RENEWAL OF THE GODHEAD in the sense of something between memorial for the dead and the dutiful promise of youth in a very effective way. The uncomplaining nature of these heroic celebrations and the idea of the 'eternal guard' underline the Nordic spirit, whose model is not a lazy and cowardly peace in the beyond with Hallelujah and waving palm fronds, but THE ETERNALLY RENEWING MOTIVATION TO JOYFUL BATTLE FOR THE HIGH AIMS WHICH WE DRAW FROM THE GODLY SOURCE WITHIN OURSELVES [...] The Volk will, consciously or unconsciously, be more willing to follow this direction if we speak to them in the language of our times [...] rather than trying to grab their attention with some tasteless piece of theatre magic.

(Dürr 1935, cited in Behrenbeck 1998: 51–2)

In the light of this statement from December 1935, it seems hardly plausible that usage of the terms *Thing* and *Thing* site were forbidden in the context of the Party, party-political events or State enterprises simply because terms like 'cult' and 'cultic' could not be applied to the National Socialist *Weltanschauung*. What happened here was evidently a kind of religious ritual so that the reproach that the *Thingspiel* plays bordered on cult or the cultic cannot seriously be taken as an argument to be used for discrediting them in the eyes of the Government.

As the comparison with the celebration of the Memorial Day suggests, rather the opposite assumption seems to make sense. The celebration of new official holidays followed well-known ritual patterns, mostly Christian-Catholic, but also those of civil and military ceremonies. In this way, they were able to serve the religious needs of the people, to arouse quasi-religious feelings in them towards the *Führer* and the Fatherland and to unite the *Volk* in a kind of religious congregation.

We have seen that the *Thingspiel* plays also unfolded the potential to evoke quasi-religious feelings in the spectators and to unite actors and spectators into a community. What makes the decisive difference, however, is that here those feelings were directed towards the nation, towards the Fatherland and not to the *Führer*. The new religion of the National Socialist state – to use Durkheim's words – was a religion based on and celebrating a particular relationship between the *Führer* and his followers. As the description of the commemorative ritual shows, the National Socialist community, as the model and ideal of the *Volk* Community, was constituted by this particular relationship. The *Führer* appeared as the mind of the *Volk* Community and his followers as its body. That is to say that it was organized according to the *Führer* principle. He not only leads the march and directs others towards the future, but he is also the only one to establish a link between the living and the dead, to incorporate the dead into the *Volk* Community and to secure their blessings for the community by presenting offerings and holding a silent dialogue with them, thus linking the movement/nation's past to its present and future.

Since the *Thingspiel* plays represented and partly brought forth a self-organizing and self-organized community, they did not serve the confession of the new religion, even if they spread faith in the rebirth of the nation and brought a quasi-religious community into being. However, the myth they re-enacted involved not the National Socialist Party and its *Führer* as someone who brought about the rebirth, but rather it came about through the will of the people of one nation to common labour and unity. Thus, they were not suited as rituals of the new religion. Its rituals and ceremonies were the celebrations of the new official holidays, in particular May Day, the Summer Solstice, the *Reichsparteitag*, the Harvest Thanksgiving and the Reich Party Memorial Day. The community enacted and brought forth by them did not recognize any conflicts between itself and its individual members, because all were equal as followers of the *Führer*. They formed the body of the *Volk* Community by serving different functions in a way and to a purpose foreseen and intended by the *Führer*, its mind. While it was forbidden to have the *Führer* represented on stage by an actor, in the celebrations of the official holidays the *Führer* himself took the leading part. He acted his own role. And he played it in such a way – supported by modern technology – that he appeared as the incorporation of Light in defeat of Darkness, as can be gathered from Leni Riefenstahl's propaganda film on the *Reichsparteitag* from 1934, *Triumph des Willens* (*Triumph of the Will*). Thus, it was these celebrations which were much better suited to the purpose of representing and bringing forth the *Volk* Community in the sense of the National Socialists, i.e. as a community composed according to the *Führer* principle, than the *Thingspiel* plays could ever be.

In this respect, there was an enormous difference between the *Thingspiel* plays and other genres of National Socialist cultural performances. Thus, it is small wonder that the government withdrew its support. That is not to say that it allowed the *Thingspiel* movement to die at the end of 1935. Rather, it let it survive as a weakly flickering flame that was supposed to blaze up once more before dying away slowly. Such a blaze was planned for the Olympic Games.

Since the National Socialists did not believe in any kind of internationalism they were at first strongly opposed to the idea of holding the Olympic Games in Berlin. But they soon understood that the Games would grant them a unique opportunity to present Nazi Germany as the legitimate heir and actual successor of Ancient Greece. Such a view of Germany was supposed to emerge in the ceremony of igniting the Olympic flame in the sacred precinct of Ancient Olympia and by constructing the *Reichssportfeld* according to the

topography of Ancient Olympia.[10] The planned cultural programme
was also meant to contribute to it.[11] The *Oresteia* was performed at the
Staatliches Schauspielhaus, directed by Lothar Müthel, and starring
Hermine Körner as Clytemnestra, Hans Georg Laubenthal as Orestes
and Pamela Wedekind as Electra. In the programme notes parallels
were drawn between Greek monuments and those of the Nazis. The
Theatre of Dionysus was shown side by side with the newly finished
Thing site adjacent to the *Reichssportfeld*, the Dietrich-Eckart Stage and
Greek statues from the archaic and early classic period were juxta-
posed to the monumental sculptures on the *Reichssportfeld*. In this
way, it was insinuated that the arts in Nazi Germany followed Greek
models that they even could rival; that the *Thingspiel* movement could
be regarded as a modern version of ancient Greek tragic theatre.

As an early climax to the cultural programme, on 2 August, i.e. on
the day following the opening ceremony, Wolfgang Eberhard
Möller's *Das Frankenburger Würfelspiel* (*The Frankenburg Game of Dice*)
was performed on the Dietrich-Eckart Stage. It was a new *Thingspiel*
commissioned for this very purpose by Goebbels. That is to say, right
from the first preparations it was clear that this play was to be performed before an international audience and that the performance
had to demonstrate that a new theatrical genre had been invented
which met the demands of a totally new theatre – a choric theatre
like the Greek theatre, a theatre without an apron that was able to
unite actors and performers into a community again. Considering
the occasion on which the performance was to be held, it was understood as a matter of fact that such a community, if it should actually
come into being would not, under any circumstances, be the *Volk*
Community.

The Frankenburg Game of Dice, in fact, differs from the previous
Thingspiel plays – from those re-enacting the ritual pattern of death
and rebirth of the German nation as well as from those enacting the
transformation of individual people into members of a community,
of a *Volk* Community. The play is a historic play. The historical game
of dice took place on 15 May 1625 on the Haushamer Field near
Frankenburg/Austria. Rise to it was given by the resistance of the
Protestant peasants to the measures taken by the governor of Upper
Austria, Count Herbersdorf, himself a former Protestant, to return
the province to the old faith. Protestant teachers and priests were
expatriated. In May 1625, a Catholic priest was assigned to Frankenburg. The peasants beat him and chased him away. By order of the
Austrian representative, Count Khevenmüller promised the peasants
that no Catholic priest would be assigned and that they would not be

punished. On 14 May, however, Count Herbersdorf marched with 650 soldiers, three canons and the hangman and summoned the peasants to the Haushamer Field the next day under threat of seizure of their property and of leading away the women and children. First, he talked to thousands of unarmed peasants about the Grace and the rites of the Catholic Church and demanded that the ringleaders be handed over. Since no one appeared, he had 36 peasants selected at random. He commanded them to play a game of dice in pairs on a black coat spread on the soil, one against the other. The winner was free, the loser was hanged immediately. Later, the corpses were transferred to the church towers of Frankenburg, Vöcklamarkt and Neukirchen. After three days, they were impaled at the roadside. This act of violence caused a revolt among the peasants, the last peasants' war. The army of the peasants was completely wiped out. Between 3,000 and 7,000 peasants were killed. The end of the resistance cleared the way for the reintroduction of the Catholic faith in Upper Austria.

Möller's play re-enacted this event as part of a tribunal. Using the architecture of the Dietrich-Eckart Stage, three different levels were played. The Judges were seated on the top level; the plaintiffs and the defendants: the Emperor, his Advisors and Maximilian of Bavaria stood on the middle level; and the re-enactment involving Herbersdorf, the peasants and mercenaries unfolded on the lowest level.

The play opened with a 'Prologue', a kind of introduction: 'listen to this play which is a play and a tribunal' (Möller 1974: 339), followed by the indictment of the plaintiffs against the Emperor for the crime committed against the people of Upper Austria:

> We sue Ferdinand the Second
> The emperor of Austria and the empire,
> Who seemed to serve God, but actually serves
> The Devil, who has stolen the best strengths
> Of the empire in his hatred, murder and arson
> These thirty dreadful years. We sue
> The emperor for never bringing peace
> And insatiably abusing the trust of the people,
> The honesty of the peasants and the courage
> Of the leaders, and violating the land.
> (Ibid.: 341; translated by Jo Riley)

In order to clarify the case, the Judges demand a visit to the scene – and the events of the past are replayed. Fanfares and storm warnings are sounded and tumult breaks out on the lowest level. The dead peasants rise out of their graves and the past events unfold. When half of the 36 peasants have forfeited their lives, the peasants revolt in outrage:

> Give us our dead who have gone before
> Back to us!
> We are no longer beggars and children
> We are a new people, a new army,
> And beware to any who betrays us.
> We are one will and one cry,
> And no temptation can divide us.
> We will liberate ourselves
> In God's name from all slavery,
> From all yokes and tyranny.
>
> (Ibid.: 373)

When Herbersdorf calls for the hangman, a figure dressed in black armour appears instead. He demands that the Emperor, his advisors, Maximilian and Herbersdorf play a game of dice for their lives. The worst result is the Emperor's, the best Herbersdorf's. However, the figure in black armour threatens them all with 'infinity'. Now the Judges pronounce their sentences. They damn them all into eternity.

The play ends with a hymn sung by the chorus. The same hymn has been repeated over and over again since the first appearance of the peasants – and by the peasants:

> *Chorus* (from above):
>   O God how marvellous thou art.
> *Peasants* (withdrawing)
>   You send the storms
>   And break the towers
>   Of false tyranny
> *Chorus*
>   You offer your blood to the people.
> *Peasants*
>   And come to those in distress,
>   The downcast,
>   And raise them up again.
> *Chorus*
>   And die for us, so that we should live.
>
> (Ibid.: 376)

The play can undoubtedly be regarded as a kind of religious play, albeit an ambiguous one. Möller himself named the *Oresteia*, the medieval *Ludus de Antichristo* (Play on the Anti-Christ) and other mystery plays as models that he followed. The allusions to medieval Weltgerichtsspiele (Plays of the Last Judgement) are obvious. It is quite probable that the performance did evoke religious feelings in the spectators, in particular in those of Christian faith or, at least, familiar with the Christian religion, who probably formed the majority of the audience. It was principally the oft-repeated hymn 'O God how marvellous thou art...!' which triggered or, at least, contributed to quasi-religious feelings.

The performance was directed by Matthias Wiemann (who also played the part of the figure in black armour) and Werner Pleister (who directed the *Ludus de Antichristo* in Berlin 1932). The choruses were composed by Carl Orff and Werner Egk. In order not to get lost in the vast space of the Dietrich-Eckart Stage, the performers wore buskins and padded, exaggerated costumes.

According to Möller's own assessment, which is not necessarily reliable, the unity of performers and spectators did actually come into being:

> It was one of the greatest experiences I have ever had in my life when Count Herbersdorf, played by Alexander Golling, paced the whole orchestra below when the chorus accused him, passing by the spectators in the round and shouting up: 'Who says that? Who dares to give warning? Who frightens my sheep?'. It was a breathtaking moment; 20,000 people literally stopped breathing. Simply this confrontation between the spectators and the actor; it was something never seen before in theatre. The unity of the theatrical process in the sense of Greek theatre was recreated for the first time ever. The people participated directly, and the actors spoke [...] directly to the spectators.
>
> (cited in Rühle 1977: 193)[12]

It seems that the critic of the *Berliner Tageblatt* did not share this experience. He writes:

> At this first performance, perhaps the audience was simply 'audience', rather than a homogeneous mass with the performers feeling directly addressed by each word. However, this kind of

communication is one of the essential prerequisites of this kind of performance and of such an ultimately political theatre.

(E. Pfeiffer-Belli, 'Das Frankenburger Würfelspiel', in *Berliner Tageblatt*, 3 August 1936)

Thus, it is hard, if not impossible, to decide whether the performance succeeded in uniting performers and spectators into a community and establishing an emotional bond between the participants or not.

Perusing the reviews, one has to state that the critics judged the play and the performance very differently. Even among the National Socialists there was little agreement. The reviewer of the *Völkische Beobachter* was quite enthusiastic: 'One may say with proud delight that he has recognised the most important elements of the German cultic play as we want it and brought these together in a purifying and convincing way for the very first time' (cited in Eichberg *et al.* 1977: 51). The Berlin theatre scholar Hans Knudsen in the *Angriff* even went so far as to announce a 'turning point in the history of theatre'. The Rosenberg fraction, which was committed to Germanic mythology, however, sharply criticized the Christian tendencies of the play which they principally identified in the hymn 'O God, how marvellous thou art ...'. The Catholic Church, in its turn, understood both play and performance as a Protestant attack that represented the repression of religion in the Thirty Years War from a prejudiced viewpoint. Thus, they included the play in the index of prohibited material.

The foreign press mostly dealt with aesthetic questions. The *Nieuwe Rotterdamsche Courant* praised the spatial and acoustic effects highly; however, in the end, the critic felt that the play was a failure: 'The art contained within the play is not new, and that which is new, is not art' (ibid.: 52). *Le Temps* found the course of the action too static, but was also quite impressed by the spatial and acoustic effects. It came to the conclusion: 'Despite its weaknesses, the play is a success for it shows the readiness of the audience to accept new forms of art' (ibid.). The English critic and scholar of German literature Geoffrey Evans was enthusiastic about the performance:

It is impossible to give an idea in words of the effectiveness of the staging. Those who have seen our Tattoos know the peculiar emotional effect that is evoked by sheer magnitude, mass movement, flooding colour and reverberating sound [...]. For in it for the first time all these means were welded together into dra-

matic and artistic whole. That is why I see in this piece the seeds
of something new.

(Evans 1937/38: 203)

Generally speaking, appreciative judgements prevailed in the
domestic as well as in the foreign press.

During the Olympic Games, four performances of the production
were shown, attracting more than 72,000 spectators. It seems that
the performance fitted perfectly into the overall scheme of the
Olympic Games – not only from the perspective of the organizers
but also in Coubertin's view. For it contributed considerably to the
quasi-religious atmosphere of the Games that Coubertin regarded as
essential, as well as reinforcing the particular community of individuals from most diverse nations and cultures brought forth by the
Games, albeit of prevailingly Christian religion.

For the Nazis, the performances worked as a kind of showcase, as
an emblem which affirmed their claim and official self-image that
the government supported the arts and, in particular, innovative
aspirations opening up new possibilities. Thus, they evidently served
their purpose satisfactorily.

When the Olympic Games took place, the government was consol-
idated in terms of domestic and foreign politics. Open opponents –
social democrats, communists – were in prison; the Nuremberg Laws
which decided who might belong to the *Volk* Community were
passed. For the duration of the Olympic Games, homeless people,
Sinti and Roma had been transferred into special camps in Berlin-
Marzahn, in order to present a 'clean' city. In March 1936, Hitler's
army marched into the de-militarized zone of the Rhineland without
any protest from the Western democracies. The National Socialist
state felt stable and safe. It seized the opportunity of the Olympic
Games to present the image of a culturally and technically advanced
nation to the international community gathered in Berlin. There was
much ado about the modern metro leading to the *Reichssportfeld* as
well as the automatic scoreboard in the stadium. On the whole, the
Olympic Games served the purpose of improving the international
reputation of Nazi Germany.

After the Games were over, there was no need for the *Thingspiel*
movement any more. So Goebbels officially withdrew the so-called
Reichswichtigkeit – importance to the Reich – from it. This meant that
it lost special State subsidies. A few representative *Thing* sites such as
Segeberg (1937), Annaberg (1938) and Loreley (1939) already
under construction were finished, however; some smaller *Thing* sites

were erected through private and local initiative. In other words, some interest for the *Thingspiel* movement was still alive amongst certain National Socialist circles, as various later performances in Segeberg (1937), Düsseldorf-Gerresheim (1938) and Passau (1939) demonstrate. But it was no longer regarded as a suitable means by which to propagate and promote important political goals. These goals were now directed towards the preparation of war. It was assumed that they were better served by the sumptuous celebrations of the official holidays than by the *Thingspiel* plays.

From 1937, the Reich Dramaturgy propagated the heroic tragedy as the most important dramatic form and this Möller, and some other former *Thingspiel* authors, tried to realize. Möller's heroic tragedy on Struensee *Der Sturz des Ministers* (*The Minister's Fall*) premiered on 25 April 1937 in Leipzig and *Der Untergang Carthagos* (*The Fall of Carthage*) on 23 October 1938 in Hamburg. The return to bourgeois culture, to its traditional theatre, was accomplished. In 1939 Hermann Wanderscheck stated: 'The theatre has no political or any other kind of goal [. . .] It is not the aim of theatre to teach people. The climax of a drama should lie in elevation and redemption, which is educational in an indirect way' (cited in Gilman 1971: 102/8).[13]

In fact, the new mass medium radio, and partly film too, seemed to be the most effective means of political agitation alongside the rituals of the new religion. For even if thousands and thousands participated in the rituals, the number of 'participants' amounted to millions when broadcast or recorded. While the fusion of theatre and ritual resulted in the *Thingspiel* movement that advocated, realized and propagated the idea of a self-organizing and self-organized national community brought about by the autopoietic feedback loop of the performance and having its identity in its will to unity and common labour, the fusion of ritual and the modern mass media propagated and actually brought forth a *Volk* Community in the sense of the *Führer* Principle excluding all those regarded by the Nazis as non-German and un-German. Thus, it became one of the most important means of attuning the people to the sacrifices they had to make for the sake and welfare of the *Volk* Community, i.e. for the war to come.

6 Towards the rebirth of a nation – American Zionist pageants 1932–46

In 1932 in Chicago, a pageant was performed at the Hanukkah Festival which, in many respects, formed a link to the tradition of the pageantry movement developed in the 1910s. It took place on 25 December, the second day of the Hanukkah Festival week, which commemorates an important event in Jewish history: the revolt of the Maccabees against the Greek oppressors in 165 BC. The revolt was provoked by a decree issued by the Greek King Antiochus in 168 BC to worship Zeus of Olympia. This historical event formed the subject of a pageant which bore the title *Israel Reborn*. Isaac van Grove acted as Master of the Pageant; he was the former Director of the Chicago Civic Opera, Chief Manager of the Cincinnati Summer Opera and served as Musical Director of all the American Zionist pageants discussed here. Van Grove wrote the play, composed the music and conducted the performance. When asked about the model he was following, he did not name a pageant of the 1910s, but explained instead that he had in mind something in the line of Max Reinhardt's spectacular productions such as *The Miracle*, which toured the United States in 1924. As was usual in a pageant, the cast was made up of professionals and amateurs – hundreds of Jewish schoolchildren formed the chorus. All the Jewish communities in Chicago were involved in the preparation of the performance. Volunteers sewed the costumes, organized publicity and sold the tickets. In one respect, however, the pageant deviated from the tradition of the 1910s. The action did not unfold on the historical, authentic site where the event to be depicted had actually occurred, but instead in the Chicago stadium; 25,000 spectators attended and the performance was an overwhelming success.[1]

Never before had the Hanukkah Festival been celebrated in America through the performance of a pageant. This first American Zionist pageant was initiated by Meyer W. Weisgal, a committed

Zionist, who worked in the Chicago office of the Zionist Organization of America (ZOA).[2] The Maccabees played an important role
in the Zionist movement in terms of the development and assertion
of a particular Jewish national identity. Theodor Herzl's treatise *Der
Judenstaat* (*The Jewish State*, 1896; 1946) ends with the words: 'The
Maccabees will rise again'.[3] Some years earlier, the Jewish American
writer, Emma Lazarus, glorified the national heroism of ancient
Jewish warriors in her poem *The Banner of the Jew* (1882), composed
in the aftermath of the Russian pogroms of 1881–82,

> Wake, Israel, wake! Recall today
> The glorious Maccabean rage,
> The sire heroic, hoary-grey,
> His five-fold lion-lineage:
> The Wise, the Elect, the Hep-of-God,
> The Burst-of-Spring, the Avenging Rod [. . .]
> Let but an Ezra rise anew,
> To lift the banner of the Jew!
> (Lazarus 1982: 35–7)

The connection between the Maccabees and Hanukkah suggested
by the All-Chicago Hanukkah Festival and presupposed in general by
the Zionists, was by no means founded on a traditional interpretation of the festival. The Talmud is not exactly outspoken about such
a connection. The Talmud highlights the 'miracle of the cruse of oil'
which was found in the Temple after the victory of the Maccabees as
the central subject of Hanukkah. The amount of oil it contained was
sufficient for one single day. However, it provided enough fuel to
burn in the candelabrum for eight days. This is why Hanukkah is
traditionally celebrated by lighting the Menorah (the candelabrum)
for eight days.

From the very beginning of the organized Zionist movement,
however, Hanukkah was reinterpreted as a festival commemorating
the revolt led by Judas Maccabaeus. Instead of celebrating it at home
with the family, as was the custom, it was chosen as a special time to
hold conferences and parties.[4] The Zionists regarded Hanukkah as a
celebration of political activism and national awakening. However,
because of ideological differences, the revolt commemorated at
Hanukkah was interpreted in two different ways. The Revisionists
regarded it as an example of heroism in battle and self-sacrifice for
the cause of national independence. The Labour Zionists, in their
turn, heralded the revolt as a popular uprising of peace-loving peas-

ants who had to defend themselves against their cruel oppressors. Irrespective of their differences, they all viewed Hanukkah as a festival that commemorates and celebrates the victorious struggle of the people for self-liberation and self-redemption which is achieved through their own efforts and not through divine intervention.

Both these images of the Jew referred to the Maccabees: the Jew as warrior and the Jew as peasant clearly contradicted traditional anti-Semitic stereotypes. In this respect they were preceded by the idea of a *Muskeljudentum* (Jewry of muscles) as propagated by Max Nordau at the turn of the century. Interestingly, it was these two images which American Zionists saw come to life in the members of the Yishuv, the Jewish community in Palestine.[5] As early as 1917, in an article in the *American Hebrew*, Israel Friedlaender, a communal leader and rabbinical scholar, sketched a picture of the Yishuv as an ideal for a self-organizing and self-organized community: 'In one generation [... the Jews of Palestine] have evolved a new form of Jewish self-government, a self-government without an army, without police, without jails and without coercion – and without a single theft and without a single murder' (Friedlaender 1917: 888). The members of this community are building up their homeland by toiling at the soil to make it fertile, by planting trees and by harvesting crops. And they defend their homeland against outward foes as armed guards.

The image of the New Jew in Palestine, portrayed in countless drawings, etchings and photographs and disseminated through books, postcards and on certificates for the 'tree fund' and other special causes, was either a bronzed peasant leading a pair of oxen and ploughing the soil and working with other simple tools in the field, or a Jew on horseback clad in a keffiyeh and holding a rifle in his hand. As the Socialist Zionist writer Zerubavel (Yaakov Vitkin) remarked as early as 1911, there was a striking contrast between the martyred Jew in the Diaspora who became the helpless victim of pogroms, and the new Jew who bore arms and fell in the defence of the homeland.[6]

For the Yishuv, Hanukkah became a festival that provided 'symbols of solidarity, national cohesiveness, and political mobilization, and was intended to imbue the Jewish population (and the younger generation in particular) with the virtues of heroism and a readiness for self-sacrifice in the pursuit of national goals' (Don-Yehiya 1992: 14). The connection to the Maccabees was expressly emphasized, as, for instance, by a pilgrimage to Modi'in, the village of the Maccabees. Here, members of the youth movement, Maccabi, lit a torch and relayed it, marathon style, to light Hanukkah candles along the way. When such a ceremony took place for the first time, the audience was told that the torch would be carried in the relay marathon by descendants of the Maccabees 'not only to light the Hanukkah candles but to light up the hearts of Hebrew youth and to herald unity and national action' (ibid.: 16). The Modi'in marathon became part of a series of sport events, held during Hanukkah week.

The kindling of the torch to light the candles of the Menorah not only symbolized the awakening of the Jewish people. By igniting it in Modi'in and carrying it through the country in order to light the candles, moreover, a living bond was established between the heroic past of the Maccabees and the heroic present and future of the Jewish people which was physically sensed and experienced by all those who participated in the event.

Thus, it is small wonder that underground organizations such as the Haganah or the Irgun also adopted symbols associated with Hanukkah and the Maccabees and claimed the title 'new Maccabees' which the Yishuv conferred on pioneers and defenders of the national cause.

As celebrated by the Yishuv, the Hanukkah festival commemorating the revolt of the Maccabees greatly contributed to the shaping of a new national identity as it was also formed and confirmed by the widely disseminated images of the New Jew as peasant and as warrior, which the pioneers in Palestine, the *haluzim*, also seemed to embody.

In the early 1930s, this image gradually entered mainstream American Jewish popular culture. As the historian Raider explains, there were mainly three factors that influenced this development:

> the Depression, antisemitism at home and abroad, and the Labor Zionist movement's political ascent in the Yishuv and the World Zionist Organization. [...] In the 1930s, American Jews experienced severe economic hardship, and they were also the victims of university quotas and virulent antisemitic attacks by the radio priest Father Charles Coughlin. The Yishuv, however, in inverse proportion to the fortunes of diaspora Jews, experienced a social and economic boom.
>
> (Raider 1998: 111–12)

By the end of 1932, however, Zionism was a weakened movement struggling to survive within the American Jewish community. The major American Zionist organizations claimed a combined membership of slightly over 65,000 from among the five million or so Jews living in the United States.

> In the midst of a major depression, Zionists vainly fought to convince American Jews to join a movement that seemed to be doing little to uplift the Jewish condition either at home or abroad. To make matters worse, within the United States powerful American Jewish organizations, such as the American Jewish Committee and the entire reform Judaism establishment, refused even to accept the very concept of nationhood.
>
> (Berman 1990: 11)

Considering the weakness of American Zionist organizations at the beginning of the 1930s on the one hand and the growing attraction of the image of the *haluzim* among young American Jews on the other, it seemed to be a promising idea to exploit the Hanukkah festival to further the national cause. By performing a pageant which featured the revolt of the Maccabees, the new image of the Jew that was just in the process of becoming popular among young American Jews was propagated with emphasis. Moreover, the idea of a rebirth of the Jewish nation, as achieved by the Maccabees in former times, was instilled in all participants. Since the pageant was a huge success, it can be assumed that all those participating in it as actors and spectators were able, at least to some extent, to identify with the fighting heroes who liberated their nation and slowly begin to accept the new national identity suggested by the pageant. Its title *Israel Reborn,* of course, not only implied the liberation of the nation as brought about by the Maccabees in 165 BC, but also, if not foremost, conjured up the idea of the rebirth of the Jewish nation through the return to Eretz Israel from exile, now and in the future.

The performance took place at a religious festival connected to the revolt of the Maccabees. It used traditional music known from the synagogue. Therefore one might suppose that the pageant was able to transfer religious feelings on to the idea of a Jewish nation, a Jewish homeland and a new national identity. Since, however, there are no documents supplying more detailed information regarding this issue, it is hardly possible to provide more evidence for substantiating such speculation. However, it seems justified to assume that the pageant contributed to shaping a new collective Jewish identity as a national identity which was acceptable and even attractive to American Jews.

After the overwhelming success of *Israel Reborn* Weisgal felt encouraged to continue his work promoting the national cause by producing pageants. He initiated and produced the pageant *The Romance of a People* for the 1933 World Fair in Chicago. That is to say that the context and framing of the new pageant was significantly different from that in *Israel Reborn*. While the Hanukkah pageant addressed members of the Jewish community only and was meant to instil at least a yearning for national identity, *The Romance of a People* was conceived as a contribution by Chicago's Jewish community to an international exhibition. This opened up the possibility of claiming a Jewish nationhood and to present a particular image of the Jewish nation to other nations.

On the other hand, the preparations for the pageant started when the Nazis had just seized power in Germany. The performance was scheduled for July 1933. In April, the 'Aryan paragraph' was issued. The persecution of Jews by the Nazis became obvious and public. It forced many German Jews into exile. This new situation had to be taken into account – if not by the pageant itself, at least by the framing programme.

As in the case of *Israel Reborn*, Weisgal involved all Jewish communities in Chicago and its surroundings in its preparation. He asked the same staff for cooperation. Van Grove wrote the script, arranged the music, taken mostly from traditional Jewish songs and liturgical music, and directed the play. Harry Beatty from the Chicago Opera served as technical director, the architects Oman and Lilienthal as stage designers and Lazar Galpern as choreographer. The cast comprised more than 5,000 people, including professional opera singers, cantors, actors and dancers, professionals and amateurs. The chorus was made up of 3,000 Jewish schoolchildren. The pageant 'would have everything, religion, history, the longing for Zion, the return to Zion. [...] It would have something for everybody, Zionists, non-Zionists, the religious, the nationalists, everybody' (Weisgal 1971: 109).

The Romance of a People was performed on 3 July 1933, the 'Jewish Day' at the World Fair, in an open space – the Soldier Field Stadium, where 150,000 spectators were assembled. On a huge multi-levelled stage, six episodes of Jewish history unfolded over three hours – from the creation of the world through the rise and fall of the Hebrew kingdom, the expulsion from the Jewish homeland, life in the Diaspora and the return to Zion in modern times. The actors did not speak while playing. Their dialogue as well as the narrator's[7] voice and the music were transmitted over a loudspeaker from a studio to the stadium.

The unfolding of the history was embedded within a framework of a synagogue ritual. Each episode opened with a reading of a portion of the Torah in Hebrew. The voice of an invisible cantor emerged from a giant Torah scroll which was placed, unrolled, on an illuminated altar at one end of the vast playing area.[8] The performance, thus, was realized as a particular fusion of theatre and religious ritual.

The pageant presented Jewish history as a national history bound to a particular land – to Zion. Life in the Diaspora appeared as but one episode in the thousand-year-long history of the people, an episode that must now be ended: Jewish national history would continue in Zion.

The performance did not allude directly or openly to the persecution of Jews in Germany. It was the task of the speeches by prominent Zionists opening the evening programme to address the issue and establish a link between the actual political situation and the pageant to follow. Chaim Weizmann – later to become the first President of the newly founded State of Israel – made a fervent appeal to Jews in Germany to leave their country without delay and emigrate to Palestine where they could contribute to the great project of rebuilding their ancient homeland.

The Romance of a People was not only an artistic success but also a political – and a financial – one. The Chicago press was full of praise for every aspect of this monumental production, commending van Grove as 'a master artist who ranks with Reinhardt and with the greatest stage directors' (Rabbi I.L. Brill, 'A People Tells Its Story', in *The Daily Jewish Courier*, 6 July 1933, cited in Citron 2000: 204–5). Many a critic found resemblances to Reinhardt's work and *The Miracle* in particular. Despite their enthusiasm for the artistic achievements of the pageant, they did not ignore its political dimension. The critic of the *Chicago Daily News* emphasized the sense of 'spiritual kinship' between Christians and Jews who witnessed the event. It had enormous political meaning: 'In Hitler's Germany, the news of this fine fellowship will carry rebuke to those who oppress the Jew, and a courage of a new hope to those who suffer anew the agony of Pharaoh's cruel bondage' (*The Chicago Daily News*, 4 July 1933, cited in Citron 2000: 205). A columnist in the *Daily Jewish Courier* regarded the pageant as 'a fitting answer to Hitler and Hitlerism' and, at the same time, it carried an important message for American Jews: 'it told the doubters and the sceptics that the Jewish people are an undying people' (Brill, cited in Citron 2000: 205). Thus, it seems that *The Romance of a People* was a significant factor in placing the issue of the persecution of the Jews in Germany on the American public agenda.

This becomes even more obvious in the light of the reception of the performance in New York. The New York tour was sponsored by New York's *Daily News*. As in Chicago, Weisgal involved Jewish communities and schools in the production. Once more, local Zionist organizations were busy selling tickets in advance and were authorized to keep 50 per cent of the income for their own work. The relationship of the pageant to the developments in Germany – on which the critics later focused – was not established in Chicago until the speeches, that preceded the performance, addressed it, yet determining its preparation in New York. Mayor O'Brian proclaimed the day of the first performance 'Jewish Day'. In a radio address, he urged Christians to take some part in the pageant since it offered 'a concrete opportunity to make public affirmation of their horror of every manifestation of racial hatred' (the address of 12 September was reported in the *New York Herald Tribune* on 13 September 1933, cited in Citron 2000: 206). And, in fact, the cast of volunteers included Christians as well as Jews. The pageant's 'Committee of Christian Friends' appealed to ministers in the city to deliver Sunday sermons on the subject of 'Four Thousand Years of Jewish Contribution to the Progress of the World'. Community leaders were asked to make 'some reference to Jewish Day, to the pageant, and to the purpose of raising funds to enable German Jews to settle in Palestine' (*The Bronx Home News*, 9 September 1933, cited in Citron 2000: 206). Not only *The Daily News* but also the other newspapers in the city promoted the pageant as a major event. It seems as if the whole community of New York, Jews and Christians alike, was involved in the event, as had been the case in the pageants of the 1910s. Because of this, the pageant turned into a massive demonstration of Jewish–Christian solidarity against Nazi anti-Semitism.

The performance had been planned, as in Chicago, in an open space – the Polo Grounds. Because of bad weather conditions – it rained for days – the pageant was transferred to the Kingsbridge Armory in the Bronx, a military depot that had to be rebuilt for this special purpose within ten days. Thus, instead of 14 September, *The Romance of a People* premiered in New York on 24 September. On its opening night, 25 aeroplanes, flown by volunteer pilots, circled in a 'V'-formation over the City Hall in honour of Mayor O'Brian's proclamation of 'Jewish Day'. Then they flew to the site of the performance. Here, they trailed banners on which was printed 'The Romance of a People'.

The Armory offered space for 20,000 spectators – 35,000 less than the Polo Grounds. When the spectators entered they were already surrounded by the sound of Jewish melodies played on the organ and carillon of Riverside Church nearly five miles away, broadcast to the Armory via a special transmission system. At the same time, they were reminded of the Jews' persecution in Germany. In the aisles, young men handed out anti-Nazi pamphlets, calling 'Read about Hitler, man or beast?' and 'Hitler, the butcher, only fifteen cents!' Young girls carried collection boxes through the aisles raising donations for the relief of German Jewish refugees. Two prominent refugees invited by the Mayor were among the spectators as guests of honour – the conductor Bruno Walter and Albert Einstein who had just arrived in the United States one day earlier.

The critics were unanimous in their enthusiasm and praise. *The New York Evening Journal* (25 September 1933, cited in Citron 2000: 206–7) described the pageant as 'the most striking and gigantically beautiful spectacle ever presented to the eyes of New Yorkers'. Approximately 400,000 spectators participated in the 20 performances of the pageant in New York, which means that they were all sold out. Thus, Weisgal was able in turn to donate the enormous sum of $100,000 from the box office income to Chaim Weizmann, who accepted it on behalf of The Central Refugee Fund. Weizmann had launched this fund to pay ransom to the Nazi regime for German Jews who were emigrating to Palestine.

The extraordinary success of *The Romance of a People* was not only due to its artistic achievements but also, if not foremost, to its miraculous ability to respond to the new political situation and to activate the masses against Nazi anti-Semitism. It was able to accomplish this mainly as a result of two strategies. The first implied the involvement of Jewish communities in Chicago and New York as well as the involvement of Christians from the New York communities. The second strategy aimed at particular framing devices – in Chicago the opening speeches by prominent Zionists and in New York the Mayor's proclamation of 'Jewish Day', his radio address, the Sunday sermons by the ministers as well as the preparatory articles in the different newspapers which all thematized the persecution of Jews in Germany. Thus, for instance, an interview with the dancer Frances Chalif appeared in *The New York World Telegram* from 10 September. In it Chalif, who danced the part of Moses' sister Miriam, related how she was not thinking of the Egyptians whose horses were drowned in the Red Sea while she danced but of the 'brown-shirted Germans rolling down the Kurfurstendamm in motor trucks'. The interview was titled 'Hatred of Hitler, Not of Pharaoh, will inspire Dancer' (*The New York World Telegram*, 10 September 1933, cited in Citron 2000: 206). Such framing devices, including the boys selling pamphlets and the girls collecting donations before the beginning of the performance, guaranteed that each and every spectator would refer the stage events to the current situation of Jews in Germany, although it was not expressly alluded to.

The political achievements of the pageant, thus, were manifold. Through the framing devices, they were able to place the persecution of the Jews in Nazi Germany on the American public agenda. Through the story unfolding on stage, the Zionist claim to nationhood was spread and the return to the Jewish homeland, i.e. the rebirth of the nation, was promoted both to Jews and gentiles. And through the strong emotional impact it had on the audience, it allowed the spectators to identify with the people presented on stage who, at the end of the performance, finally returned to Zion and organized themselves in and as a community, the Yishuv, in order to reconstruct their ancient homeland as peasants, defend it against enemies as warriors and accomplish the rebirth of the Jewish nation. Moreover, the community that came into being between actors and spectators in the course of the performance appeared to be an anticipation of the Yishuv, a kind of promise that all would be incorporated into it one day, all would become an integral and integrated part of it.

On the other hand, the pageant was able to make the Zionist claim acceptable to non-Zionists. Through the framing device, Palestine appeared to be a secure haven for the refugees and therefore their immigration, their 'return' to Palestine seemed to be the best possible solution to the refugee problem. Thus, the pageant propagating the return of the Jews to Eretz Israel and the rebirth of the Jewish nation in its homeland could, in fact, be received in the summer of 1933 as 'a fitting answer to Hitler and Hitlerism'. As such, it not only united thousands and thousands of thoroughly heterogeneous Americans in 'their horror of every manifestation of racial hatred'. It also served the Zionist cause by making the idea of the return of the Jews to their ancient homeland more acceptable to non-Zionist Jews and to gentiles.

With *Israel Reborn* and, in particular, *The Romance of a People*, it had become obvious that a pageant could work as an effective propaganda instrument; that it harboured enormous potential for promoting and furthering the Zionist cause. Thus, it comes as no surprise that Weisgal decided to continue the series of exceedingly successful pageants.

While I was working in Chicago on *The Romance* I read an item in the paper that Max Reinhardt had to flee Germany. In one of my inspired moments I sent off a cable: To Max Reinhardt, Europe: IF HITLER DOESN'T WANT YOU I'LL TAKE YOU. The cable never reached him, but the idea stayed with me. Its purport, to put it simply, was to put together a Reinhardt-directed spectacle on a theme resembling *The Romance*, as a sort of answer to Hitler; but unlike *The Romance* it was to be the project of some of the greatest artists of our time.

(Weisgal 1971: 116)

The new project, later to be called *The Eternal Road*, differed from the previous ones in two important aspects. First, instead of taking recourse to experienced staff who had proven their effectiveness, Weisgal wanted to win over 'some of the greatest artists of our time'. And second, instead of involving New York's Jewish communities, a well-tried practice, he relied completely on some wealthy Jews in the States and Great Britain as the sole sponsors for his project – an act which might have negative influences on the project of building a national Jewish community.

After handing over the $100,000 from *The Romance* to Weizmann in London, Weisgal continued his journey to Paris where Reinhardt was working on a production of the operetta *Die Fledermaus*. Reinhardt was not very enthusiastic about the idea of directing a biblical play. On the one hand, he was opposed to any kind of politics and propaganda in art, even propaganda for a good cause. On the other, he was afraid of being trapped in kitsch. 'I'm not going to deny my Jewishness, but I can't put on a biblical variety show! Not even Cecil B. De Mille could get me to do that', Reinhardt objected. He was afraid that the project would be 'taking us from the creation of the world via the dance around the golden calf to every well-known alpine peak of kitsch. An opportunity for De Mille which, alas, I could not seize for all De Millions in the world' (Reinhardt 1979: 246). Why Reinhardt did accept in the end is not quite clear. Weisgal's assertion that he was free to choose his collaborators might have been a strong argument; the calculation that the production might provide the basis for a second career in the United States, an even stronger one.

Reinhardt asked Franz Werfel to write the play and Kurt Weill to compose the music. Both were, as Reinhardt himself, somewhat estranged from Jewish life. Since his youth, Werfel felt strongly attracted to Catholicism. Although his knowledge of Hebrew, the

Bible and the Talmud was extraordinary, he felt uncomfortable with Judaism. It was only the Third Reich sending his books to the flames in the late spring of 1933 that kept him from being baptized. His novel *The Forty Days of Musa Dagh* – the story of the 1917 Armenian massacre by the Turks – won him international acclaim. It made it seem most probable that Werfel would be the best choice if the suffering of Jews through the ages was to be depicted. But it did not secure a Zionist play. Werfel thought it was ridiculous for Jews to embrace nationalism, which 'they have so despised and mocked in other nations'. Even after his visit to Palestine in 1925 he maintained his anti-Zionist position.

Kurt Weill, like Weisgal the son of a cantor, had to flee Germany not only because he was Jewish but also because of his collaboration with Bertolt Brecht. He composed the music for the *Threepenny Opera* (1928) and *The Rise and Fall of the City of Mahagonny* (1930). While Werfel at least loved the Old Testament, Weill had turned his back on religion altogether.

Reinhardt entrusted Oskar Strnad, with whom he had worked together on many productions, with the stage design. After his untimely death, Norman Bel Geddes, who built the cathedral for Reinhardt's American *Miracle* in 1924, took over. He was a gentile and notorious for his anti-Semitic utterances. Even if one would not go so far as Reinhardt's son Gottfried, who called the project 'a grotesque business!', it seems most unlikely that the result of a collaboration between a writer who was Catholic at heart, a composer who had done his best work in collaboration with a Marxist and a stage designer unable to conceal his dislike of Jews[9] would be a *Zionist* pageant.

Nonetheless, Weisgal promoted the project as a Zionist undertaking. In the summer of 1934, he published the following news item:

> Weisgal says Herr Reinhardt will devote the proceeds of the production to the establishment of a 'theatre in exile', which Reinhardt himself will head, and in which artists banned from Germany will find opportunity for expression. A fund will be set aside as well for the erection in Palestine of a theatre that will be a permanent home for the Reinhardt spectacle, and a center for Jewish dramatic talent. The Reinhardt spectacle will be an annual event in Palestine, and it is expected that thousands will make the pilgrimage as thousands have visited Oberammergau and the Salzburg Festival.
>
> (*The New York American*, 20 August 1934, cited in Citron 2000: 211)

The second difference from the previous projects makes it doubtful that the undertaking might be labelled *pageant* at all. The pageants of the 1910s – as also *Israel Reborn* and *The Romance of a People* – were deeply rooted in the community. Usually, the whole community was involved, either in the preparation and/or as performers. When Weisgal deviated from this well-tried practice, he not only endangered the financial success of his project but also, it seems, its reception as a pageant. However, the concept of pageant had changed so much over the last 20 years that the press unanimously called the production a pageant: 'a glorious pageant of great power and beauty',[10] 'a reverent pageant of Old Testament Lore',[11] 'pageantry of gigantic proportions',[12] 'a racial pageant',[13] even 'the greatest of pageants'.[14] Gilbert W. Gabriel, who provided the last superlative, saw himself as an expert on the genre of pageants. He elaborated on the genre problem as follows:

> A pageant is a pageant, and no usual man has the power to make a play of it. Most pageant-producers, realizing that large limitation, keep them out of theatre and let them run wild over stadiums, baseball fields and public parks. But when Max Reinhardt produces the pageant of 'The Eternal Road', he chooses the biggest possible theatre, the Manhattan Opera House, and confines it there, a magnificent specimen, for theatre-goers to examine and exclaim upon. This is the first time I have ever seen a pageant which could lay claim to the extra virtues of a proper drama too.
>
> (Gilbert W. Gabriel, *The New York American*, 24 January 1937)

The Eternal Road was obviously received as a pageant even if it was a pageant that transgressed the usual boundaries of genre. Irrespective of this, the critic found the constitutive characteristic of a pageant realized in it – a particular fusion of theatre and ritual that caused many a critic to talk about the performance as 'a religious experience'.[15]

In the contract drawn up between Weisgal and Reinhardt, Werfel and Weill, 'three of the best-known un-Jewish Jewish artists', however, the term 'pageant' – somewhat unfamiliar to the Austrian/German artists – did not appear. Here, the work to be elaborated by them was called 'a musical biblical morality play to express the spiritual origin, the earliest mythical history and the eternal destiny of the Jewish people to whom they belong' (Weisgal 1971: 121).

The Eternal Road, originally *Der Weg der Verheißung* (*The Road of Promise*) was scheduled to open in New York not later than March 1935. After ten postponements it premiered in January 1937. That is why Reinhardt called the production his 'eternal road' and Weisgal even his '*via dolorosa*'. The delay was caused primarily by 'structural alterations' to the Manhattan Opera House which Bel Geddes demanded.

> What he did with that ancient, dilapidated Manhattan Opera House was beyond human imagination. He had begun by tearing out the proscenium to make room for a synagogue which was the bottom level of action; above that he had constructed a five-tier stage for the historical action and the mass scenes. Somewhere close to heaven, six stories above the ground level and in full view of the audience, was the choir. We had built elevators in a semi-circle to the rear of the stages to transport the scenery. Miles and miles of electric cables had been installed to achieve the most visionary lighting effects [...] Then it was Reinhardt's turn. He decided that the synagogue was too small and not deep down enough. '*Der Kontrast zwischen Erde und Untererde muß unterstrichen werden*, the contrast between the world and the underworld must be emphasized', he said. I had held out against Bel Geddes's last flash of techno-megalomania; I succumbed to Reinhardt's latest explosion of theatrical insight. His expanded and deepened synagogue, added about $75,000 to production costs and reduced the income from each performance by several thousand dollars. It had been necessary to rip out the first three or four rows of the orchestra – my best seats – while the depth of the synagogue reduced to nil the visibility from certain seats in the balcony.
>
> (Weisgal 1971: 132)

The 'structural alterations' took quite a long time and swallowed up enormous sums. The production was planned to cost between $150,000 and $200,000, in the end, it cost more than half a million dollars. Extravagant expenditure on this scale seems to have been somewhat counterproductive to the political aims of the project.

At the beginning of February 1935, the Actors' Union forced the rehearsals to stop. Forty members of the chorus had not been paid for a week. Moreover, the management announced that the actors could not be paid either, since there was no money left. It was bankrupt. The disaster seemed complete.

After Weisgal recovered from this blow and succeeded in raising new funds, rehearsals began again in October 1936. Quite a number of actors had accepted other engagements and new actors had to be employed. Thus, in some respects, they had to begin once more right from the start. Meanwhile Sidney Lumet, who had rehearsed the part of Isaac, had outgrown his part. His voice was breaking and some hair appeared on his upper lip. He took over the part of the 13-year-old Son of the Estranged One. Harry Horner, a former assistant of Strnad, replaced Bel Geddes, who 'would have gone on improving the stage and delaying the opening till old age overtook both of us' (ibid.: 134), and finished the sets.

Now the opening was set for the end of December. It had to be postponed once more to 4 January 1937 and finally took place on 7 January.

> We had no curtain, all the effects were based on lighting – $60,000 worth of it. When the first lights went on dimly they revealed only the small synagogue, and the Jews, men, women and children, huddled together in fear – nothing more. Then the *chazan* – a marvellous singer – [. . .] began to chant 'And God said to Abraham . . .'. Slowly the stage began to light up, revealing the depth and height of five broad ascending tiers, and, finally, at the top, the choir – one hundred singers in the robes of angels, a heavenly host. The audience caught its breath and one could hear a collective 'A-ah'. I knew the play was made.
>
> (Ibid.: 135)

What unfolded on the stage over the next three hours was a permanent blurring of present and past times. In a synagogue of 'timeless congregation Israel in a timeless night of persecution' the members of a Jewish community seek refuge from the threat of a pogrom. Their rabbi stands at the reading table. In order to remind them of the road travelled by the people of Israel from the beginning of all times until the present day and to give them strength for the new road they will have to travel the next morning, he reads to them from the Bible – the stories of the Patriarchs, Moses, the Kings (the fourth part on the Prophets was left out). These stories were acted, danced and sung on the different ascending levels that filled the depths of the opera house and together formed a huge winding road leading from the synagogue up towards heaven. They were followed and interrupted by members of the congregation who commented upon them and referred them to their own present situation.

The performance had an 'enormous emotional vitality' (Atkinson 1974: 343). This was primarily due to its sophisticated display of well-known Reinhardt devices: the occupation of the space by the masses; dynamic and energetic bodies moving in space; the creation and effect of atmosphere. As expected, these three devices in *The Eternal Road* appeared indissolubly intertwined with each other. The critics, at least, felt unable to separate the dynamic and energetic bodies of individual actors from those of the masses. Burns Mantle remarked: 'Principals are admirably chosen, both for voice and type. But these melt so completely into the picture that few individuals stand out.'[16] And Richard Watts commented: 'It is not the easiest thing in the world to identify the actors in a work that concentrates on its vastness rather than on individual performances.'[17]

Thus, it was the dynamics and the energy of the masses occupying the space – 245 actors, singers and dancers performed on the different levels – which electrified the spectators. 'For one thing the crowds are never merely crowds, and no matter how complicated the groupings may be, one never loses the sense of form and organization. For another, there is inexhaustible variety; so that the spectacle which ordinarily grows so quickly monotonous, seems continually fresh.'[18] In particular, the critics refer to the rhythm of the movement which was accentuated by the music accompanying it. 'Reinhardt has never before had Kurt Weill at his elbow to give his mobs the lift of song, and that is a privilege devoutly to be cherished.'[19] Thus, it can be concluded that the dynamic and energetic bodies of the masses occupying the space – in this case only on the different levels of the stage and not in the auditorium as well – worked on the senses of the spectators, forced them into a certain rhythm and thereby transferred their energy to them. In this way, a particular community of actors and spectators was formed.

As Atkinson's remark suggests, the creation and changes of atmosphere in *The Eternal Road* were closely linked to the device of occupying the space. Beside the bodies of the performers, it was – as so often in Reinhardt's productions – principally the lighting and the music that were decisive in this respect. Bel Geddes, 'a superman in his own right',[20] had created the complicated lighting system, controlled it himself and managed to bring forth 'wonderful light effects'[21] that had a kind of magical impact.

And what he works with paint and canvas and streaming lights and levels which burrow down towards the subway and climb towards the clouds must be hailed as the garnerings of genius

[...] I cannot hope to do more than hint here at the rich felicity of many of the lighting effects, at the magnificence of the colors and movements those lights imprison.

(Gilbert W. Gabriel, *The New York American*, 24 January 1937)

There can be no doubt that the lighting effects had an immediate, physical impact on the spectators.

Following the reviews, it seems that music worked as the most impressive atmospheric factor in *The Eternal Road*. Brooks Atkinson writes full of admiration: 'Mr. Weill's music, instrumental as well as vocal, invests the spectacle with vitality and exultation. It is the principal life-giving force along *The Eternal Road*.'[22] It was particularly the combination of different musical forms that carry their own atmosphere like operatic forms which underlined the mass scenes as in the dance around the golden calf or in the final march, psalmodizing singing like that of the rabbi, and smaller musical forms such as dances, small-scale choirs or short instrumental movements which endowed his music with such atmospheric power. John Anderson rejoiced: 'If I were a musical critic I would risk superlatives on Herr Weill's music, so powerful did it seem in its influence on the scheme, so strong in its design and effect, so continuously alive and vital in its accent.'[23] Arthur Rundt, the New York correspondent of the *Neues Wiener Tageblatt*, emphasized the particular effects caused by the blending of recorded music and that played by the small orchestra on stage; effects which apparently contributed greatly to the creation of atmosphere:

A melodic film strip played by the fully complete Philharmonic Orchestra of New York rolls invisibly from somewhere, but permeating the whole space. As if emanating from a distant land, floating, fantastical music. And deep within it faint but true, the music of a tiny orchestra placed on the side stage – that is just one of the many innovations tried out in this play: a mixture of conservative and 'fresh' music.

(Arthur Rundt, *Neues Wiener Tageblatt*, 22 January 1937)[24]

Of course, 'operatic recitation, Protestant polyphony, Jewish cantorism, American jazz, Tristan and Isolde, music hall ballads, a bit of chanson réaliste, even Elizabethan madrigal-and-willow-song style (David)',[25] they all contributed a different flavour, another atmosphere to the performance. However, it seems that it was not just the rabbi's reading but the music accompanying it that gave rise to a specific religious atmosphere which, following Atkinson's second review, permeated and dominated the whole performance. Here, he singled out Weill's 160 minutes of music as 'the most moving part of *The Eternal Road*', which 'the composer of the raffish *The Threepenny Opera* endowed [. . .] with religious exaltation' (Atkinson 1974: 347).

The well-tried Reinhardt devices enhanced, in this case, by Weill, Bel Geddes and, to a certain extent, Benjamin Zemach, the choreographer, to appear even more refined and powerful, had an enormous emotional impact on the audience as can be gathered from the reviews. Thus, it can be assumed that a transformation of the individual spectators into members of a community was accomplished. It was a theatrical community, however, i.e. a community based on common experiences lived through in the course of the performance and dissolving the very moment the performance is over, as was the case in *Electra, Oedipus Rex* and *The Oresteia*. It was not a community founded on shared values, attitudes or ideologies etc. In contrast to *Israel Reborn* and *The Romance of A People, The Eternal Road* did not contribute to shaping and asserting a particular collective identity – let alone a Jewish national identity as envisaged by the Zionists. The three scenes, which were almost unanimously singled out as the most impressive and emotionally powerful by many critics, even openly contradicted the Zionist position. These were Abraham sacrificing Isaac in the first part, the dance around the golden calf in the second and, at the end of the third, the final scene of the performance.

In Reinhardt's Production Book (*Regiebuch*) the scene of the sacrifice reads as follows:

HEAVENLY HOSTS AND VOICE IN CAVERN *powerfully*:
Abraham

(simultaneously Light)
ABRAHAM   *stammers gasping   terrifyingly short and strong*
Here I am . . .

Sound: A brief terrific peal of thunder
VOICE IN CAVERN *unaffected, clear*
mild and without pity
Bring me thy son, the delight
of thy heart and thy comfort
the one son thou hast. In the land
of Moriah afar on the heights a
sacrifice shall be become to me.

Light: *The scene suddenly*
darkens

Abraham stands immobile, as stone,
then he falls screaming with pain to the floor.
In the darkness one hears Abraham sobbing
wildly and sighing. Deep silent emotion in the congregation.
The women weep. Now they all crouch
next to each other on the floor,
then murmur to each other. Single voices, (dejected)

> Sound: The receding sound of Abraham's
> weeping and moaning

CONGREGATION *voice* RICHMAN
   Timid Soul
A mountain falls upon us. Why
upon us? Upon us of all men?
. . .

RABBI *raises his head*	Abraham, Isaac, Eliezer
and Abraham lifted up	and a serving man on
his eyes and saw the place	(Middle Stage) *as they climb*
atop Moriah	Light: (above only)

General tension in the congregation
ABRAHAM, *sways, covers his eyes,*
Looks timidly at his son.
Clears his throat, draws himself up with effort,
Speaks hoarsely, disjointedly to Eliezer,
Yonder the wood . . . the fire . . .
the knife! *gulps violently*
<u>Abraham</u> *receives the butcher's knife from Eliezer*
and tucks it in his belt with a shaking hand,
in his left hand he takes the torch
whilst the servant puts the wood on his
back and ties it fast.
Then he puts two logs across Isaac's   Music: Theme 2.9
back, speaks heavily, softly   ends (Time 2:45)
Trying to control his movements
My son and I, we climb to the peak . . .
He takes the innocent's hand in his right hand
And when we will have adored the
Eternal *He falters again, sobs,*
looks ahead then we will descend *pauses repeatedly*
He looks to the ground,

finishing suddenly and hoarse,
to be with you here . . .
Isaac looks at his father in amazement.
Abraham releases him, quickly returns to
the altar. Isaac follows. At the altar
he throws down the logs and
piles them neatly.
ISAAC *follows him, calls in a clear child's voice*
My father . . . my father . . .

Eliezer and Serving man behind
disappearing in a shadow.

ABRAHAM *deeply moved,*
trying to control himself:
Here I am, my child (*His voice cracks*)
The Son of the Estranged One stands
on the path among the congregation in
front of the crowd, *who follow the procedure,*
ISAAC *brightly, innocently, excited:*
Lo, father, kindling and wood are ready.
He looks around unconcerned, asks cheerfully:
But where is the lamb for the burnt offering?
ABRAHAM *looks at his son,*
then, trying to contain his voice
God will select the lamb to be offered
ISAAC *lifts his head, understands,*
suddenly serious and afraid
Father . . .
ABRAHAM *aghast, opens his arms*
Come hither, my son, my beloved
sobbing
Isaac races to his arms crying loudly
Abraham embraces him tightly, kisses him,
Torn by inner sobs,
then he grabs hold of him with sudden violence
and lies him down on the rock.
He covers Isaac's eyes, the knife flashes
(Rembr.[andt])
Amongst whispers in the congregation, several briefly:
Listen Israel
At the same moment
2.11
slicing violently

pause
HEAVENLY HOST
Abraham . . . Abraham

⌊Light: All light on
Abraham and Isaac

Abraham remains in position,
raises his tear-streaked, sobbing
face up to the light

Time from and of Theme 2.9 here
0:30 Music: Theme 2.11 starts

ABRAHAM *raw, gasping*
Here am I . . .
HEAVENLY HOST *bright, clear, decisive:*
Hold! Stay! Lay not they hand on
the lad thou lovest. Take him nor
do any harm to him!
Abraham stretches out his hand lets
the knife fall;
Repeated whispering in the congregation below
Among many a short prayer of thanks
VOICE OF GOD *forgiving and*
transfigured floating in space announcing

Light:

13 Heads of
the Heavenly
Hosts appear
against a
ground of gold
a shining
youth amongst

I know now that thou
fearest God and lovest him
and therefore thy children
the stars shall outnumber
and they shall triumph
against all that hate them.
Isaac stands up
Jumps from the rock into
Abraham's arms who, overcome,
Holds him in his arms.
(The golden horns of a ram on the rock)?
The congregation stand with lifted heads leaning back
the light of mercy reflects on their faces
(with backs to the audience). In front
of them all the Youth, whom the experience
has sent far up on the path

the angels who
holds up a
flashing mirror.

⌊Light: *Dazzling light*
from the mirror of mercy

– So that on high
the Angel (with the mirror) in a similar
pose as Isaac, Isaac in the centre
and below him the Thirteen-year old
Son of the Estranged One stands.
Isaac moves for a second away from   *Abraham falls back,*
Abraham, so that only the three boys   *prays to God.*
Seem related to one another
A JUBILANT ANGEL
In the beginning God made earth and heaven.
ANOTHER ANGEL
And man he created in his image.
Abraham lifts his son up high,
THE CHOIR OF THE HEAVENLY HOST
In His image created He him.
The vision is extinguished and fades away

> Exit: at 12: Abraham and Isaac at 7:
> Eliezer and serving man
> Time to Theme 2.11 is 2:15.
> (Kowalke 2002: 50–6)[26]

The scene of the sacrifice, which is the centre and the climax of part I, appears in the Production Book overflowing with ambiguity. However, it seems quite clear that, despite his deep despair, Abraham is ready and willing to sacrifice his beloved son, his one and only, because God has commanded it. And it is solely because of God's intervention that Isaac is saved from the sacrificial knife of his father. Even here, the sacrifice is dealt with as a test of Abraham's obedient fear of God, of his firm faith and unquestioning trust in God. Although deeply shocked and utterly desperate, Abraham does not hesitate to do as God has told him, without asking why and to what end he should do so.

Such a sacrifice had but little, if anything, in common with the idea of self-sacrifice in the pursuit of national goals as propagated by the Zionists. This idea did not so much originate in trust in God but in trust in man and his own strength. Thus, self-sacrifice as it was understood and propagated by the Zionists was never unquestioning, it could not be commanded but had to be offered voluntarily. It was up to the individual to decide whether he found it necessary for the survival of the Yishuv and the Jewish people. What made the scene even more provocative from a Zionist point of view is revealed when it is considered that the Jews labelled themselves 'Abraham's children' and 'Isaac's progeny'. With this in mind, the scene of the sacrifice could be understood as an image of the Jews' fate. It is God who has doomed them to suffer as a test of their trust in Him and it is only by His intervention that they can be saved. This interpretation would be unacceptable to Zionists for it totally contradicted the new national identity they envisaged. However, it is hard to imagine that there was anyone in the audience who was not emotionally stirred and deeply moved by the scene.

The scene of the dance around the golden calf which ended with Moses arriving and smashing the tablets with the Ten Command-ments openly opposed another idea fundamental to Zionism – the idea of the Yishuv as a self-organizing and self-organized community. After Moses, their leader, has left the people, they are unable to organize themselves. Seduced by the Adversary they seek to imitate foreign – Egyptian – customs and worship a golden calf. In a parallel action, Moses receives the tablets with the Ten Commandments high up on the Heavenly Stair, while deep down in front of the cavern, his people begin to dance around the golden calf. In his Production Book, Reinhardt described the dance – choreographed by Zemach – as follows:

> *Dance around the golden calf, at first the _Priests_ alone then the _women_ and finally the _old_, the drunk _men_ and _women_ of the _crowds_ which as a trailing procession finally weaves its way up the road behind the golden calf which those in front are carrying. The _Priests_ bow forwards and bend backwards, raising their hands. The _women_ sway and rock and finally _men_ and _women_ spin ever faster, racing in a frenzy (like the dancing Dervishes.) Up above, Moses receives the highest spiritual and moral monument of all time, whilst the people sink down into bestial primitiveness. In a parallel action the angels and their singing voices dominate up above, while the orgy continues in full below without, however, even one note being heard in the final climax, totally without sound, dream-like, eerie.*

(Ibid.: 142)

While members of a self-organizing and self-organized community act as embodied minds, here, mind and body are split apart. The mind is Moses, the leader, who receives 'the highest spiritual and moral monument of all time' from God whilst his people act as mindless bodies. To make matters worse, it seemed that the syna-gogue congregation sided with the mindless dancing people: '*Even the male members of the community are drawn into the frenzy. They begin to sway in time to the music*' (ibid.). Thus, the scene could by no means be accepted or even well received by Zionists.

This was also the case of the final scene of the performance which made most critics jubilant. As other members of the congregation are sleeping, the Son of the Estranged One has a vision of the Angel of the Last Days (in former versions of Werfel's text called the Messiah) who spreads his arms over the sleeping congregation.

> VOICE *gasping*
> Justice my son, is great, great . . . *sweet*
> Love is greater, is boundless.
> THE ESTRANGED ONE'S SON (*still whispering*)
> *Highly agitated   cheering quietly   shouting feverishly*
> It is your voice . . . Yes, it is your voice, Messiah . . . I feel it in all
> my body . . . *glancing over them* The others are asleep . . . We are
> alone, you and I . . . *Why* must we always suffer? Answer me?
> Why?
> *begging   listens intently   penetrating*
> NOW THROUGH THE WINDOWS OF THE SYNAGOGUE
> THE DAWN WEAK AT FIRST, BUT GROWING STEADILY,
> BEGINS TO BREAK
> VOICE
> Be grateful for pain, for the things that are ill
> Are sent by the Lord to strengthen your will . . .
> THE ESTRANGED ONE'S SON
> *thoughtful, rests his head on his arms   looks at the windows*
> Oh, I understand you, Messiah . . . Your voice is still far off . . .
> But the light is growing . . . I love you, my redeemer . . . Speaking
> where lies your way?
> *Whispers softly   burning*
> VOICE *half sung*
> I meet you: wander, set free from all harm
> Into the Kingdom of my strong arm. *The voice disappears.*
>
> (Ibid.: 304)

The King's messenger arrives and announces the expulsion of the congregation. The Estranged One's Son leads the congregation along with all the Biblical characters up the Road, towards the light, towards the outspread arms of the Angel of the Last Days. The Angel's eyes are directed to the Biblical people as well as to the congregation, overlooking the whole history. The Heavenly Hosts appear behind his back. Before the Boy meets the Angel, the light goes out.

The finale undoubtedly bore an eschatological and messianic message, interpreting the aeon of redemption in terms of a christo-logical soteriology. Nothing could be farther removed from the self-liberation and self-redemption of the Maccabees and the *haluzim*. The message of the pageant understood by the critics – and probably also the audience – was the complete opposite of the Zionist posi-tion: 'That is the Jews' eternal destiny, to be the nomad bearing peace and good-will among all warring nations and to suffer all insults and suspicion that this nobly passive role accords will reap.'[27] Even non-Zionist critics wondered why this lamentation lacked 'the defiance and the fighting fury that should accompany its message'.[28] The image of the Jew conveyed here could not be reconciled with the image of the peasant reconstructing his homeland and the warrior defending it. Whatever the effects of the pageant might have been – and all critics agreed on its extraordinary emotional impact – they did not contribute in any way to the shaping and assertion of a new Jewish national identity. In this respect, *The Eternal Road* cannot really be regarded as a *Zionist* pageant.

This production revealed, more clearly than any other Reinhardt production before it, that a problem exists which is inherent in the communities created on stage and brought about between actors and spectators by him as purely theatrical communities. In accord-ance with his insistence that theatre as art should not mingle with politics, such communities remained politically without substance or contour. Before World War I, this allowed for the possibility of a people's theatre, i.e. a theatre for all social classes, irrespective of their political interests and intentions; a theatre that was able to unite people of most heterogeneous backgrounds. However, what opened up new possibilities before the war, even in terms of the existing social order, appeared as a drawback by the 1930s. The pro-duction did not take a clear stance in a political situation that seemed to demand it.

Furthermore, it is striking that the critics – with a few notable exceptions – did not draw any connection between the pageant and the persecution of Jews in Nazi Germany – a connection that seems obvious considering its 'message' as well as the fact that Reinhardt, Weill and Werfel were themselves victims of the Nazis. One of these exceptions was the critic from *Time Magazine*: '*The Eternal Road* would provide a symbol of solidarity around which to rally world Jewry to the defense of fellow Jews suffering the lash of Nazi persecution.'[29] Another critic of quite the opposite opinion wanted to find such a connection, but could not. He blamed the performance for its timelessness. The lack of any outspoken protest was, in his view, the main obstacle which prevented the pageant from causing a wave of sympathy for the Jewish people.[30] A similar stance was taken by a third critic. He assumed that the performance was intended to be a demonstration against the Nazis and criticized it for having failed (N. Buchwald, 'Reinhardt's Eternal Road', 7 February 1937, cited in Fiedler 1991: 55).

Most of the critics, however, did not even mention this context. Some even commended the pageant for *not* making political allusions. Brooks Atkinson, who was quite enthusiastic about the performance emphasized: 'Although the event may have had a political motive originally, it is now the story of the ages, told with great dignity, power and beauty'.[31] And the *New Yorker Staatszeitung*, published in German, stated:

> And a final thought: when this work was planned, there was unquestionably a political and propagandist idea behind it. As it took shape, this morass has completely disappeared and what we came to see had not even a trace of that – it was just a wonderful combination of the most pure, noble, artistic and human powers of theatre.
>
> (Walter A. Reiss, January 1937, cited in Fiedler 1991: 55)

It seems strange that the critics insisted on receiving the pageant as 'pure' and 'genuine' art without connecting it to the persecution of the Jews in Nazi Germany although its main subject was the suffering and the persecution of the Jews. The people huddled in the synagogue throughout the performance constantly reminded the spectators of a pogrom, even if it did not directly draw on the situation in Germany. Even *The Romance* did not have this effect. While the truly Zionist *Romance* was still able to put the persecution of the Jews in Germany on the public agenda in America, *The Eternal Road* seems to have encountered quite another situation. It was no longer high on the public agenda if at all, even though things had grown worse in Germany. The Nuremberg race laws were passed in September 1935. Whether the persecution of Jews in Germany was not 'news' any more as it had been in 1933, or whether the Olympic Games in Berlin had left an imprint on American public opinion, the pageant in 1937 dealing with the persecution and suffering of the Jews was unable to trigger a public discussion of what was currently going on in Nazi Germany, let alone inspire a re-thinking of the immigration regulations or 'only' a public demonstration against Nazi anti-Semitism. And this was certainly *not* because it was 'genuine art'!

Thus, the explanations given for the apparent paradox that a pageant almost unanimously hailed by the critics as one of the great moments of American theatre history was not a box office success, prove somewhat unconvincing. In a letter to Reinhardt in February 1937, Rudolph Kommer, Reinhardt's business representative wrote: 'It is perhaps too artsy for New York, for the little Jews it is perhaps not obvious enough, for the big Jews – too Jewish. The Catholics are just crazy about it' (Max Reinhardt papers at the State University of New York, Binghamton, cited in Citron 2000: 217). And van Grove who was Musical Director to the production commented in a letter to Weisgal on 2 December 1937: 'I don't think a professional show of even Reinhardtean calibre and his incomparable art would accomplish financially what a job, smelling of the same crudities that was the folk-feeling of our *Romance* could accomplish' (Weisgal Papers at the Weizmann Institute of Science, Rehovot, cited in ibid.). It hardly seems plausible that the financial disaster was solely due to the loss of the best seats, Union demands and the gap between the production costs per week and the income from nine fully booked performances, as Weisgal (1971) suggested. He failed to mention the fact that the performances were not all sold out. Nor does the explanation given by later scholars that the box office failure was the consequence of not involving the Jewish communities of New York seem likely.[32] Perhaps one also has to take into account that at that time Americans were not much interested in what happened to Jews in Germany.

Thus, despite the long standing ovations given by the first night audience to the performance and, in particular Max Reinhardt; despite the euphoric reviews which, with only a few exceptions, were not merely positive but downright enthusiastic, even jubilant, *The Eternal Road* was forced to close in May 1937 after 153 performances. It was Reinhardt's last great piece – and the last 'Zionist' pageant initiated and produced by Weisgal.

In the following year, the situation for European Jews grew worse and worse. In March 1938, Hitler annexed Austria, welcomed by cheering masses who longed to come '*heim ins Reich*' (home to the Reich). Now the Nuremberg laws were also valid in Austria. A pogrom of unheard atrocities, the *Reichskristallnacht* took place on 9 November, i.e. on the anniversaries of the declaration of the Weimar Republic in 1918 and the Reich Memorial Day since 1933. Anyone who was able sought to flee over the next months.

But where to find refuge? Between 1933 and 1945, the United States was not willing to change immigration regulations which only allowed 27,230 Germans and Austrians to immigrate each year. To make matters worse, Palestine, the seemingly secure haven for refugees, was almost closed. On 17 May 1939, the British Government issued a White Paper which partly repudiated the Balfour Declaration of 1917 by declaring that

> His Majesty's Government believe that the framers of the Mandate in which the Balfour Declaration was embodied could not have intended that Palestine should be converted into a Jewish state against the will of the Arab population of the country [. . .] His Majesty's Government therefore now declare unequivocally that it is not part of their policy that Palestine should become a Jewish State.
>
> (cited in Berman 1990: 66)[33]

In order to reassure the Arab population that a Jewish State would never come into being, the British Government announced that they would not allow more than 75,000 Jews to enter Palestine over the next five years. Thus, what had seemed the best possible solution to the refugee problem, because it not only provided a secure haven for the refugees but also furthered the national goals of Zionism, was only available from now on to a very small number of refugees – emigration to Palestine.

On 1 September 1939 the German Army marched into Poland. Two years later, when huge parts of Europe were already occupied, it was decreed that any Jew older than six years should be marked by attaching a yellow 'Star of David' to his clothes. By October, all emigration of Jews was prohibited. On 20 January 1942 the Wannsee Conference took place. Here, the total extermination of European Jews, already planned and discussed for more than a year, was finally decided upon and worked out in detail. Systematic mass murders began shortly afterwards.

The first news of deportations was transmitted to the Roosevelt Administration and Rabbi Stephen S. Wise in August 1942. The Administration did not believe it and explained the deportations as labour measures. Rabbi Wise was asked to keep such news quiet in order not to irritate the Jewish population. Wise followed the instruction, but when the Government gave no signal that it would undertake anything, he held a press conference on 24 November 1942 informing the leaders of various Jewish organizations. The response of the press was disappointing. Either they did not report the information at all or they printed it in the back pages together with other items that were of somewhat subordinate importance.

Rabbi Wise then managed to arrange a meeting between leading representatives of Jewish organizations and President Roosevelt at the beginning of December. It did not take more than thirty minutes. Wise presented documentation of the mass murders and strongly appealed to the President to take measures to save the Jews. The only measure taken was that the United States warned Hitler's Germany against committing further war crimes. Wise once more informed the press and handed over a copy of the documentation. *The New York Times* placed the item on page 20, *The Washington Post* proceeded in a similar way. Thus, the average American citizen was not even aware of what was going on in Europe. A representative Gallup Poll from 7 January 1943 proves a shocking ignorance. One question was formulated thus: 'It says that since the beginning of the war two million Jews have been assassinated in Europe. Do you believe this is true or just a rumour?' Only 27 per cent held it to be true, 49 per cent to be a rumour and 24 per cent had no opinion on the issue. Most Americans did not know and, obviously, did not want to know what was happening to Jews in Europe.[34]

This was the situation in New York when another Zionist pageant was staged: *We Will Never Die. A Memorial. Dedicated to the Two Million Jewish Dead of Europe.* It was initiated by Ben Hecht, a writer, famous for his Broadway plays and Hollywood scripts. Until the outbreak of World War II he did not seem to care much about the fate of the Jews; but then he turned into an ardent Zionist and a belligerent campaigner to help the persecuted Jews. He allied himself with the underground organization Irgun and to Peter Bergson and his 'Boys', the Palestinian militants who pursued the project of organizing a Jewish army. Hecht had received information about the extermination of the Jews in Europe from the editor of the Labour Zionist *Jewish Frontier*, Hayim Greenberg. Immediately, i.e. in February 1943, he published a detailed account of the continuing genocide in *American Mercury* and, in this way, brought it to public attention. His article reappeared in a condensed version the same month in the *Reader's Digest*. Entitled 'Remember us', it formed the third part of the pageant to be performed the following month.

Hecht persuaded Kurt Weill to compose the music (taken, to a great extent, from the score of the fourth part of *The Eternal Road* and from traditional Jewish music). Weill had just had an enormous Broadway success with *Lady in the Dark*, for which Ira Gershwin wrote the lyrics and which was directed by Moss Hart. Hart also would direct the pageant *We Will Never Die,* and Billy Rose would produce it.

Hecht wanted to involve the Jewish communities in the preparation and promotion of the pageant. At a meeting arranged by Peter Bergson with representatives of nearly three dozen Jewish organizations, Hecht quoted the prophet Habakkuk ('They shall never die'), read from his script and succeeded in moving his audience deeply. Nonetheless, they unanimously declined to sponsor *We Will Never Die.* The American Jewish Congress even refused to accept it as a joint project. Billy Rose's efforts to receive a statement of support from the White House also failed. The only success was to persuade Governor Thomas Dewey of New York to declare 9 March, the day of the performance, an official day of mourning for victims of Nazi terror.[35]

The performance took place in Madison Square Garden. Although it was neither supported by the Government nor any Jewish organization, the crowds flocked to attend the memorial service so that it had to be repeated the same night. Each performance was attended by 20,000 participants. Even after the beginning of the second performance 'still thousands were waiting in the cold, hoping in vain, that, maybe, a third performance would follow' (Weill-Lenya Research Center, New York, cited in Schebera 2000: 202).

Two narrators were placed centre stage, Paul Muni and Edward G. Robinson. At the back of the stage, two huge 40-foot tablets inscribed with the Ten Commandments in Hebrew were erected. Over these was hung an illuminated Star of David. The performers – among them John Garfield, Ralph Bellamy and Frank Sinatra – the chorus and the orchestra were placed in front of the tablets as well as at the sides of the auditorium thus, in a way, surrounding the audience. At the beginning, a cantor chanted *Kol Nidre* and then an actor playing a rabbi appeared from between the tablets. He spoke the words:

> We are here to say our prayers for the two million who have been killed in Europe [. . .] We are not here to weep for them [. . .] We are here to honor them and proclaim the victory of their dying. For in our Testament are written the words of Habakkuk, prophet of Israel, 'They shall never die.' They shall never die though they were slaughtered with no weapons in their hands.
>
> (Ben Hecht, 'We Will Never Die', typescript 1, in Folder 8A, Box 36 of Ben Hecht Papers, cited in Whitfield 1996: 241)

Then twenty rabbis, who had managed to escape from Europe, stepped forward holding Torahs as the cantors chanted the watchword of Judaism *Sh'ma Yisrael.*

The performance lasted one and a half hours and unfolded in a tripartite succession of narrated tableaux. The first part, entitled 'The Roll Call', recorded Jewish contributions to the arts, sciences and social life, as the two narrators recited the names of 119 prominent Jews, starting with Abraham and Moses, including Michel de Montaigne, Nostradamus, Felix Mendelssohn, Karl Marx, Sarah Bernhardt, Benjamin Disraeli, Marcel Proust, Niels Bohr, Franz Werfel and ending with Albert Einstein. The second episode, called 'Jews in the War' commemorated the sacrifices which the Jews had already made as soldiers fighting for the United States, Great Britain, Russia, France and the Netherlands in the battle against the German Armed Forces. It began with the touching last life sign of a Jewish soldier who served in World War II in the Philippines. It was his last radio message before the Japanese army overran the Americans. The episode ended with a dialogue between two Jewish soldiers who concluded from this partly tragic-sentimental, partly belligerent scene that the Jews had to set up an army of their own. (In the performance of the pageant at the Hollywood Bowl in Los Angeles in July, a newly conceived scene followed, entitled 'The Battle of Warsaw', which depicted the revolt in the Warsaw ghetto of the same year. It aimed to commemorate the death of Jewish people who fell in the battle against the Nazis defending their people and, at the same time, formed a desperate appeal to the American nation for a quick and effective fight to prevent the genocide continuing and which required the organization of a Jewish army.)

The first two (and in Los Angeles three) episodes presented the Jews as significant contributors to human civilization and as heroic soldiers who were willing to sacrifice their lives for the rescue of their people from genocide. The last part, headed 'Remember Us' was devoted to the genocide itself, to the suffering of the Jews. The massacred Jews appeared to recount their fate, recite the atrocities committed by the Nazis and plead for mourning and remembrance. A Dead Man related how 'the Germans came when we were at prayer. They tore the prayer shawls from our heads. Under whips and bayonets they made us use our prayer shawls as mops to clean out the German latrines. We were all dead when the sun set. [...] Remember us.' A Dead Woman reported from Poland, where 'we hung from the windows and burned in basements. [...] We fill the waters of the Dnieper today with our bodies. [...] Remember us.' After such a litany of atrocities and suffering, a narrator stepped forward to explain that such suffering was not a typically Jewish fate, that it was something the whole world had to deal with: 'The massacre of the Jews is not a Jewish situation. It is a problem that belongs to humanity. It is a challenge to the human soul.' The chorus – comprising two hundred rabbis, including the 20 survivors, and 200 cantors – chanted a prayer while the actors who had spoken for the murdered Jews left the stage. The narrator contrasted the fate of the Jews with the inertia of the Roosevelt administration: 'The Jews have only one voice left to raise among the governments of the world. It is the voice of prayer [. . .] Perhaps the dying will hear it and find hope. Perhaps the Four Freedoms will hear it and find their tongue' (Ben Hecht, 'We Will Never Die', typescript 21–7, cited ibid.: 241). The cantors recited the *kaddish* and the performance ended with the singing of the national anthem.

The impact of the pageant was enormous. A tour through the whole United States was called for. Next it was shown in Washington's Constitution Hall on 12 April where the audience included Supreme Court justices, Cabinet officers, about 300 members of Congress, military and naval commanders, and foreign diplomats. The First Lady was also present and hailed the performance as 'one of the most impressive and moving pageants I have ever seen. No one who heard each group come forward and give the story of what had happened to it at the hands of a ruthless German military, will ever forget those haunting words "Remember us"' (cited ibid.: 242). Afterwards *We Will Never Die* played in Philadelphia's Convention Hall, the Chicago Stadium, the Boston Garden and the Hollywood Bowl. More than a hundred thousand Americans attended the pageant, even more heard it when it was broadcast on the radio.

We Will Never Die accomplished what Rabbi Wise's press conferences failed to provoke. 'The news and pictures of the pageant in the press were the first American newspaper reports on the Jewish massacre in Europe', as Hecht recalled. Even in the run-up to the pageant, it produced political effects. In December 1942, the editorial of the *New York Times* still insisted that the Allies were helpless to do anything for the Jews. Yet six days before the pageant opened in New York, the same newspaper urged Washington to 'set a good example [. . .] in the interest of humanity' by undoing 'the chilly formalism of the immigration regulations'. The same day, the editorial of the *New York Herald Tribune*, entitled 'They Will Never Die', welcomed the pageant scheduled for March and called it a consecration of 'the memory of men, women and children killed, not in combat, but in cold blood' (cited ibid.: 242–4). And as a consequence of the pageant, the *New York Sun*, the *New York Post* and *The Nation* called for action to save the Jews before V-E Day. As historian Deborah Lipstadt remarked, *We Will Never Die* had 'energized the press and other prominent personalities into asking whether it was really true that nothing could be done. The more they asked, the more politicians and bureaucrats recognized the growing political danger of appearing to do nothing' (Lipstadt 1986: 201–2).

What *The Romance* accomplished in 1933 with respect to the persecution of Jews in Germany, *We Will Never Die* succeeded in doing ten years later regarding the mass murder of the Jews in Europe – putting it on the American public agenda. It could no longer be ignored. Unlike *The Romance*, *We Will Never Die* expressly addressed the issue – the massacre of the Jews. And like *The Romance* in New York, it provoked the press to report on it as a major event before it even happened. Just as the day of *The Romance* by the Mayor was proclaimed a 'Jewish Day', the Governor declared the day of the premiere of *We Will Never Die* an official day of mourning for the victims of Nazi terror.

With these analogies in mind, one difference appears more than striking. In *The Romance* the Jewish and Christian communities of New York were involved, but the Jewish organizations refused to sponsor *We Will Never Die* or even to label it as a joint project. Moreover, the response of the Jewish press – Zionist as well as non-Zionist – to *The Romance* was unqualified praise, but this was not the case with *We Will Never Die*. As the historian Wyman concluded, it drew

> almost no support from the established Jewish leadership. Coverage of the pageant in Anglo-Jewish weekly newspapers was widespread but generally less enthusiastic than in the regular daily press. The New York Yiddish newspapers tended to be critical. Most English language Jewish magazines failed even to report on the event.
>
> (Wyman 1984: 91–2)

A report in the German-language Jewish magazine *Aufbau – Reconstruction* focused on what might be appropriate artistic means to direct the attention of the American public to what happened in Europe. Under the headline: 'We Will Never Die – Two Critics – Two Opinions' a dispute was published which discussed the theatrical means by which the tragedy was (re)presented at great length. The favourable critique of the pageant praised its enormous impact on different audiences, and attributed its success to its artistic achievements:

> The effect of this political-Jewish show by Ben Hecht [...] was something only theatre can release. It was not just an effect on the broad masses [...] but also in individual hearts [...] the sense of the poetry, accusation, outcry and demands – could not have been better illustrated than it was here through the well-rehearsed presentation of the masses.
>
> (*Aufbau – Reconstruction*, 12 March 1943, cited in Kuhnt 2000: 230)

While this critic regarded the pageant as *theatre* – and undoubtedly as great theatre, his opponent saw in it an attempt to perform a *ritual* which, in his view, it was not authorized to do: 'The sacred outer covering seemed almost blasphemy: the sounding of the Schofar like a clever director's gag, the bearded Ghetto Rabbis like naïve statues, the theology procession dressed in white seemed like a silent, but ancient blessing of choir boys' (ibid.). For this critic, fusing theatre and ritual seemed to be a sacrilege.

The pageant provoked contradictory responses in the Jewish press because it bound together things which were usually conceived as opposites. It presented the Jews as brave soldiers ready to sacrifice their lives to save their people as new Maccabees and, at the same time, brought the suffering Jews, the victims of an unparalleled brutal persecution, to light. It was a memorial service for the two million European Jews slaughtered by the Nazis, a truly religious ritual and, at the same time, a belligerent political demonstration, a searing accusation against the government and its incomprehensible inactivity and a passionate call for the organization of a Jewish army. It seems that it was this particular blend that made *We Will Never Die* a success with the American public.

Kurt Weill, however, did not recognize it as a success. He stated that 'the pageant has accomplished nothing. I know Bergson calls it a turning point in Jewish history, but he is stage-struck. Actually, all we have done is make a lot of Jews cry which is not a unique accomplishment [...] There is too much silence still' (Hecht 1954: 576). There might indeed have been too much silence. However, the pageant was indeed a unique accomplishment. It had an immediate and strong impact on public opinion. It not only informed America's public of what was going on in Europe; it also made the daily press urge the government to change their politics in order to save the lives of European Jews. It presented to American audiences, both Jews and gentiles, an image of the Jews as a warring nation that does not rely on the activity of other nations alone but is willing and able to rescue its own people – as part of the allied armies if there is no other possibility, but preferably as an army of its own. Even if *We Will Never Die* neither brought about a change in American politics nor established the founding of a Jewish army, it was not ineffective. It changed public opinion and it spread and justified the Zionist concept of nationhood among non-Zionist Jews and gentiles.

By the end of World War II about six million European Jews had been killed. The film reports from the liberated death camps shocked and moved the American public in a profound way. No one could understand why the surviving Jews could not immediately emigrate to Palestine but instead were kept in so-called displaced persons camps operated by the Americans and the British. And those who managed to board a ship that would bring them to Palestine did not often reach their destination. The British navy captured the ships and transported the refugees to Cyprus where they kept some 50,000 Jews in custody. The Zionists felt the only possible solution to the problem was to secure the ancient Jewish homeland in Palestine for the survivors by the immediate foundation of a Jewish State.

In order to urge the American government to intervene in London and to persuade the British to give up Palestine, Hecht and Weill (who borrowed again from *The Eternal Road*) mounted another pageant in New York directed by Luther Adler and produced by Billy Rose. *A Flag is Born* premiered on 5 September 1946, i.e. 50 years after the appearance of Herzl's *The Jewish State*, at Broadway's Alvin Theater. The foreword to the book edition states:

> It is a propaganda play – frankly and deliberately a propaganda play. It is not, however, a chest-beating, tear-jerking play, but a proud play, one that cries out in pride, with tears, but with pride nevertheless that the day of liberation, not from German barbed wire to British barbed wire, but the complete liberation of Palestine is approaching and asks the world to be ready for it.
>
> (Bercovici 1946: n.p.)

The protagonists of the pageant were three survivors of the Shoah, the elderly couple Tevya and Zelda, the now aged protagonists of Sholem Aleichem's Yiddish novel *Tevje der milchiger* (*Tevya the Milkman*), and the young man David, who managed to survive the concentration camp at Treblinka. The performance was opened by a narrator who told the tragedy of the Shoah. Throughout the whole performance he remained on the right side of the stage to comment on the action from time to time. After his prologue, Tevya (Paul Muni) and Zelda (Celia Adler) appeared on their way from Treblinka to Palestine. Sabbath is approaching and they make a halt in a Jewish cemetery somewhere in Europe – 'in a part of the earth where Jews once lived and live no more' (Hecht 1946: 3), as the narrator comments. He also explains why the old couple takes the strain of such a long tiresome journey upon themselves instead of returning to their old home: 'Does one open a shop under the gallows where one's father was hanged? Does one return to picnic near the lime pit where one's children were slain?' (ibid.: 4).

While Tevya is praying, he sees biblical beings such as Saul, David and Solomon. In answer to Solomon's question as to who are the enemies of the Jews he says: the whole world. And Solomon tells him that in this case the whole world must be confronted: 'Be not afraid of its mighty councils' (ibid.: 29). The vision ends with a tribunal resembling the United Nations. This is the forum where Tevya challenges the international conscience to grant the Yishuv its independence from Great Britain.

While Tevya is praying to God to show them the way to Palestine, David (Marlon Brando) steps forward. He is also on a journey to the Promised Land without knowing his way. David openly attacks Great Britain's policy on Palestine: 'The English have put a fence around Palestine. But there are three things that the English fence can't keep out of Palestine – rain, the wind, and a Jew' (ibid.: 8). He also accuses the wealthy and well-established Jews in the United States and England of not having done anything to prevent the mass murder of their co-religionists. He reproaches them for not having been brave enough to unite and rebel together against the genocide. In this speech, Brando directly addressed the audience and it aroused enormous emotional response.

The old couple dies. David takes Tevya's prayer shawl and turns it into a flag, fastening a Star of David to it. Raising the flag, David decides to join the men and women who will liberate Jews from the British Empire. 'We battle the English – the sly and powerful English', the soldiers tell him, 'We speak to them in a new Jewish language [...] We fling no more prayers or tears at the world. We fling bullets' (ibid.: 46). The Maccabees have risen again. The rebirth of the nation is about to begin.

The sound of the *Hatikvah* and guns brought the pageant to its grand finale – recalling in some way the grand finale of the Russian mass spectacles. At the end of every performance, 'when the Hebrew warriors called for young Jews to come "and fight for Palestine"', where death could be met on a battlefield instead of a crematorium, 'the audience rose in enthusiastic applause, and a call for funds brought in thousands of dollars', as a historian of Zionism noted (cited in Whitfield 1996: 246). Eliahu Epstein of the mainstream Jewish Agency felt annoyed that the audience left 'the theater excited and impatient with everything that is not based on Irish methods of national struggle' (cited ibid.).

Such utterances imply the conclusion that the Jewish audiences were now more than willing to accept the new national identity, putting emphasis on the Jew as warrior, on the 'new Maccabees', in the current situation. Such willingness was also proven by the financial success of *A Flag is Born*. After 120 performances in New York, a month-long run in Chicago – where Jacob Ben-Ami replaced Muni and Sidney Lumet took over from Brando – and performances in Detroit and Philadelphia, the pageant raked in nearly a million dollars for the Irgun – which was partly spent on a ship to bring refugees to Palestine. The Zionist concept of nationhood and a Jewish national identity was no longer approved and propagated by a small minority of American Jews alone but by quite a large number. This is also mirrored in the membership figures of the Zionist organizations of America. From 1933 to 1945 it climbed from barely 65,000 to one million – i.e. by the end of the war, a fifth of America's Jewish community openly subscribed to Zionism. It would seem that *A Flag is Born* granted American Jewish audiences the opportunity of consciously adopting their new collective identity and symbolically acting it out – declaring themselves new Maccabees.

Israel Reborn, the first American Zionist pageant, performed at the All Chicago Hanukkah Festival in 1932, represented the revolt of the Maccabees and thereby instilled into the largely non-Zionist members of Jewish communities the idea of a national Jewish identity – that of self-liberators, i.e. liberators of their own oppressed people. The story of the Maccabees appealed to young American Jews to become new Maccabees themselves – to build up and defend their ancient homeland. That which in *Israel Reborn* appeared as a vision, as an appeal, had turned into reality by the time of *A Flag is Born*. Young American Jews seemed to imagine themselves as new Maccabees, to have adopted a particular Jewish national identity.

When *Israel Reborn* was staged, the Nazis had not yet seized power in Germany; the persecution of the Jews, culminating in the extermination of six million European Jews, had not yet begun. By the time

A Flag is Born was performed, Europe was liberated from the Nazis and the survivors of the death camps had been saved, but were still prevented from emigrating to Palestine. Shortly after the tour of the pageant through the States in February 1947, the British Government announced that it would allow the United Nations to solve the Palestine problem. After sending a committee to the Middle East, the United Nations decided on the partition of Palestine into Jewish and Arab states. In May 1948, David Ben-Gurion declared the independence of the new Jewish state of Israel. A Jewish state had finally come into existence; the Jewish nation was reborn.

The question arises as to whether the years between the two pageants, *Israel Reborn* and *A Flag is Born*, or between the Nazi seizure of power and the foundation of a Jewish state can be considered as liminal times for American Jews. Such a question is not answered easily. From a Zionist point of view, the period between envisaging a Jewish state until its actual foundation is to be regarded as in-between time, as liminal time. It was such liminal time that made a pageant such as *Israel Reborn* possible. However, there are also good reasons for singling out the time span between the first and last American Zionist pageant as liminal time in particular. For these were the years when many American Jews who, for different reasons, had been more or less opposed to Zionism, were converted to the Zionist cause. They began to believe in the concept of nationhood and adopted a new collective identity which was no longer foremost a religious, but a national identity. They underwent a transformation from American citizens of Jewish religion or even only of Jewish descent to people of a Jewish nation. The Zionist pageants, therefore, appear as products of liminal times which, in their turn, greatly contributed to this process of transformation. They not only presented the image of a Jewish nation as a self-organizing and self-organized community of peasants and warriors and incited the spectators to identify with them. They also enabled a kind of anticipation of such a community by uniting actors and spectators in common, shared experiences, even in common impulses. The Zionist pageants propagated the new national identity and strongly appealed to the performers and spectators to adopt it. And finally, as can be witnessed with regard to *A Flag is Born*, they also brought about a transformation. It was in and through its course that the spectators began to feel, imagine and experience themselves as new Maccabees. The transformation was accomplished. This holds true even if – as was usually the case – they remained American citizens and did not emigrate to the newly founded State of Israel.

Conclusion

The Russian mass spectacles 1917–33, the German *Thingspiel* movement 1933–36 and the American Zionist pageants 1932–46 emerged and unfolded in utterly different cultural and political contexts and served very different goals. The Russian mass spectacles sprang up after the October Revolution and lasted until the end of the Civil War, i.e. until the final victory of the revolution. Their aim was to celebrate the revolution as liberation from oppression. The German *Thingspiel* movement developed out of various open-air and amateur theatre movements after the Nazis seized power. It lasted until the Olympic Games when the government felt stable in terms of domestic and foreign politics. The *Thingspiel* plays celebrated the beginning of the Third Reich as the rebirth of the German nation and pursued the goal of bringing forth the *Volksgemeinschaft* as a living community. The American Zionist pageants came into being not as a consequence of a particular historical event, but in the context of the American Zionist movement with the aim of propagating the idea of Jewish nationhood. After the Nazis seized power, the plays also served the purpose of raising public awareness in America about the persecution of the German Jews and, ten years later, the extermination of European Jewry. The last Zionist pageant was performed shortly before the foundation of the State of Israel.

Despite such enormous differences which, at first glance, seem to imply any further comparisons would prove far from promising, let alone productive, our investigations into the three different kinds of mass spectacle have brought to light an incredible number of characteristic features common to all.

They can all be regarded as a particular fusion of theatre and ritual which pursues political goals. In this sense they are rightly considered as propaganda. For they did in fact propagate political changes and ideas – social or national revolution; the idea of *Volk*

Community or nationhood; the rebirth of a nation and even the foundation of a new state. However, even if they can be deemed propaganda, they cannot be denounced as manipulation of the masses – not even when performed within a totalitarian state system. They were political and propagandist, but they were not manipulative, if manipulation means to force certain convictions upon the audience and demand actions from them against their own will and intentions. As we have seen, the audiences contributed to the performance by their response.

All the mass spectacles examined here propagated comparable concepts of a new community – a self-organizing and self-organized community, which does not need a leader and can do without a watching eye. In such a community, all are equal; there is no split between those who represent and act as the mind of the community and those who are considered its body. Rather, each and every member acts as embodied mind. There is no individual who has the power to force particular convictions and actions on others. Each member of the community co-determines its decisions and actions and is willing to let him/herself be determined by them to a certain extent. And this kind of community was not only represented on stage, but in many cases also actually came into being during the performance as a community of actors and spectators. This was the *promesse de bonheur* presented by all the mass spectacles between the wars, examined here. This seems to be one of the most remarkable results – the Russian mass spectacles, the German *Thingspiel* plays and the American Zionist pageants all propagated and celebrated an idea of community, that, in a very important aspect, was similar. But since this was an imagined community, the only place where it could come into existence was the spectacle itself.

Promoters of the mass spectacle also shared in the conviction that such a community cannot emerge or be maintained without the individual members being ready for self-sacrifice. Whether they have to shed blood to liberate themselves from oppression or in defence of their homeland, or whether they have to renounce positions, privileges, fortunes, conveniences, habits etc. in order to unite in common work, to build up their homeland or their fatherland, the community demands sacrifices from those who create it as well as later from its members. It is based on the idea of sacrifice. However, it is a very special kind of sacrifice. It does not mean sacrificing a scapegoat or some other outsider. The sacrifice is exacted from each and every individual member – whenever s/he becomes convinced that it is vital for the community to make it. That is to say, the sacrifice depends on the decision of the particular individual who offers it. Despite such structural affinities, however, there are important differences in terms of contextualization and semiotization, which endow the idea of community with very different meanings. Besides, it has to be stressed that neither the Russian communists (after the end of the Civil War) nor the Nazis (after 1935) allowed the idea of a self-organizing and self-organized community to be promoted even in a performance.

All mass spectacles under investigation here propagated and contributed to shaping a new collective identity for the members of such a community. This identity was always conceived as participatory; the identity of self-liberators as in the Russian mass spectacles and in the American Zionist pageants (the new Maccabees) and the identity of those who build up their homeland and their fatherland by uniting in common work as in the *Thingspiel* plays and in *The Romance of a People*. A prominent role was played by peasants who were turned into warriors. In the Russian mass spectacles it was the peasants – and the labourers – who became soldiers, which enabled them to become self-liberators. This was also insinuated by *Israel Reborn* and the *Frankenburg Game of Dice*. It was the peace-loving peasants who rose up against the oppressors in defence of their faith and turned into fierce warriors. In the Russian mass spectacles, the new collective identity was not meant to be a particular national identity but to appeal to and provide a model to be followed by the people of other capitalist countries. The new collective identity propagated and shaped by the *Thingspiel* plays and the American Zionist pageants, however, was expressly meant as a particular national identity. By adopting and acting it out the people were expected to bring about the rebirth of the nation.

This is to say that fundamental transformations took place in the course of and through the mass spectacles – from the identity of oppressed and exploited people to that of self-liberators; from the self-image of a defeated, fragmented, humiliated and betrayed people to that of a nation that will be reborn when people unite in common work; from the identity of the persecuted, martyred Diaspora Jews to that of the new Maccabees – the liberators of the nation who will accomplish its rebirth.

While the self-organizing and self-organized community as an imagined, theatrical community could only come into existence in and through the performance and was unable to survive beyond it, we can assume that the new collective identity brought forth in its course might have outlasted the performance for some time – at least for the duration of liminal time.

To a great extent, such common characteristic features were due to particular theatrical means which, as we have seen, were applied in different kinds of mass spectacle. They were all forms of choric theatre, presenting speaking, singing and moving choruses. The choruses, i.e. the masses occupying the stage, whether marching in through the auditorium or encircling the audience, represented the new ideal of community. Individual actors could confront the chorus, step out of it for a moment without, however, running the risk of ever causing a fundamental opposition between individual and community.

In order to extend the community represented on stage into the auditorium, to incorporate the spectators into it, the different kinds of mass spectacle all displayed Reinhardt-style devices – occupation of the space, working of an atmosphere, presenting energetic and dynamic bodies moving in and through the space. They were able to bring a community of actors and spectators into existence by marking the performance space as a common space shared by actors and spectators, by allowing the spectators to immerse themselves in a particular atmosphere, by circulating energy between actors and spectators, by transferring it from the actors on to the spectators – by opening up the possibility of shared, lived experiences.

Time and space in which the community was brought forth appeared, in some respects, as sacred time and sacred space. The unfolding of the performance in time often followed liturgical principles and borrowed heavily from well-known liturgies and mythologies – the Russian mass spectacles took recourse to Christian mythology and Orthodox Easter liturgy, the *Thingspiel* plays borrowed from the Catholic liturgy and Christian mythology, the American Zionist pageants drew on Jewish mythology and liturgy. In this way, the liminal time of the performance could be experienced by spectators who were familiar with the different mythologies and liturgies used as something hallowed, as some kind of sacred time, like the time of a divine service – as a time of transformation, even of redemption.

The space of performance was not only 'sacred' because it took place on the Square in front of the Winter Palace or at the *Thing* site at Heiligenberge (Sacred Mountain), for instance, but also because of the particular form of the stage. Many of the mass spectacles such as *The Storming of the Winter Palace*, all the performances at *Thing* sites, *The Romance of a People* and *The Eternal Road* were all performed on a multi-levelled stage. The different levels were connected by stairs or winding roads so that the performers could not only move on different levels but also between them, were able to climb and to descend.

That is to say, the very construction of these stages marked the vertical line and not so much the horizontal one. In European theatre history, this kind of stage had been used in theatre forms conceived to be religious such as the medieval mystery and miracle plays or, in the seventeenth century, the Jesuit and other Catholic theatres – but also Protestant school theatre. Here, the action went back and forth between Heaven and Earth, Earth and Hell, Heaven and Hell, featuring the ongoing battle between God and the Devil, which necessarily ended with God's triumph in the final apotheosis.

The recourse to well-known mythologies and liturgies as well as the construction of multi-levelled stages not only added a religious flavour to the performance. Moreover, in some ways, it turned it into a religious play itself; for such devices were able to arouse quasi-religious, if not actual religious, feelings in the participants to be transferred on the community that was represented and came into being in the course of the performances as well as on the political goals which it propagated. That is to say that in the mass spectacles between the wars, a self-organizing and self-organized community was represented and came into being that was a religious as well as a political community. That which Smith, Frazer, Harrison and Durkheim had discussed theoretically from the turn of the century to World War I, by taking recourse to archaic and so-called primitive societies in order to find a solution to the problems of modern societies, became reality in the mass spectacles in modern societies between the wars. However, here, the idea of sacrifice reappeared in a changed version – it was no longer a year god, a scapegoat or a totem animal or plant that had to be sacrificed in order to bring about a community or to guarantee its survival. The sacrifice was conceived as self-sacrifice by the members of the community.

Whether the mass spectacles actually provided solutions to the problems of modern societies as addressed by scholars at the turn of the century, which were even more virulent after World War I, seems rather doubtful. We must not forget that the communities which they represented and brought forth were theatrical communities, i.e. brought about by theatrical means and did not survive beyond the end of the performance.

The new collective identity acquired in this process may have outlasted the performance, it is true. But since it was now dissolved from the self-organizing and self-organized community in the process of whose self-organization it was brought forth, the risk was that it could be attached to another community – that it was, for instance, detached from the *Volk* Community as a self-organizing and self-organized community emerging in the performance of a *Thingspiel* play, and transferred onto the *Volk* Community structured according to the *Führer* principle.

Last, but not least, we must take into account that the time period when mass spectacles brought about this self-organizing and self-organized community was limited. It was exactly the time span which I have called liminal times. In Russia, the end of the Civil War also meant the end of the mass spectacle. Instead of becoming a self-organizing and self-organized community, Russian society turned into a society divided into those who watched and those who were watched, whose mind – first Lenin, later Stalin – split up from its body, the people. The idea of self-sacrifice for the liberation of the oppressed was distorted into the idea of self-sacrifice for the sake of the all-knowing Party, over whom those who watched and, finally, Stalin decided. In World War II, the idea of self-sacrifice was rehabilitated, to a certain extent, since now it was needed for the liberation of the fatherland from a brutal aggressor and occupier.

In Germany, the liminal period was over by 1935, if there had ever been one at all, which I doubt. From now on, the need for sacrifices to be made for the sake of the *Volk* Community became more and more demanding. In particular, indoctrination of youth to be ready to sacrifice themselves for *Führer* and fatherland in the war to come permeated and dominated society on all levels. By the *Reichskristallnacht* (1938) at the latest it became obvious even to the rather ignorant general public that sacrifices were completely senseless and that they even served criminal goals. Thus, after World War II, the concepts of community and sacrifice became deeply abominable concepts, even the very words 'Gemeinschaft' (community) and 'Opfer' (sacrifice) became taboo words for the next thirty years.

The situation of American Zionists was completely different. For here the liminal time stretched out over many years and did not end before the foundation of the Jewish state. It was common opinion that the self-organizing and self-organized community as represented and brought about by *Israel Reborn* and *A Romance of a People* was not an imagined community, that it had, in fact, already come to life in the Yishuv in Palestine; that the ideal community of the pageants was not the anticipation of a not yet extant utopian community, but modelled after the Yishuv. In order to guarantee its survival and expansion on a long term basis, a Jewish state was mandatory. The persecution of the Jews by the Nazis first in Germany and later, across Europe, strengthened the Zionist belief that a Jewish state was the only possible solution to the problem of anti-Semitism. Thus, before and during the war they pursued the policy of following any-thing which furthered this issue and avoiding everything that might hinder it.

After the end of the war, when the magnitude of the Nazi slaugh-ter came to light, American Zionists faced the problem of reconcil-ing their policy with the brutal fact of six million murdered European Jews. They solved it by interpreting these deaths in terms of their own struggle for a Jewish state.

After a meeting with some death camp survivors, Judith Epstein, President of the Hadassah, the organization of Zionist women, told an American Zionist audience that

> They had not been afraid to die because they knew that life was [. . .] worth living with dignity and with beauty [. . .] and what made life beautiful? The fact that there was a Palestine; that the Jews could look forward if not to personal happiness, to future happiness for their descendants, that there would be a collective Jewish future which was well worth dying for.
>
> (cited in Berman 1990: 154)

In this way, Epstein reinterpreted the death of European Jews as a kind of sacrifice for a collective Jewish future in Palestine. As Berman, a historian of Zionism comments, there were many Amer-ican Zionists who shared this view. He reports that in November 1945, the entire annual convention of the ZOA stood in a moment of silent tribute 'as a mark of respect for those who suffered and died in the cause of freedom – our cause'. Berman explains that

> American Zionists, believing themselves engaged in a holy crusade to change the course of Jewish history, knew that in all wars, soldiers fell. The Jewish nation, just like the Allied nations, had to be willing to make huge sacrifices in the struggle against tyranny. Thus, American Zionists tended to perceive of the Holocaust victims as fallen soldiers of a great Zionist army.
>
> (Ibid.)[1]

Therefore, the struggle for a Jewish state still had to be continued, whether through a determined policy, performing a pageant such as *A Flag is Born*, running the British blockade and smuggling refugees into Palestine or by military actions in Palestine. When the new Jewish state Israel was finally founded in 1948 and, from a Zionist point of view, the liminal times had passed, it was hoped that the

Yishuv, as a self-organizing and self-organized community would develop and become Israeli society.

Finally, at the end of part II, the question arises how it might be explained that despite the striking cultural and contextual differences which determine the three kinds of mass spectacles examined here, such affinities between them in terms of aesthetic preferences and strategies or mechanisms of community building were possible. On the semiotic level of performance, the differences stand out and yet the performances clearly followed more or less the same devices on the performative level – devices which Reinhardt developed before the war. The context in which such devices were elaborated was the situation of modern societies at the turn of the century as diagnosed by Durkheim. The devices of Reinhardt's new people's theatre – or even of the English and American pageants before the war – aimed to satisfy the people's growing yearning for communal experience, the generally felt need to regain a sense of belonging without, however, proclaiming any particular ideology or politics of communality that would demand a social and political change. (This was the strength of Reinhardt's apolitical theatre at that time.)

After devastation, destabilization and disorientation, the re-evaluation of values as brought about by the war and, later, the crisis caused by the collapse of world economics, such devices still remained effective, though now only in the framework of a particular ideology and various politics of communality that promised the people a very particular community as well as a stable collective identity linked to it – such as Marxism, Socialism, Zionism, Fascism. Thus, it happened that the mass spectacles were all similar on a performative level although very different on the semiotic one.

This also had far-reaching consequences for the similarly structured concept of community conceived as a self-organizing and self-organized community. For in each case the concept was embedded in clearly different contexts and discourses that also have to be considered. For performance and context can only theoretically be separated from each other. Performance and the concept of community which it realizes is always placed in, and forms, an integral element of a particular context, thus being part of, referring and contributing to particular discourses. This might offer one possible explanation for the fact that the three different kinds of mass spectacle exposed impressive similarities on the performative level, while on the semiotic level, i.e. in terms of cultural, political contexts and prevailing discourses, they seem almost incomparable.

Part III
Dismembering tradition

7   Bringing about a crisis

In the 1960s, many Western countries faced serious challenges to the political, social and moral order established or re-established after World War II. President Kennedy was assassinated in November 1963. One year later Congress authorized President Johnson to allow the United States to enter the Vietnam War. This is why the 1960s can rightly be regarded as the years of the Vietnam War and fierce protest against it. It was also the age of the Civil Rights Movement. Riots sprang up in New York, Newark, Chicago, Detroit, Washington and Los Angeles. Martin Luther King was assassinated in May 1968, which resulted in another outburst of riots. In 1968, the Civil Rights Movement and the protest against the Vietnam War reached a peak. Robert Kennedy was killed in June 1968 – the last hope that a president could be elected by the following November who would end the war was shattered. A mighty anti-war demonstration was held at the Democratic Convention in Chicago in August but it was brutally put down by the police.

On the other hand, the 1960s also witnessed a growing women's liberation movement as well as the emergence of a new youth culture. Young people were not only committed to political causes such as the anti-war demonstrations and marches for the Civil Rights Movement. They also experimented with new forms of life-style and cultural expression that undermined the social and moral order of the establishment. They found expression in rock music and ecstatic dances; they experimented with psychedelic drugs; they grew their hair long and wore multi-coloured clothing.

The year 1968 also saw the peak of different rebellious movements in Europe. In May, millions of French students and workers put up barricades and demanded decisive changes in the French educational system. In Germany, riots had already broken out in 1967. In June, when the Persian Shah visited Berlin, students at the

Free University organized an impressive demonstration against his dictatorial reign. When the police tried to control the protest, one student was shot. This was the beginning of the students' rebellion, led by Rudi Dutschke, who later fell victim to an attempt on his life by an assassin; he survived, but suffered from its consequences until his untimely death. The Baader-Meinhof gang which later developed into the RAF terrorist movement (Red Army Faction) was born, first terrorizing huge department stores with arson, later robbing banks and kidnapping key figure-heads from important firms and banks, humiliating them in public and killing them. On the other hand, the student movement also meant trying to live together in groups, so-called communes, instead of in the family or in university dormitories, and to practise sexual liberation. Wilhelm Reich became the most popular author among German students. The students' movement also resulted in a deep generational conflict. Young people attacked their parents for not having resisted the Nazis and their crimes or even for having contributed in one way or another.

In August 1968, Catholic civil rights marches took place in Derry, Northern Ireland. These marches are usually regarded as the beginning of a new outbreak of violence between Protestants and Catholics, between the British occupying forces and the Irish people, a kind of civil war that lasted for about 30 years. The same month, the Prague Spring, which seemed to announce a democratization in Czechoslovakia, was quashed by Soviet tanks.[1]

Bearing such examples in mind, it seems justified to label the 1960s times of transition. Focusing on the cultural changes, one might subsume them under the term 'cultural revolution' as it was coined by the philosopher Herbert Marcuse:

> In the West, this term first suggests ideological developments which rush ahead of the development of the social *basis*. Cultural revolution – but not (yet) political or economical revolution. Whilst changes have occurred in art, literature and music, in forms of communication, in morals and customs, which cause new experiences, a radical re-evaluation of values does not seem to alter the social structure and its political forms of expression very much, or at least lags behind cultural changes. 'Cultural revolution' implies, at the same time that radical opposition today extends in a new way to the region beyond material needs and aims towards wholly reorganizing traditional culture in general.
>
> (Marcuse 1973: 95)

The term 'cultural revolution' as applied to the 1960s foregrounds the radical transformation of, even total break with, traditional culture.

Another aspect of the decade comes to the fore when the focus shifts to the violence that was committed through assassinations, in the confrontation of demonstrators and police at riots, protests, marches etc., and even in a kind of civil war. A deep crisis is revealed through this perspective. Such a crisis is described by René Girard in his seminal study *La violence et le sacré* which appeared in 1972, i.e. was conceived in the late 1960s. As Girard explains, in a situation where the potential of violence which exists more or less latently in any given society multiplies to a degree that marks a special moment, an odd mechanism is triggered: a victim is found. In this way, the violence of all against all turns into common violence against one victim. The guilty party has to be annihilated. The lynch murder of an allegedly guilty victim brings unity and social peace is reinstated. Girard calls this violence 'cathartic'. For it prevents the 'unclean' violence of members of the community to each other. This is why Girard argues that the sacrifice protects the whole community from its own violence. For it directs the community to other victims beyond itself. The sacrifice relates the first signs of quarrel to the victim and, at the same time, dissipates them by temporarily appeasing them. In sacrificial rituals in which an animal replaces the original reconciling victim, this ur-scene of founding violence is repeated and re-enacted anew. It is not only the original sacrifice but also the symbolically re-enacted sacrifice that is endowed with almost magical power to bring about a community and to sustain it.

As Girard goes on to argue, the symbolic sacrifice loses this power in times of crisis in the sacrificial cult. In its place, other phenomena and institutions may step in temporarily. This is how Girard explains the emergence of Greek tragic theatre. According to him, theatre was an attempt to overcome a crisis in the sacrificial cult by symbolically representing the mechanism which underlies the reconciling sacrifice. Girard demonstrates this with recourse to *Oedipus Rex* and *The Bacchae*. Through its symbolical representation, theatre succeeded in serving the purpose of the reconciling sacrifice at least temporarily, i.e. in preventing a relapse into mutual violence.[2]

The theories on sacrifice developed by Smith, Frazer, Harrison and Durkheim at the turn of the century by referring to so-called primitive and archaic societies responded, as we have seen, to a particular problem in modern industrial societies, namely the loss of solidarity among members and growing disintegration. At the same time, they entailed a very specific proposal for a remedy. It seems that Girard's theory also responded to the situation in which he elaborated it, i.e. the outburst of violence in modern Western societies which went hand in hand with the transition of industrial to post-industrial societies. Perhaps Girard's theory even implied a suggestion of how to overcome the crisis – a suggestion, however, that has to be taken with care. For modern societies that dispose of an institutional jurisdiction, that have declared violence to be a monopoly of the state, can hardly be identified with archaic communities which need the sacrificial cult in order to prevent mutual violence and secure unity among their members. However, perhaps that which might have worked in such societies in times of a crisis in the sacrificial cult could also work in times when the state's monopoly on violence is seriously challenged and a crisis emerges in a modern society.

At the turn of the century, theatre dealt with the problem of how to bring about a community and the subject of sacrifice at approximately the same time as scholars of religion, anthropology, sociology and the classics. But by the 1960s, the performing arts were ahead of theory. Even by the early 1960s, when Western societies still seemed far removed from outbursts of violence, the Viennese actionists took up issues of violence and sacrifice. Whereas Rudolf Schwarzkogler did violence to his own body, almost sacrificing himself, Hermann Nitsch performed a kind of sacrificial ritual by committing violence on a victim's body. Nitsch's so-called *Orgy Mystery Theatre* can be regarded as a particular fusion of theatre and ritual that was meant to bring about a catharsis in participants, performers and spectators alike.

Nitsch was educated in graphic design and developed the later so-called action art by way of painting actions in which he poured red colour on a canvas in the presence of onlookers. After first attempts at concrete poetry and drama, Nitsch inaugurated his *Orgy Mystery Theatre* in a series of actions. He performed his second action on 16 March 1963, in the Dvorak gallery in Vienna. It already included almost all the elements which became constitutive of his *Orgy Mystery Theatre* and which were constantly repeated regardless of whether the performance lasted 30 minutes – as the second action – 15 hours (as his seventh action, which took place on 16 January 1965 in his apartment and studio) or even six days (as the performances which would take place much later on the estate of the Prinzendorf Castle). The 'score' for the second action reads as follows:

the walls of the main room are covered in white hessian splashed with paint, blood and bloody water. on a meat hook, on the end of a rope suspended from the ceiling, hangs a slaughtered, bloody, skinned lamb (head down). a white cloth is spread out on the gallery floor beneath the lamb, and on it lie the blood-soaked intestines. the lamb is swung across the room. the walls, the floor and the spectators are splashed with blood. blood is poured out of buckets over the intestines and the floor of the gallery. the actor tosses raw eggs against the walls and onto the floor and chews a tea-rose. the bloody lambskin hangs on the blood-spattered hessian wall. more blood is splashed over it.

(Nitsch 1979: 50)

The action was accompanied by music by the Greek composer Logothetis: the composer created loud noises as he drove his hand in rubbing and pressing movements over the taut skin of a drum. The spectators were involved in the action – in later actions they even acted as performers. They were splashed with blood, excrement, dishwater and other liquids and were given the opportunity to do the splashing themselves, to gut the lamb, to mould the intestines, to trample barefoot on them, to consume the meat and the wine. In a way, we are reminded here of Smith's sacrificial meal. But while there, the point was the common consumption of the sacrificial animal, here it is the violence acted out in common on its corpse.

The dominant element of the second, as of all Nitsch's actions, was the corpse of a lamb. In Western Christian cultures, the lamb may symbolize Jesus Christ and his sacrifice. Sacrificing a lamb – even the corpse of lamb – may be understood as re-enacting Christ's Passion and the ultimate sacrifice that led to his resurrection, and to the redemption of mankind. Thus, it comes as no surprise that although Nitsch's actions were somewhat marginal when performed, since they took place in small galleries or in apartments and studios of other artists without the press taking much notice of them, sometimes by just publishing a small item he was sued for blasphemy – which provided a certain kind of publicity.

Although Nitsch probably did not strive to re-enact Christ's sacrifice, he insisted that transformation be the 'mythical leitmotif of the orgy mystery theatre (mythical expression of the collective need to abreact)'. He expressly referred his actions to the ritual of communion:

communion: TAKE, EAT, THIS IS MY BODY, BROKEN FOR
YOU FOR THE REMISSION OF SINS . . .
DRINK YE ALL OF THIS, FOR THIS IS MY BLOOD OF THE
NEW COVENANT; SHED FOR YOU AND FOR MANY . . .
the crucifixion of jesus christ
the dismemberment of dionysus
the blinding of oedipus
ritual castration
the killing of orpheus
the killing of adonis
the castration of attis
ritual regicide
killing and consuming the totemic animal
the primitive excesses of sado-masochism
consuming food:
meat and wine in sumptuous measure.

(Nitsch 1979: 87)

Undoubtedly, Nitsch draws heavily on the Christian Catholic
Eucharist as well as on examples of ritual violence provided by
Frazer. All the elements used by Nitsch in his actions are connected
to ritual violence – both in the sensual impressions which they cause
as well as in the symbolic meanings which may be attributed to them
in Western culture. Nitsch himself has listed a number of symbolic
associations that can be assumed for any of the elements as well as of
the possible sensual impressions. To the element 'blood' he assigns
the symbolic associations: 'red wine, Eucharist, the blood of Christ,
sacrifice, human sacrifice, animal sacrifice, slaughter, archaic sacrifice, sacred killing, life juices' and the sensual impressions 'body-
warm, warm from the slaughter, blood-soaked, wet, bright, blood-red
liquid, to be splattered, poured, paddled in, salty taste, wounding,
killing, a white dress smeared with blood, menstrual blood, the
stench of blood'. With regard to 'flesh' Nitsch names the following
symbolic associations: 'bread, Eucharist, the transformation of bread
into the body of Christ (flesh), sacrifice, animal sacrifice, human sacrifice, sacred killing, slaughter, wounding, killing, war, the hunt'. He
cites the corresponding sensual impressions as being: 'body-warm,
warm from the slaughter, blood-soaked, wet, raw, bright blood red,
malleable, resilient, the taste of raw meat, wounding, killing, the
stench of raw meat'. Concerning the entrails, Nitsch specifies the
symbolic associations: 'slaughter house, sacred killing, slaughter,
animal sacrifice, human sacrifice, archaic sacrifice, the hunt, war,

surgical operation'. Amongst possible sensual impressions he mentions: 'blood-warm, blood-soaked, malleable, resilient, stuffed to bursting, puncture, crush, a stream of excrement, the intensive odour of raw meat and excrement' (Nitsch 1990: 103–4).

The elements which Nitsch employed in his action belong to the realm of taboo in Western cultures of the early 1960s, and in particular in the Austrian culture: blood, raw flesh, intestines, which normally, i.e. physical integrity provided, were regarded as part of the inaccessible inner zone of the body. They are to be sensed exclusively by way of inner physical processes such as pain or by feeling through the skin. Only in the case of illness, menstruation, violence or wounds do they appear on the surface and can be perceived by the senses. In terms of the blood, raw meat and intestines of animals, they are in a raw state, i.e. not processed, banned to particular precincts such as the slaughterhouse, butcher or kitchen. They will give grave offence to the public until they are cooked, pickled, roasted, boiled or otherwise processed – only then is it sure that they will not infect the members of society with violence.

That this is, in fact, a permanently impending danger is implied by Nitsch's list of symbolic associations and sensual impressions. They all point to acts of violence such as hurting, wounding, slaughtering and so on. While the sensual impressions undoubtedly stem from the realm of totally forbidden experiences, the symbolic associations (with the notable exception of the Eucharist and Christ's blood which are so to speak legalized by the Bible and the church) refer to acts of violence performed on other men or animals such as war, the hunt, killing and sacrifice. The taboo word 'sacrifice' which could only be pronounced and heard in the holy precinct of the church with reference to Jesus Christ at the beginning of the 1960s in Austria as in Germany is repeated here over and over again. It seems that a contagious force is inherent even in the word itself.

Thus what actually occurred in Nitsch's actions was the infection of the participants with violence, bringing about a crisis. By doing violence to the corpse of the 'sacrificial animal', the lamb, by splashing it with blood, by moulding its intestines, by trampling on them barefoot, the potential of violence that lurks in each and every member of society – according to Girard – was released in the participants, acted out, and thus 'abreacted' in a kind of 'catharsis', as Nitsch stated – which, from today's point of view, seems rather dubious.

In any case, Nitsch's actions opened up the possibility, on the one hand, for participants to transgress the carefully watched and guarded boundaries of the taboo zone in public, to bond together with others to share forbidden sensual impressions and to endure bodily experiences which were usually locked up and prohibited, experiences that are able to cause 'ur-excess' (Nitsch 1979: 87) that led to a cleansing of the individuals from violence.

On the other hand, since Catholic Austria in the early 1960s would undoubtedly interpret the lamb in association with Christ's sacrifice, the violence done on the corpse of the lamb could also be understood as violence directed symbolically towards a social and symbolic order that claimed to be Christian. In this respect, a dismemberment of their own cultural tradition was symbolically performed in the action.

Moreover, since such acts of violence were performed together by various individuals assembled here by chance, they were able to bring about a community: a community made up of individuals who dared to violate strong taboos publicly – i.e. before the gaze of other spectators, and in this way to revolt against the existing social and symbolic order. The common meal of meat and wine at the end of the action renewed and confirmed the community of individuals 'cleansed' by their common acts of violence. The meal, as Nitsch expressly states, recalls the Christian Catholic ritual of communion but also Smith's meal community. But whereas the communion as well as the meal community of the hunters is meant to lead to a permanent confirmation of the community, in Nitsch's actions, the meal was the last common act before the community dissolved. Whatever community might have come into being during the performance, it ended, at the latest, the very moment the performance was over.

The 'sacrifice' of the lamb did not aim to bring forth a community – this was a rather subordinate aspect. Its goal was the 'catharsis' of the individual participants. By actually acting out their potential to violence, by symbolically dismembering their cultural tradition, they entered a state of liminality and were transformed. They were 'cleansed' from their own violence. If Girard's argument is thought valid, one could argue that, in addition, society was protected in this way from an outburst of violence by some of its members. The action induced a crisis in individual participants that led to a 'healing' of their disease 'violence'. This, in turn, prevented violence from infecting society and hindered the outbreak of a social crisis. But this is as doubtful as Girard's argument itself. The dismemberment of the lamb in Nitsch's action broke crucial taboos and, thus, pointed to the violence which society does on its members by demanding the observance of such taboos. However, quite unlike blasphemy or revolt it did not question the existing social order in principle. Thus, Nitsch's 'Orgy Mystery Theatre' reintroduced the concept of sacrifice so abominable after the war into Austrian culture as a means of cleansing the individual from his own violence, of bringing about his 'catharsis' – a claim which in some respects more closely resembled an almost pubertal provocation than the demands of particular 'priesthood'.

As already mentioned, it was another Viennese actionist of the early 1960s, namely Rudolf Schwarzkogler who, by doing violence on his own body, reintroduced the concept of self-sacrifice so prominent in the mass spectacles between the wars. Whereas at that time his work remained even more marginal than that of Nitsch, by the end of the 1960s, early 1970s a number of performance artists appeared who also did violence on their own bodies. These included, for instance, the American artists Vito Acconci, Dennis Oppenheim, Chris Burden and the European performance artists Michel Journiac, Gina Pane and Marina Abramović. Obviously, they did not sacrifice themselves for the sake of a community, a common cause or the shaping of a new collective identity. So, the question arises as to what they did achieve by doing violence on their own bodies, as to what the impact of their self-sacrifice actually was.

In her performance *lips of St. Thomas,* performed in the Krinzinger gallery in Innsbruck, Austria, on 24 October 1975, Marina Abramović maltreated her own body for two hours in various ways. She undressed before the performance began so that everything she did was performed naked. At the beginning of the performance she went to the back wall, where she fastened a photograph of herself and framed it by drawing a five-pointed star around it. Then she went to a table, placed at the right side somewhat before the wall. The table was covered with a white cloth and set with a bottle of red wine, a glass of honey, a crystal glass, a silver spoon and a whip. Abramović sat down and began to slowly eat through one kilo of honey with the silver spoon. She poured red wine into the crystal glass and drank it. After swallowing the wine, she broke the crystal glass in her right hand. Blood poured out. Abramović stood up and went to the back wall where her picture was fastened. Standing before the photograph and facing the audience, she took a razor blade and cut a five-pointed star into the skin of her belly. Then she seized the whip, knelt down under the picture with her back to the audience and started to flog herself violently on the back. Bloody welts appeared. After this, she lay down with outstretched arms on ice cubes laid out in a cross. A radiator hanging from the ceiling was directed towards her belly. Through its heat, the slashed wounds of the star began to bleed copiously again. Abramović remained on the ice, apparently willing to undergo the ordeal until the radiator had melted the ice completely. She held out on the cross of ice for thirty minutes without being ready to end the torture when some spectators were no longer able to bear her agony. They hurried to the cubes of ice, seized the artist and took her away from the cross. In doing so, they ended the performance.

During the two hours of the performance, Abramović did violence on her body in various ways. She fed it excessively with substances which, enjoyed in small doses, even have a strengthening effect but consumed in such enormous quantities will lead to nausea and indisposition. Nonetheless, it seemed strange that neither the artist's face nor her movements betrayed any such symptoms. Moreover, the artist hurt herself in a way and to an extent that the spectators must conclude that she was suffering unbearable physical pains. However, in the action of violating her hand, cutting her skin or flogging her back, she did not produce any signs which would express pain – she did not moan, she did not cry, she did not even pull a face in pain. Abramović avoided any kind of bodily sign which an actor might show in order to express the pain of a dramatic figure. She confined herself to performing the actions that did perceivable violence on her body.

In this way, Abramović transferred the spectators into an extremely upsetting, deeply disquieting, even agonizing situation. Norms, rules and securities that had been taken for granted up to then seemed invalidated. Traditionally, in a visit to a gallery or theatre, the part of the visitor/spectator is defined as that of an observer. The visitor of a gallery views the exhibited works from a closer or greater distance without ever touching them. The visitor of a theatre looks at the actions unfolding on stage without ever intervening even in the case of a deep inner empathy, or even if on stage a character (Othello) sets out to murder another (Desdemona). For he knows quite well that the murder is only acted, i.e. pretended and not actually performed and that the actress playing Desdemona will reappear together with her colleague who played Othello at the end of the performance in order to receive the applause. In everyday life, however, it is a rule to intervene immediately when someone sets out to hurt himself or another – unless that intervention would seriously endanger one's own body or life. Which rule applied for the spectator in Abramović's performance? Obviously, the artist did actually hurt herself and was willing to continue her self-torture. If she had done so in another public space in the city, no spectator would have hesitated to intervene. But here? Did respect for the artist demand that she should carry out what seemed to be her plan and artistic intention? Would intervening not run the risk of damaging her work? On the other hand, was it compatible with the laws of humaneness to watch her calmly with simple human compassion while she was hurting herself in such a horrible way? Did she even intend to pressure the spectator into taking over the part of a voyeur? Or did she test him in order to find out what else she must do before a spectator would end her ordeal? What rules could be applied?

In and by her performance, Abramović created a situation that put the spectators between the norms and rules of art and everyday life, between the aesthetic and the ethic. In this sense, she plunged them into a crisis that seemed impossible to overcome by referring to generally accepted and common patterns of behaviour. The previous standards were no longer accepted, new ones not yet articulated. The spectators were transferred into a state of radical 'in between', into a state of liminality.

First, the spectators responded by displaying precisely those physical signs which the artist refused to produce – signs that could be interpreted in terms of disbelieving amazement as the artist ate the honey and drank the wine; or the horror which was caused by breaking the glass in her hand. At the moment when the performer set out to cut into her own flesh with a razor blade, one could literally sense how the spectators held their breath in complete shock. And at the end, some spectators decided to end the situation of in-between and their own state of liminality by invalidating the rules of art and complying with the ethic rules of everyday life. They transformed themselves into performers, carrying out the action of taking the artist away from the ice before the gaze of other spectators.

Blood and wounded flesh, elements that infected the spectators with violence in Nitsch's *Orgy Mystery Theatre*, here also induced a crisis in the spectators. However, the paths opened up by the performance to overcome it, were quite different. And this is not to be deduced from the circumstance that blood and wounded flesh appeared here in another symbolic context. Of course, the elements Abramović employed to do violence on her body not only entailed a different symbolic meaning from the lamb, they were even more ambiguous. The five-pointed star, for instance, may be interpreted in various mythical, metaphysical, cultural-historical and political contexts – even as a fixed symbol of a socialist Yugoslavia. When the artist framed her photography with a five-pointed star and later cut a five-pointed star into her skin, some spectators might have received these actions as signs of inescapability from a state that encircles the individual with its laws, decrees and wrongdoings, as signs of violence done by the state on the individual and inscribed in the individual's body. When the artist employed a silver spoon and a crystal glass for eating and drinking sitting at a table which was covered with a white cloth, some spectators might have perceived this as an everyday action in a bourgeois environment – perhaps interpreting the excessive consumption of honey and wine as a critique of the bourgeois-capitalist consumer and squandering society. Or, he discovered in such actions an allusion to the Last Supper. In such a context, he would probably interpret the whip and flogging with reference to Christ's Passion and to the medieval Christian practice of flagellants – although in another context he might refer them to punishment and torture practices of the state or to sado-masochist sexual practices. When Abramović lay down with outstretched arms on the cross of ice, some spectators will most likely have related this act to Christ's crucifixion. Through their own action that took her from the ice, they might have understood them-selves as preventing a historical repetition of the sacrificial death or as a repetition of the taking down from the cross. It might well be that some spectators interpreted the performance entirely as an encounter with violence, done on the individual by the state or on behalf of the state or political or religious community, as well as with the violence the individual feels forced to do to herself. In this case, the spectator would have understood the performance as a critique of political and social conditions that allow the individual to be sacri-ficed by the state, or which press her to sacrifice herself.

Such interpretations might seem plausible in retrospect; during the event of the performance, however, they seem completely incommensurable. For it is rather unlikely that during the perform-ance the spectators will have embarked on such hermeneutic attempts. For the actions which Abramović carried out did not only mean, 'to eat and drink excessively', 'to cut a five-pointed star in the skin', 'to flog oneself' etc. Rather, they performed exactly that which they meant. They were 'real' actions. As such they were not so much interpreted by the spectators, but first and foremost experienced. They triggered amazement, horror, shock, fright, disgust, vertigo, fascination, curiosity, compassion and agony in the spectators and made them carry out real actions themselves. One can assume that the emotions triggered that were evidently so strong as to cause some spectators to intervene finally, far exceeded the possibilities and efforts of reflecting on what was going on, to interpret, to search for meaning. It was not understanding the performance that was at stake here, but experiencing it and dealing with such experiences without being able to come to grips with them through reflection.

By transferring the spectator to an in-between situation, to a state of liminality, the performance destabilized his perception of himself, the others and reality. In this sense, the crisis induced by the performance can be understood as a crisis of identity as it is experienced in rites of passage. However, quite unlike such rituals – and similarly unlike the mass spectacles between the wars which strived towards a collective identity – the performance destabilized the identity of the spectators and transferred them into a state of liminality not so as to let them acquire a new stable identity to be accepted by society. Rather, the liminal or transformation phase lasted until the very end of the performance. It is even questionable whether those who decided to take the artist from the ice without asking for her consent even acquired a new identity by this very action. They were transformed from spectators into performers, it is true. But it is impossible to decide whether by this very action they actually mastered the crisis, i.e. the experience of total destabilization in terms of their perception of self, others, reality or in terms of the annulment of valid rules and norms; whether the transformation they underwent by/in such experiences as well as by taking over the role of performers, actually brought about a new identity rather than released another crisis.

The self-sacrifice of the performer caused a crisis of identity in the individual spectators – and probably in the artist herself, too – by permanently transgressing the allegedly fixed borderline between art and 'reality'/'life', aesthetics and ethics, and by forcing the spectators to transgress them too without showing them a way out of the crisis. By completely different means and to completely different ends, Abramović even surpassed the self-sacrifice committed by the actress Gertrud Eysoldt when she played Electra.

In the 1960s, when action and performance artists re-introduced the concept of sacrifice or self-sacrifice, they did not strive to bring about a community or shape a collective identity. Rather, it was the individual they were concerned about. Nitsch's actions in the *Orgy Mystery Theatre* infected the spectators with violence and opened up the possibility for them to act out their own violent potential, to undergo a catharsis. Abramović's performance, in its turn, destabilized the spectators' identity in terms of their perception of self, other and reality by transferring them into a situation of conflicting frames, rules and values and, thus, put their self-image and self-understanding to a searing test.

Moreover, the sacrifice of the lamb as well as the self-sacrifice of the artist symbolically performed a dismembering of tradition. Whereas Nitsch's actions symbolically dismembered the Christian Catholic symbolic order as founded on taboos, Abramović's performance actually dismembered the traditional understanding of identity. What kind of symbolic order would arise in place of the old one? And what kind of identity would emerge?

8   *The Bacchae* – dismembering the text

In the 1960s and 1970s the issue of sacrifice was not only re-introduced into Western culture through action and performance art that radically questioned the traditional social and symbolic order. It was also put on the agenda by taking recourse to the oldest theatrical form that deals with sacrifice and which is the oldest form of choric theatre as well, to which Reinhardt took recourse when creating his new people's theatre: ancient Greek tragedy. Since Nietzsche's *The Birth of Tragedy*, the relationship between tragedy and sacrifice and, particularly, Dionysus' dismemberment, is at the heart of any discussion on the relationship between theatre and ritual. In the 1970s, performances of Greek tragedy experienced a veritable boom. This not only included tragedies that already had a long performance history on modern European stages such as *Oedipus Rex* or *Antigone*, but also tragedies that had almost no performance record at all – for example, Euripides' *The Bacchae*. Before the 1960s, this play had only been performed very rarely. At the beginning of the century, Gilbert Murray's fascinating translation seemed to spur a performance history. In 1908, William Poel, famous for his Shakespeare productions, staged the play at London's Court Theatre. However, no other performances followed. *The Bacchae* was performed twice in the Ancient Theatre of Syracuse in 1922 and in 1950 (this time starring Vittorio Gassman as Dionysus). The tragedy was never performed in an American professional theatre.

On 7 June 1968, Richard Schechner's version of *The Bacchae*, *Dionysus in 69* opened in New York in his newly founded Performance Garage, i.e. one day after Robert Kennedy was assassinated. It ran until July 1969, closing one month before the notorious Woodstock festival took place. Schechner's production was followed by a whole series of *Bacchae* performances. The most famous and discussed productions were those by Hansgünther Heyme in the

Cologne Theatre (1973), by Luca Ronconi in the Vienna Burgtheater (1973), by Klaus Michael Grüber in the Berlin Schaubühne
(1974) and a version by Wole Soyinka, commissioned by the London
National Theatre, published in 1973 and performed at the London
National Theatre. This version was also staged by Carol Dawson in
Kingston, Jamaica in 1975.[1] The same year Ronconi restaged the
tragedy in Prato and Tadashi Suzuki's version premiered in Tokyo in
1977.[2] Considering such an impressive record, one could label the
years 1968–77 the decade of *The Bacchae*.

And indeed there does seem to be a striking parallel between the
tragedy and the situation of the 1960s and 1970s outlined at the
beginning of the previous chapter. The play deals with all kinds of
transgression, change and loss of identity, violence, madness, ecstasy,
release of libidinal energy, transformation, relations between individual and community, challenges to authority. This seems to
explain its sudden and unforeseen popularity. For these are exactly
the problems which sparked the social and political crises of these
years and contributed to the ongoing cultural revolution. Bearing
this in mind, it cannot be overlooked that the tragedy moves towards
a sacrifice from the very beginning: to the dismemberment of
Pentheus which, in a way, recalls Dionysus' dismemberment, but
unlike the latter, is not followed by a rebirth. At the end of the
tragedy, the dismembered body remains in pieces scattered on the
ground.

Moreover, *The Bacchae* is precisely the tragedy which Murray took
as an example in his contribution to Harrison's *Themis* to show that
tragic theatre developed out of the sacrificial *eniautos daimon* ritual.
It is also the tragedy to which René Girard refers to explain how
ancient Greek theatre sprang from a crisis in the sacrificial cult by
representing the mechanism underlying sacrifice.

Thus, the question arises as to how the performances responded
to the political and social situation and how they viewed the crisis at
stake. Of particular interest in our context is, in addition, the question of which role, importance and meaning they accorded the sacrifice. I shall discuss these questions with reference to two
performances – to the productions by Schechner and Grüber. One
can hardly imagine two performances as different as these, as we
shall see. Still, they have two features in common that seem to be
particularly relevant with regard to the focus of our study. First, they
both allow the performance to emerge out of a dismemberment of
the text, which is to say that it was the 'sacrifice' of the text that
made this particular performance possible. And second, they feature

exactly those themes and problems dealt with in the mass spectacles celebrating self-sacrifice between the wars: the problem of how to bring about a community and how to create a collective identity. Moreover, both took place within Western culture at a time when the crisis was extremely virulent – even if for very different reasons.

Dionysus in 69 is generally regarded as the beginning and exemplary representative of a new ritualistic theatre that can be seen as a very special fusion of theatre and ritual.[3] It was meant to bring about actual transformations both in the performers and the spectators. Schechner (1973: 197) proceeded from the assumption that people living in industrial societies lack essential dimensions which define humanity such as: 'Wholeness, process/organic growth, concreteness, religious, transcendental experience'. Interestingly, he sees the reason for this lack in the inability of modern societies to reconcile individualism with communality – a diagnosis that, in a way, recalls Durkheim's statement on the disease of modern societies. Therefore, Schechner concluded that such dimensions can only be regained by developing a new cultural identity which allows for reconciliation:

> Links must be discovered or forged between industrial societies and non-industrial ones, between individualistic and communal cultures. And a vast reform in the direction of communality – or at least a revision of individualism – is necessary. This reform and revision will leave no aspect of modern society untouched; not economics, government, social life, personal life, aesthetics, or anything else. Theater takes a pivotal position in these movements because these movements are histrionic: a way of focusing attention and demanding change. The marches, demonstrations, street and guerrilla theaters, arrests of well-known and unknown people were for show: symbolic gestures.
>
> (Ibid.: 197–8)

A utopian dimension is clearly attributed both to the theatre and the movements. They will bring about something that was lacking at the end of the 1960s.

However, theatre will only be in a position to fulfil such goals when – as Herrmann already declared – it turns from text to performance. In Schechner's view this entails a critique of textual culture in general: 'Because our tradition is written, it has become a burden. An oral tradition quite naturally takes its shape from the changing culture which transmits it. A written tradition, however, tends to solidify and become reactionary' (Schechner 1969: 227). That is to say that a new performative turn is needed that will transform the solid and fixed textual culture of the past into a fluid, ever-changing performative culture of the future which will grant the missing dimensions. Theatre can contribute to the performative turn required when it sets out to treat 'the text as if it were part of an oral tradition' (ibid.). The fixed text has to be dismembered in order to allow the ever-changing performance to emerge.

In *Dionysus in 69*[4] the dismemberment of the text mainly served three purposes, namely to redefine the relationships (1) between role and performer, (2) between the performers and (3) between performers and spectators.

With reference to Grotowski, Schechner refused the idea that the performer has to represent the role and, in this sense, to embody it. 'Rather, there is the role and the person of the performer; both role and performer are plainly perceivable by the spectator. *The feelings are those of the performer as stimulated by the actions of the role at the moment of performance*' (Schechner 1973: 166). In *Dionysus in 69* the performers used the roles in order to act out their wholly personal problems and feelings. Each actor rewrote the role or roles for himself (since a change of roles among the performers was usual) working his personal experiences and private biography into it. One performer gave his personal view on how the process worked:

> I am not interested in acting. I am involved in the life process of becoming whole. I do many technical exercises which organically suit that process. They act as a catalyst for my ability to let essence flow, to let my soul speak through my mind and body [...] I am acting out my disease, the disease that plagues my inner being, that stops the flow [...] *Dionysus* is not a play to me. I do not act in *Dionysus*. *Dionysus* is my ritual.
>
> (Schechner 1970: n.p.)

Here, performing meant undergoing a rite of passage that might lead to a new individual identity which will encompass all the dimensions which Schechner listed as lacking in people living in industrial societies. Thus performing very much resembled the actions in Nitsch's *Orgy Mystery Theatre*. In both cases it was all about acting out the individual's 'disease' – either his potential to violence or 'what stops the flow'.

Since it was the performer's individuality that was at stake here, the performers introduced themselves to the audience by using their proper names:

> My name is Jason Bosseau. I am the son of Damar Bosseau and Jessie Bartoletti. I was born twenty-seven years ago in a small, boring, typical Midwestern town in southeastern Kansas called Pittsburg [. . .] I've come here tonight for three very important reasons. Number one is to announce my divinity. I mean: I am a god. Number two is to establish my rites and my rituals [. . .] And number three is to be born – in this, my birth ritual, if you'll excuse me.
>
> (Ibid.)

During the performances, the performers called each other by their proper names as well as by the names of the dramatic figures whose role they played.

In this way, a new individual identity came into being. It was no longer that of the person before embarking on the production nor that of the dramatic character. It was the identity of the performer – an in-between identity, i.e. the one as well as the other. It came into being by permanently transgressing the boundaries between the person and the dramatic character without ever identifying one with the other. And since the performers changed parts over the thirteen month run of the performance, they permanently changed their in-between identity as well. The transformation they underwent in the course of the performance run was not the transformation from Identity A to Identity B. Rather, it was a permanent process of being transformed from one in-between identity to another. The in-between identity that was in the process of emerging and disappearing at all times was the result of performative acts that the performers carried out during the performance.

Thus, the idea of a stable, fixed individual identity – as well as the idea of a stable, fixed text – became obsolete. This appears to be a prerequisite for the emergence of a community – a community formed by the members of the Performance Group as well as a community of performers and spectators. And it does not come as a surprise that the dismemberment of the text was the basic condition for it. The scene after Dionysus' arrest by Pentheus' guards in which the king's palace collapses because of an earthquake was replaced in *Dionysus in 69* by the so-called 'Dionysus Game':

We turned to exercises from the workshop. We had been playing an encounter game in which one performer challenges another. A question or statement is made which, according to the rules of the exercise, must 'cost something.' An answer is given that is equally revealing and difficult. And so on, until everyone has contributed at least once [. . .] After everyone in the Group had participated in the encounter, people could turn on Shephard, who was playing Pentheus at this time. Shephard had to answer the questions, but could not ask any. The game continued until Shephard's opacity was sufficiently pierced so that he could not respond to a question. Then he said, 'This is mortifying,' and the scene was over. Once the questioning went on for more than an hour.

(Ibid.)

Even if Schechner (1973: 225) conceived the group as a 'viable dialectic between solitude and being-with-others' and praised it as 'an attempt to create a family, but a family structured from the assumption that the dominance of the parents can be eliminated and that repression can be reduced if not eradicated', the 'Dionysus Game' is reminiscent of Girard's ur-scene: a victim is found to be expelled from the community, to be sacrificed. However, there are at least three significant deviations from it. First, the question-and-answer game challenges everybody taking part in it, it must 'cost something' for everybody. That is to say that the aggression of the members of the group was not only directed towards the 'victim', but spread to all members. Second, it was declared to be a game which means that whoever was intended as the victim, so to speak, only took over the role of the victim for the duration of the game. And third, the game was played as part of a fictitious play. The intended victim played the role of Pentheus, the ruler, the man of law and order who brutally suppressed the others. Thus, the game oscillated. It blurred the boundaries between the social reality of the Performance Group, the reality of the game and the fictitious reality of the play. Everyone involved in the game permanently transgressed the boundaries between different realities, was situated in an in-between state, a state of liminality.

The same holds true of the sacrifice at the end of the play, Pentheus' dismemberment. A particular ritual was designed for the beginning and end of the performance – a birth (Dionysus) and death (Pentheus) ritual. It was modelled after the adoption ritual of the Asmati people of New Guinea. Five men lay on the floor side by side whilst four women stood over them with legs spread out, leaning slightly forward so that a tunnel was formed representing the birth canal. At the beginning of the performance the performer playing Dionysus was reborn as a god – he was pushed through the 'birth canal' by the rhythmic hip movements of the men. As Shephard reports, the birth ritual was essential 'not only in our work but also in our collective existence'. For it 'gave us the opportunity of experiencing and expressing our common bonds in non-rational symbolic form' (Shephard 1990: 88). That is to say that it was the birth ritual which brought forth and confirmed the community of the group – a ritual that was also meant to represent the fictitious event of Dionysus' birth.

The dismemberment of Pentheus was performed as a reversal of the birth ritual. Shephard was pushed in reverse direction through the tunnel; Pentheus was symbolically swallowed by the community that, as an individual, he had tried to dominate. In this way, the death ritual accomplished two different things simultaneously. On the one hand, by carrying out the same performative acts as in the birth ritual and by allowing for the same physiological, affective, motoric and energetic experiences, it confirmed the Performance Group as a community, including Shephard. On the other, it performed the sacrifice of Pentheus not as an expulsion from the community, as dismemberment, but as a symbolic act of incorporation. He became physically one with the community he had terrorized. That is to say that the Performance Group did not come into being as a community or was confirmed as such through sacrifice, but by performing particular actions in common and by sharing the same experiences. The sacrifice performed was, literally, a theatrical sacrifice – a symbolic gesture. The performance expressly brought forth a community of performers without demanding the sacrifice of one individual – although in the 'Dionysus Game' it came close to that – but by performative acts carried out in common.

This also holds true for the community that might come into existence between performers and spectators in the course of the performance. In order to enable performers and spectators to carry out the same performative acts in common, do the same actions, audience participation was encouraged. It was dependent on two conditions:

> First, participation occurred at those points where the play stopped being a play and became a social event – when spectators felt that they were free to enter the performance as equals

[...] The second point is that most of the participation in *Diony-sus* was according to the democratic model: letting people into the play to do as the performers were doing, to 'join the story'.

(Schechner 1973: 44)[5]

This kind of audience participation was enabled by the perform-ance space. The division between stage and auditorium was abol-ished – the whole theatre became an 'environment'. The spectator could choose a place to sit – high up on a tower, relatively distanced on the scaffoldings at the walls or rather close on the carpeted floor. The audience was able to change seats during the performance changing the perspective and the relationship to the performance and to other spectators. Thus, it was up to the individual spectator to decide whether to join the performers, for instance, in the circle dance after the birth ritual or in the procession which ended the performance as a kind of rite of incorporation. The doors of the Performance Garage were opened wide and the participants, per-formers and spectators alike marched out through the streets of New York. Thus, any community that might have come into being between performers and spectators was due to common actions that the spectators decided to perform together with the performers. Of course, such a community could only exist for the time span in which the common actions were performed and the same experi-ences shared. It was, by definition, a temporary and ephemeral community.

In this way, *Dionysus in 69* presented a new model of community – a community in an industrial society that was already on the verge of changing into a post-industrial society, a community which actually seemed to be a 'viable dialectic between solitude and being-with-others'. It was based on two conditions: on the dismemberment of the solid, fixed, 'written' tradition as well as on the dismemberment of a fixed, stable identity. These are the 'sacrifices' to be made in order to allow a community to come into being. That is to say that the prerequisite of any community is the state of in-between, of limi-nality. It is not due to shared beliefs, ideologies, convictions or even a fixed collective identity. Rather, it emerges out of common actions and shared experiences as a state of transition.

Without doubt such a theatrical community recalls, in many respects, the theatrical communities created before World War I in Reinhardt's performances of *Oedipus Rex* and the *Oresteia*. However, while Reinhardt used devices that overwhelmed the audiences and dragged them into the community of actors and spectators, in *Diony-*

sus in 69, it was up to the individual spectator to decide whether to join in. More importantly, whereas Reinhardt insisted on the autonomy of art, on theatre not mingling with politics, the Performance Group understood their work as clearly political, as permanently transgressing the borderline between art and life. They even proposed theatre as a model of politics. Since life had become theatrical, politics had to employ theatrical means. And whatever community came into being could only be a theatrical community. Still, it was hoped that just such theatrical communities would be able to grant its – temporary – members the much-needed experience of 'wholeness/organic growth, concreteness' as well as 'religious, transcendental experience'. It was assumed that this would not only cure individual performers – and possibly some spectators – from 'disease', but also contribute to overcoming the current crisis in political and social life. In this respect, *Dionysus in 69* cannot only be regarded as ritual theatre, but as ritual theatre and political theatre at the same time.

The Berlin Schaubühne, founded in 1970 by Peter Stein and others, was also generally acknowledged to be political theatre. (In 1968, Peter Stein directed Peter Weiss' *Vietnam-Discourse* at the Munich Kammerspiele. On the first night, after the applause died down, Stein and his actors descended from the stage into the auditorium and lounge and raised a collection for the Vietcong. This provoked an enormous scandal and Stein had to leave the Kammerspiele.) The Berlin Schaubühne was founded at a time when the Social Democratic Party had become the ruling party for the first time in the history of the Federal Republic of Germany, with Willy Brandt as Chancellor. This more or less marked the end of the so-called APO (extra-parliamentary opposition), although not the end of the Baader-Meinhof gang and the RAF. The Schaubühne overtly responded to the students' rebellion and to the change in West Germany's society and politics. Its early productions included Brecht/Gorky's *The Mother* (1970), Enzensberger's *The Havana Inquiry* (1971), Vishnevsky's *An Optimistic Tragedy* and Marieluise Fleisser's *Purgatory in Ingolstadt* (1973).

In 1973, the Schaubühne embarked on the enterprise of the *Antikenprojekt* (Antiquity Project). The year before, the leaders of the Baader-Meinhof gang had been arrested. On 5 September, at the Olympic Games in Munich, Palestinian terrorists shot eleven Israeli athletes and a German policeman – five terrorists were killed. The *Antiquity Project* opened in February 1974. Three months later, Chancellor Willy Brandt resigned because an East German spy had infiltrated the Chancellery. Helmut Schmidt took over. Some months later, in November, members of the RAF shot Günter von Drenkmann, the most supreme Judge in West Berlin. Whoever thought that the *Antiquity Project* would directly respond to the actual social and political situation was deeply disappointed. Thus, it is small wonder that the critics did not refer to it either. However, as we shall see, the production did take a stance.

The Schaubühne started preparation for the project in 1973, when members set out on a journey to Greece. Huge quantities of literature on ancient Greek culture and ancient Greek theatre were carefully studied and discussed before and after the journey. Among the literature consulted, one book seems to stand out: Walter Burkert's *Homo Necans*, which appeared a year before, i.e. the same year as Girard's *Violence and the Sacred*. In it, the Swiss philologist and anthropologist deals extensively with ancient Greek sacrificial prac- tices. He connects the sacrifice with the hunt, emphasizing the act of killing, and with the meal on which the hunters feast after a success- ful hunting expedition. He identifies three parts of the sacrifice: the beginnings (which consist of cleansing rites, dressing up in new clothes, self-decoration, often sexual abstinence, forming a proces- sion, and all the procedures right up to the killing of the sacrificial animal); the killing of the animal, accompanied by the screaming of the women, and its dismemberment (*sparagmos*); the burning of the bones on the altar and the shared meal of meat (*omophageia*).[6] Obvi- ously, Burkert's study was of great importance for the production of the *Antiquity Project*. Long passages from it are quoted in the pro- gramme. Traces of it can also easily be found in the performances.

It was decided not to perform in the small theatre building of the Schaubühne at the Hallesches Ufer, but to create a particular environment for the performances in a huge exhibition hall – the Philips Pavilion – on the Berlin Fairground. The project consisted of two performances presented on two successive nights. On the first night, there was a performance of *Exercises for Actors* directed by Peter Stein. On the second night, Euripides' *Bacchae* was performed in a production by Klaus Michael Grüber. The *Exercises for Actors*, which explored the possible origin of theatre in ritual foreshadowed *The Bacchae* in some respects. The three parts before the intermission, bearing the titles 'Beginnings', 'The Hunt', 'The Sacrifice', not only drew heavily on Burkert's study but also looked forward to and anticipated what would happen the following night.[7]

On the second night of the *Antiquity Project*, the performance of *The Bacchae*, Gilles Aillaud and Eduardo Arroyo had erected a huge, white, planked area in the exhibition hall which marked the field of play and was enclosed by the spectators on two sides in a rectangular arrangement. The back wall had four openings: on the left, a road-sweeping machine was parked, manned by figures in yellow plastic suits; in the middle were two doors, one closed, the other open to reveal a 'contemporary man', at the beginning dressed in a tuxedo, drinking a glass of champagne and watching the arena; on the right, two horses stood behind a pane of glass. (Later on, Pentheus would mount one of them in order to set out for the Cithaeron Mountains.) On the ceiling there were a number of ventilators and neon lights which lit the hall brightly. The space gave off a cold, clean, clinical atmosphere. Here, the performance would unfold out of the dismemberment of the text.

In *Dionysus in 69*, dismembering the text meant to 'sacrifice' more than 50 per cent of it, i.e. to tear it into pieces and to put these pieces together with texts written by the performers or improvised in the performance – as in the 'Dionysus Game' – with newly designed rituals. In Grüber's production of *The Bacchae*, the dismemberment of the text was carried out in a strikingly different way. The text was also shortened, although not to such an extent; it was also brought together with other texts as, for instance, passages from Wittgenstein's diaries. However, the dominant practice was another one. The linearity of the dialogue and action was broken up by interspersing them with enigmatic, self-referential images that could hardly be referred to the text, action or dramatic characters. They seemed to establish a pictorial and symbolic order of their own, an order that was highly associative, creating proliferate meanings that led far away from the text, action and dramatic characters.

Such dismemberment of the text also served a different purpose from that in *Dionysus in 69*. It was carried out as, and sparked off, a reflection (1) on the relationship between present and past, i.e. on the accessibility of the past; (2) between text and performance; and (3) on the possibility of collective identities. Here, sacrificing the text could not possibly result in a community of any kind.

The performance began with an enigmatic image. Dionysus (Michael König) was pushed onto the stage on a hospital trolley and placed directly under a lamp to the sounds of the apotheosis from Stravinsky's *Apollon Musagète*, which created a particular acoustic space that, in several ways, was opposed to the visual space. Dionysus was naked, except for a G-string – as were all the male figures in the performance. He held a woman's shoe in his hand – which he later used to dress Pentheus for his journey to the Cithaeron Mountains.

After some futile attempts he managed to stammer the words 'I' and 'am'. He began to giggle and performed some clumsy, uncoordinated movements. While continuing his monologue, his body cramped into convulsive spasms which shook so violently that the trolley tipped over.

Then, through an opening in the side wall, the Bacchae made their entrance. They were all dressed differently, each highly individually. They were not ecstatic but rather moved in a rather dreamlike way. They inspected the room, fingered the ventilators and the walls which closed the playing area at the back, turned off the lights, and began to tear up the planks from the floor to the sound of drumbeats. Clumps of soil, fruit, lettuce, wool and steaming slime were thrown up. One of the Bacchae poured grain through a pipe that came out of the wall. The chorus leader, at approximately centre stage, spoke the first *stasimon* while the Bacchae started to tie wool to the trolley and to draw the threads all over the space like a spider's web. They pounded the grain, trampled on the grapes, lit a fire. Finally, they unearthed the elderly Cadmus (Peter Fitz) and Tiresias (Otto Sander), thoroughly covered in slime, and fragments from a bust of Dionysus. It was as if they were performing a particular ritual with slow but determined movements. The fastening of the wool to the trolley recalled part three of the *Exercises of Actors* from the previous night, 'The Sacrifice' where the performers brought on an object made of animal skulls and bones. They wound woollen threads around it – which was also reminiscent of Burkert's description of how the horns of the sacrificial animal were wrapped up with bandages. Similarly, the way in which the Bacchae unearthed Cadmus and Tiresias was reminiscent of the fifth part of the *Exercises*, 'The Initiation'. Three actors were undressed, beaten, buried, unburied and smeared with slime.

The actions of the Bacchae could undoubtedly be identified as performing a ritual. Yet, it was hard to guess what the occasion and the purpose of the ritual might be, what it intended to accomplish. They remained somewhat strange and incomprehensible.

After the newly made bust of Dionysus was crowned with prepared offerings, the naked Pentheus (Bruno Ganz) appeared. His first words were taken from Wittgenstein's diaries (1979: 53), more precisely, the entries from 31 May 1915 and 8 July 1916 on the problems of describing the world by naming: 'There are only two godheads: the world and my independent I.' As Pentheus spoke, the road-sweeping machine drove onto the stage and swept away the 'filth' created by the Bacchae. The yellow figures replaced the boards and

Pentheus ordered the neon lights to be turned on again. The Bacchae, who had become immobile, slowly started moving again. They tried to combine the words 'Pentheus' and 'hybris', and they delivered exercises on Greek terms such as *orgiazein*, 'to perform a sacred act'.[8]

As the performance continued, there were many other similarly striking and enigmatic images which, superimposed on each other, intersected and cut through the linear succession of the dialogues and the choral passages. When Pentheus and Dionysus met for the first time, Dionysus stepped behind Pentheus; first Pentheus tried to catch his shadow and then allow his own shadow to merge with that of Dionysus. He turned to Dionysus so that they came very close to each other. They greeted each other with an intimate kiss, touched each other and almost melted into one person before they separated again in a kind of boxing match. In a way, this scene recalled Girard's theory that Dionysus and Pentheus are each other's '*monstrous doubles*' (Girard 1977: 16).

The messenger reporting Pentheus' death remained on the same spot to give his report, as yellow slime dripped down his naked body. He spoke torturously slowly, in a singing vocal tone, listening to each of the sounds he produced. After Agave (Edith Clever) killed her son, no dismembered body lay on the stage. One of the yellow figures took the bloody head of her son from her hands and replaced it with a stand-up collar, in which she recognized 'the greatest pain' (Bacchae 1284). Other yellow figures presented on a silver tray, 'The wretched burden of Pentheus' (Bacchae 1298), his body, ripped up in pieces: stand-up collar, tails, white shirt and grey patent leather shoes. It was not Pentheus who wore them but the contemporary spectator when, at the beginning of the performance, he drank a glass of champagne while watching the arena. Cadmus helped Agave to sew together the pieces of his suit. They sewed and sewed and sewed – and never came to an end.

Such enigmatic images revealed a particular attitude towards the past. They can be 'understood' as a kind of meditation on the fundamental strangeness of archaic as well as classical Greek culture. Grüber's production demonstrated impressively that the elements used on stage to stand in for elements of a past world are primarily related to our own world; any meaning we attribute to them concerning the past world we want to represent or revive tells more about us and our present than about the past world it is meant to represent, interpret and explain. On the contemporary stage, a revival of the ancient Greek world – or of any other past world – is impossible. No resurrection of the dead will take place here. The past is lost and gone forever. What remains are only fragments – play texts torn out of their original contexts – which cannot convey their original meaning. They are mute, distant, alien, and because of this, it is not possible to stage them as if they were contemporary plays. The past is not, in principle, accessible to us. We cannot bring about its rebirth – even when staging a text from the past. Thus, the dismemberment of the text, which has to be accomplished, is due to the past's fundamental inaccessibility.

On the other hand, the dismemberment of the text follows from the particular relationship between text and performance on which the *mise-en-scène* also reflected. In the final image of the performance, Cadmus and Agave appeared to be sewing parts of the contemporary spectator's clothes. Instead of having Cadmus put the fragments and pieces of Pentheus' dismembered body back together again, Grüber created images of a never ending process of stitching and re-stitching which was open to several different readings. It could be read as a commentary on the process of staging Greek texts – moreover, of staging texts in general. In this process the textual 'body' has to be dismembered. It is accessible not as a whole but only in its single parts and pieces. The performance, thus, will never be able to convey the text. It may pretend to put together the bits and pieces of the text and to come into being as a restoration, a rebirth even on stage. But this is a delusion. The performance can do no more than sew parts of a contemporary spectator's clothes together – sewing and sewing and sewing and never coming to an end. Not even the sacrifice of the text-body will redeem us – or admit us into the paradise of an unmediated understanding of ancient Greek tragedy. By performing a sacrificial ritual, the production of a Greek tragedy allows us, at best, to reflect on our fundamental distance to it and perhaps to include some fragments of it into our present theatre, into our contemporary culture. Our distance from the past of Greek tragedy and Greek culture cannot, in principle, be bridged – at least not by theatre and its performances of ancient Greek plays. Thus, the purpose of staging Greek – and other ancient – texts is to remind us of this distance and to enable us to find ways of coping with it individually and perhaps to insert fragments of such texts into the context of our contemporary reflections, life and culture.

That is to say that the text has to be dismembered in order to be staged. And this is what generally characterizes the relationship between text and performance. To stage a text means to perform a *sparagmos* and an *omophageia* – to perform a sacrifice. The participants, the actors, musicians, director and designer dismember the text and something totally new emerges out of the dismemberment that could not be accomplished by putting the fragments and pieces together. The text has to be sacrificed in order to allow the performance to take shape. The sacrifice is performed somewhat in the manner of a Greek sacrificial meal as described by Walter Burkert. For, the producers incorporate into the performance what a 'priest', or some ruling 'Zeitgeist', have declared to be edible. That which appears as 'bones', inedible 'innards' or even 'fatty vapour' to them is left to the 'gods'; that is, they will not be considered in the instance of this particular production. In this sense, from the late 1960s each and every production which comes into being by the process of staging a text, performs a ritual of sacrifice.

The sacrifice of the text in Grüber's production did not result in the coming into being of a community – neither a community represented on stage nor a community between actors and spectators or even among spectators. The performance highlighted differences between the members of the chorus in terms of clothing and movement. It achieved individualization among the spectators by presenting enigmatic, polyvalent, highly ambiguous images. Some images, actions, bodies and objects could be referred to the text by all, it is true. For example, Pentheus appeared at the same moment as the road-sweeping machine drove onto the stage. This device, as well as Pentheus' order to switch on the lights, could be taken as an interpretation of Pentheus as a man of law and order, with which many would agree. However, most of the images could not be referred to the text. They were self-referential in a very peculiar way. From the point of view of the spectator, they emerged in a way which was completely unforeseen and unpredictable.

The sudden, seemingly unmotivated appearance of an image drew the attention of the spectator to it; he directed his attention to these particular bodies, movements, objects, sounds. The image was such that it allowed the spectator's perception to adopt a certain quality. It excluded the question of other possible meanings, of potential purposes or of another context to its appearance. Perception was performed as a kind of contemplation on the image. In this contemplative mode of perception, free of any intention, the perceived image presented itself to the spectator in a way that it seemed to reveal its innermost mystery – it had nothing to do with the text and was different for each and every spectator.

On the other hand, these same images achieved quite the opposite effect after a while. They were able to trigger most diverse memories, fantasies, associations, to arouse various physiological, emotional, energetic and motoric responses in each and every spectator – they exploded his memory and imagination. The outcome of this process could hardly be referred to the text or the dramatic characters; it was the encounter of an individual spectator with his own memories, fantasies and associations.

Grüber's *The Bacchae* suggested the idea that the past, in principle, is inaccessible to us; that a performance can only come into being on the condition that the fixed, seemingly stable text is dismembered; that the meanings that might be generated by and in the performance will never be the same for different, individual spectators. In this way, it seriously challenged the notion of a collective cultural identity. From the end of the eigtheenth century onwards the German educated middle classes (*Bildungsbürgertum*) took Greek culture as they understood it as model for their own culture. They saw Greek culture as something characterized by 'noble simplicity and quiet greatness', as Winckelmann put it. On the other hand, they believed in theatre as a moral and educational institution which conveyed great texts from ancient Greek theatre as well as, according to Goethe's dictum, from *Weltliteratur*, world literature (which mostly implied European drama), and thereby greatly contributed to the shaping and stabilization of their own cultural identity. It was assumed that the texts were actually mediated and thereby the same meaning conveyed to each individual of each generation. The Nazis deeply despised the cultural identity of the educated middle classes. It had to merge with the *Volksgemeinschaft*, *Volk* Community, i.e. their particular cultural identity had to be given up in favour of a national identity, based on consanguinity, on race as well as on the *Führer* principle. After the disaster of the Third Reich, which the educated middle classes had been unable to prevent and to which many of their members had even contributed, there was a desire to go back to the former cultural identity. In the 1950s, the repertoire of the state and municipal theatres was dominated by the 'classics'. Performances were intended to display and convey the eternal values and meanings of these great texts. Then, from the middle of the 1960s onwards, Peter Zadek, began in Bremen 'to demolish the classics' (*Klassiker-Zertrümmerung*) with productions of Schiller's *The Robbers* (1966) and Shakespeare's *Measure for Measure* (1967) – and this was soon followed by many young, revolutionary minded stage directors. The educated middle classes took this as a malicious assault on their particular cultural identity.

Grüber's *Bacchae* went even further. It undermined the very idea underlying such a cultural identity. For if it is not possible to have direct access to the past, if the texts of the past are no longer considered able to grant such access, if a performance can no longer be taken as conveying a text and its 'common' meanings, but comes into being only on the condition that the text is dismembered, it follows that this kind of cultural identity is impossible. All that such texts may transfer from the past to the present is but bits and pieces, fragments of the past, which might be incorporated in our present culture, in our present life. The past is not alive in fixed and stable texts. It must be re-invented anew by the performance based on the dismemberment of the text. Therefore, the idea of a stable, fixed cultural identity, based on a canon of stable, fixed texts of the past, seems absurd.

Grüber's production of *The Bacchae* demanded and performed a critique of textual culture and a new performative turn. Theatre, here, appeared as a particular model of culture – as was already the case at the beginning of the century, albeit a very different model. It was not regarded as bringing forth any kind of community whatsoever. Something new emerges by dismembering the text – the performance, which has incorporated bits and pieces of the text. In this way, the performance re-invents and re-creates the past – or better: the performance invents and creates images of the past which are fluid and ever-changing, generating different meanings for each and every individual spectator, as performative processes. Tradition is not something handed down from one generation to the next unchanged in stable, fixed texts. But it comes into existence by dismembering the texts, by having them swallowed in and through performative processes, which permanently bring it forth as something ever-changing, unstable, not to be fixed. Where cultural identity is based on tradition, it can also only exist as ever changing and fluid – i.e. never as a stabilizing factor in an unstable, ever-changing world.

The new performative turn that emerged in the 1960s and early 1970s is, in some ways, reminiscent of the performative turn that happened at the turn of the twentieth century. Both performative turns came up in anticipation as well as in response to a severe crisis in modern society. Both entailed a utopian solution to the problem at stake. The earlier turn was supposed to be able to bridge the gap between elitist and popular culture; to transform individuals who made a cult of their individuality and the anonymous masses into members of a community by establishing an emotional bond between them. Two ways seemed particularly promising: the invention of a new theatre and the invention of new rituals, as suggested

by the turn from myth to ritual, from text to performance. Max Reinhardt's Theatre of the Five Thousand seems to have succeeded in
uniting actors and spectators from all social classes and strata into a
community, by employing and displaying elements and devices from
elitist as well as from popular culture. By his 'revival' of the Olympic
Games, Pierre de Coubertin founded a new religion, the 'religion of
sports', which demanded particular rituals – rituals that embodied
and displayed values, even contradictory ones, from different social
classes and strata and succeeded in transforming all participants into
members of a community. The temporary communities which
theatre and sports were able to bring about were regarded as a kind
of anticipation of a stable community yet to emerge out of modern
societies. The success of Reinhardt's Theatre of the Five Thousand
as well as of the Olympic Games across the Western world seemed to
substantiate such hopes and expectations.

The performative turn of the 1960s and early 1970s was carried
out and understood as a cultural revolution, as a radical re-
evaluation of all values. It was realized in and sparked off a number
of new forms of cultural performance such as spectacular demonstrations and marches, go-ins, sit-ins, teach-ins, happenings, inter-
rupting the course of traditional cultural performances, street
festivals and many others. These forms were, in fact, theatrical, as
Schechner stated. The new performative turn theatricalized politics,
economics, law, the arts and everyday life. Theatre became a cultural
model. When Schechner and Grüber dismembered the text in their
versions of *The Bacchae* in order to allow the performance to come
into existence, they actually and symbolically accomplished the transformation of the traditional textual culture that proceeded from the
assumption of stable, fixed texts and stable fixed identities, into a
new performative culture that would focus on transitory, ephemeral
events and allow for fluid, ever-changing identities. There was no
attempt to overcome the liminal character of the epoch by constructing new identities. Instead, the transformative tendencies of the time
were taken up and even reinforced. Criticizing the textual culture of
the past, dismembering its tradition, did not mean burning texts and
smashing monuments. Rather, as Schechner's and, in particular,
Grüber's production demonstrated, dismembering tradition meant
allowing a new order to emerge that will necessarily incorporate fragments of the dismembered tradition and, thus, breathe new life into
them. The idea of a new performative culture that would enable a
community to be a 'viable dialectic between solitude and being-with-
others', which could do without any stable individual and collective

identities, entailed another utopia of a better world to come. Theatre, once more, acted as its substitute and anticipation. One might assume that the new performative turn finally achieved that which the earlier performative turn had striven to accomplish. However, as it turned out later, the better world remained a utopia – the last utopia of the twentieth century.

9   The rebirth of tragedy out of the chorus

Although the theatricalization of Western culture brought about by the performative turn of the 1960s and early 1970s continues today so that theatre still functions as a cultural model, the utopian vision it entailed and promised to realize for the future has long since withered despite the fact that after the great transformations in 1989, the dissolution of the Communist dictatorship in middle and eastern Europe encouraged new hopes and expectations. Therefore, it seems all the more surprising that in the 1990s, new forms of choric theatre arose which recall the pageantry movement of the beginning of the century, Reinhardt's Theatre of the Five Thousand, and the mass spectacle between the wars. However, whereas all these earlier forms of choric theatre represented, propagated and even partly brought about a self-organizing and self-organized community that allowed for shared communal experience, nothing could be farther removed from the choric theatre of the 1990s. In the light of late capitalist, post-industrial societies, they radically criticized the concept of such a community and fundamentally questioned its very possibility.

At least in the German speaking countries, the theatre of the 1990s can rightly be characterized to a great extent as choric theatre. Some directors only created particular forms of choric theatre occasionally – such as Robert Wilson in his productions of Gertrud Stein's *Doctor Faustus Lights the Light* and *Saints and Singing* (Hebbel Theater Berlin 1992 and 1997), Jossi Wieler in his production of Elfriede Jelinek's *Wolken.Heim* (Schauspielhaus Hamburg 1993), Jan Lauwers in his production of the *Needcompany Macbeth* (Kaaitheater Brussels 1996) or Volker Hesse in his production of Urs Widmer's *TOP DOGS* (Theater am Neumarkt, Zurich 1997). Others have created theatre that is exclusively – or almost exclusively – choric theatre, such as the theatres of Einar Schleef and Christoph Marthaler.

TOP DOGS, for instance, dealt with unemployed head managers who assemble in a so-called outplacement office. What unfolded in the performance was a grotesque attempt to recycle the top victims of capitalist market economics back into the market – albeit with only a slight chance of success. Here, individualizing and de-individualizing the figures appeared to be nothing more than economic strategies to fit them back into the system. The choric scenes showed the climax of self-alienation of the figures. In the 'Battle of Words', consisting of 'ready-mades' taken from the language of economics and management, all figures did the same actions at the same time and yet nothing they did made any sense at all. The scene started with verbal and physical fighting between the former leading representatives of a ruthlessly competitive society trying to push each other out, but ending in chaos. Then, mysteriously, a body chorus emerged out of the chaos, which transformed the aggressive management speech into a seductive marketing sound and luring 'solidarity'[1] by harmonically flowing movements and stylized choreography.

While in *Dionysus in 69*, a community came into being by performing the same actions at the same time together, in *TOP DOGS*, the same performative actions betrayed the total self-alienation of all those participating. Even the image of a harmonious community at the end of the scene was delusive. It appeared to be nothing but a clever marketing strategy promising the consumer that the market will even fulfil his desire for solidarity, his yearning for a community, for communal experience. In Grüber's *The Bacchae*, a fluid and ever-changing identity was suggested as the prerequisite to a new performative culture emerging out of the dismemberment of the text, the dismembered textual tradition. But in *TOP DOGS*, such an identity was denounced as a necessary prerequisite that allows the individual to adapt to the ever-changing demands of late capitalist market economics perfectly, to function well in any place, in any position or for whatever purpose capitalist economics require. Here, the utopian vision of a new performative culture was debased to nothing but a prerequisite for the smooth functioning of the capitalist system in times of globalization. In the world of *TOP DOGS* there are no individuals, there is no community. What, at first glance, may appear to be an individual is the transitory result of strategies to make that figure fit some specific market demands. That which seems to be a community is actually revealed to be a group of self-alienated conformists, who neither care for each other, nor for a surrogate fabricated to satisfy the desire for communal experience. Although the spectators literally surrounded the actors, being placed on rising moveable scaffoldings, such a spatial arrangement did not invite any kind of community building. Rather, a cool, distant, analysing gaze was provoked from being moved around and being enabled to look down on the stage proceedings from different angles and perspectives.

In *TOP DOGS*, that which was presented as the world and 'fate' of top managers who fail, appears in the theatre of the Swiss stage director Christoph Marthaler as the everyday life of common people. In his production of *Murx den Europäer! Murx ihn! Murx in ab! (Bump off the Europeans! Bump them off! Bump them off!* at the Volksbühne am Rosa Luxemburg Platz, Berlin 1993) which is still running, for instance, 11 generally rather ugly, in part grotesque, filthy and somewhat unappealing figures performed identical everyday actions such as sitting at a table, drinking tea, munching a cookie, going to the toilet, cracking jokes etc. They continue in endless repetition which nonetheless follows particular rhythmical patterns. They seemed to be more or less isolated, unable to communicate with each other, almost autistic, diffusing a mood of grotesque-comical dreariness, shabbiness, or uncanny, even nightmarish atmosphere. They did not seem to be living individual characters, but almost zombies in the guise of ordinary people, as ghosts of themselves (*Wiedergänger*). The atmosphere changed suddenly when the figures came together to form a chorus and strike up a song, as happened every now and then in a certain rhythmic pattern. As a choir they sang, for instance, the old hymns 'Sicheres Deutschland, schläfst du noch' ('Germany at peace, are you sleeping still', from the year 1650, i.e. two years after the end of the Thirty Years War); 'Wach auf, du deutsches Reich' ('Awake, the German Reich'); the romantic song 'In einem kühlen Grunde' ('In a cool valley' by Joseph von Eichendorff); 'Danke' ('Thank you'), a song written and composed for the meeting of all Protestant churches which took place the year before; even Paul Lincke's 'Glühwürmchenidyll' ('Glow Worm's Paradise') and the 1950s hit 'Ich laß mir meinen Körper schwarz bepinseln' ('I shall paint my body black'). Their singing changed the atmosphere completely. It allowed the audience to forget the depressing hideousness of the waiting-room like place and the mean and venomous way the figures treated each other. Their singing seemed to carry them and the spectators away from this revolting everyday life to create an atmosphere which, characterized by fullness, richness and harmony, seemed to anticipate the utopia of redemption from the depressing vexations of a petty, paltry, everyday life. After the last tone died down and even its reverberation no longer wafted through the space, the figures departed and the atmosphere of dolefulness filled the space again and affected, partly even infected, the spectators.

Under no circumstance did the singing bring about a community between the singing figures. Rather, the singing choir served as a kind of surrogate for a community. It recalled past times or rare occasions when such a community was not only feasible, but actually came to life. It was a melancholy memory which evoked in the spectators similar melancholy memories of a time when people were able to enjoy communal experiences. In the world of *Murx*, these times were long since gone. It allowed neither individuals nor communities to come into being.

Thus, the choric theatre of the 1990s appears to be a searing critique of late capitalist, post-industrial societies. The market and the Internet have no need of individuals – of any particular identity – only consumers and surfers. Nor do they need any kind of community, either. Their purposes are best served by isolated conformists, by people who comply with their rules and demands without question. Post-industrial societies as presented and analysed in choric theatre of the nineties, rather seem to want to transform individuals who have proved resistant to new trends up to now into conforming consumers and net users. Those who, for whatever reason, drop out of society, are not regarded as victims, sacrificed on the altar of capitalism, globalization and worldwide communication, but as losers who could have performed better but did not want to. And if they were unable to perform better, it was only their own fault. The utopian vision of a self-organizing and self-organized community which unites individuals as embodied minds seems to have disappeared from the agenda of modern Western societies.

While most choric theatre of the 1990s presented and analysed this state of affairs, whether in a somewhat distanced and satirical way, or enraged and aggressively, Einar Schleef's theatre took quite another stance. It did not accept the diagnosis that there are no longer individuals and communities in post-industrial societies. Rather, it insisted on the belief that individuals and communities as well as the tension between them, are an anthropological given, that there is no society feasible that could evade or avoid it, that could do without individuals and communities.

Schleef started his career in the early 1970s as a stage director and designer in the German Democratic Republic (East Germany) at the Berlin Ensemble. In 1976, he left for the West. He pursued projects in Düsseldorf and Vienna without ever finishing them. After ten years of searching, he staged Euripides' *Suppliant Women* and Aeschylus' *Seven against Thebes* at the Frankfurt Schauspielhaus (1986). The production which lasted almost four hours was entitled *The Mothers*. In this, his first production in the West, Schleef created a new form of theatre which he further developed in all his following productions until his untimely death in July 2001. In *The Mothers* he experimented for the first time with what from now on would become the trademark of his theatre: the chorus.

Schleef created a unique space for his *mise-en-scène*. Except for the three back rows (for elderly or disabled people), all the seats in the auditorium were removed. The floor gradually rose to the back rows in shallow steps where the spectators took their places. From the stage, a kind of catwalk, also sloping in steps, cut through the middle of the auditorium to the back wall where it met with a second, narrow stage behind and above the remaining seats. Thus the acting space was spread out in front, behind and in the middle of the spectators so that they were often almost surrounded by the performers.

There were three different choruses in the performance, all consisting of women: the chorus of widows, dressed in black, meeting Theseus (Martin Wuttke) holding axes in their hands; the chorus of virgins, dressed in white tulle in the first part, red in the second and the chorus of women dressed in back overalls, like workers in an ammunition factory. They occupied and ruled the space: the stage in front of the spectators, the catwalk where, particularly in the second part, they ran, hurried, dashed up and down, wearing black metal-capped shoes, and the stage behind the spectators – recalling in some ways the dynamic and energetic bodies in Reinhardt's choruses which also occupied the whole space. The members of Reinhardt's choruses, however – as well as the chorus in Grüber's *The Bacchae* – were intentionally individualized in terms of their costume and movements. But in *The Mothers*, the members of each chorus not only wore identical clothes but also moved their bodies in seemingly the same rhythm, performing the same movements and speaking, whispering, shouting, roaring, howling, screaming, whimpering and whining the same words in what appeared to be unison. Nevertheless, this does not mean that the chorus acted as a collective body, in which the individuality of the different chorus members dissolved and merged with the others. Rather, the chorus appeared to be a permanent battleground between individuals who want to join the community while maintaining their individual uniqueness, and the community, which strives for total incorporation of all its members and threatens alienation to those who insist on their individuality.

Thus, a permanent tension existed in the chorus between the individual members and the community which they formed; a tension which caused an incessant flow within the chorus, a dynamic of transformation in terms of the individual's position in, and relationship to, the community. This tension never vanished; the chorus never transformed itself into a harmonious collective, but rather the tension intensified. It made itself felt as an act of violence done on the individual by the community as well as on the community by the individual, over and over again.

This latter violence became even more obvious whenever the chorus was confronted with another individual – Theseus or Eteocles (Heinrich Giskes). The conflict between Eteocles and the women of Thebes, for instance, was settled by a constant shift of position on the catwalk. The women lay on the steps while Eteocles stood upright above them, or Eteocles crouched while the women bent down towards him. The power struggle between the individual and the chorus was fought through a constant change of position in space and varying the force of the voices. When the women suddenly straightened themselves and, literally, shouted Eteocles down solely by the strength of their voices, he fell to his knees and cowered.

In some respects, Schleef's treatment of the chorus provides a link back to Nietzsche. For Nietzsche claimed that the chorus is the origin of theatre and tragedy is constituted by the incessant battle between two conflicting principles: that of individualization and that of its destruction, or dismemberment. This is, in fact, what could be observed in the choruses of *The Mothers*. On the other hand, it also recalled the ur-scene of sacrifice, as described by Girard. Obviously, Schleef did draw upon it, as a passage on the chorus in his book *Droge Faust Parzifal* (Drug Faust Parcifal) suggests:

> The classical chorus presents a terrifying image: figures held tightly, seek protection amongst each other although they vehemently reject each other as if the proximity of another person might contaminate the air. This endangers the group itself, it will yield to any attack, precipitously and fearfully accept the idea of a necessary sacrifice, ostracize one member to buy its own freedom. Although the chorus is aware of its betrayal, it does not readjust its position, but rather places the victim in the position of someone who is clearly guilty. This is not just one aspect of the classical chorus but also a process which repeats itself every day. The enemy-chorus is not just made up of the millions of non-whites, perishing people, looters and asylum

seekers, but also of alternative thinkers, especially those who speak our own language; they must be destroyed first, no matter how. And yet, up to this day of reckoning, the classical constellation is alive; the chorus and the individual are still at war, the relationship of the individual to others who were previously isolated from each other, continues to rumble as does the relationship among them and as a whole against the chorus, which hopes to defeat them successfully.

(Schleef 1997: 14)

Although, at first glance, Schleef's description of the situation follows the model of Girard's ur-scene, he deviates from it in one important aspect: he does not judge or even legitimize the violence of the chorus/community on the victim as cathartic violence that would save the community from its total destruction through mutual violence. Rather, he regards such violence as a permanently impending threat which, however, the community has to evade in any case. For, on the one hand, it destroys an innocent victim and, on the other, it does not save the community from mutual violence among its members. The battle between individual and community is an ongoing, never-ending process. The tension which determines the relationship between individual and community is not to be annulled by doing common violence on one individual. It is not to be annihilated.

In his view, the situation described by Schleef in the passage quoted above is not only characteristic of the classical chorus but also of modern societies, i.e. of the post-industrial society of his times. Thus, it is small wonder that the permanent tension in *The Mothers* which defined the relationship between individual and community extended into the auditorium and also defined the relationship between actors and spectators. The spatial arrangement which allowed the actors to surround the spectators or to act right in the middle of them suggested the idea of a fundamental unity between actors and spectators, of a single – perhaps even harmonious – community formed out of the two groups. But this unity was permanently challenged. Whenever it came into being, the community was immediately broken up again. Instead of unity, conflicting forces were experienced. This was partly due to the ambiguous spatial arrangement. The catwalk cut through the auditorium. This allowed the actors to perform in the middle of the audience, but it could also be experienced as a permanent threat of dismemberment in terms of the collective body of the audience, which it dissected. Moreover, it exposed the spectators to the violence done on them by the chorus when they trampled up and down the steps overhead and shouted down to them, or shouted them down, so that the audience felt physically attacked and responded, in its turn, either by retreating or aggressive defence – as, for instance, by stamping, by rhythmically clapping their hands or even by shouting comments. Here, too, a power struggle was fought between the chorus and the audience. The ecstatic chorus aimed to overwhelm the audience, to bring about a state of ecstasy which individual members of the audience opposed, either verbally or by leaving the auditorium. Others, however, seemed to succumb to the unification with the chorus either in fear or with pleasure. There were only rare moments when chorus and auditorium formed a harmonious community – moments of transition before the next outbreak of conflicting forces between the two groups that turned the house into an inferno.

In the course and wake of such battles and unifications, common actions were never performed by actors and spectators alike, nor did it happen that members of one group actually, i.e. physically, attacked members of the other. Nonetheless, battles were indeed fought between actors and spectators; despite this, for a few moments a community did come into being occasionally. Yet no audience participation occurred in Schechner's sense: the actors remained actors and the spectators remained spectators. How was that possible? It seems as if in this case the autopoietic feedback loop of interactions between the actions of the performers and the perceptions and responses of the spectators released certain energies in all those participating which endowed their perceptions, actions and behaviour with a particular quality in terms of a community coming into being. It is most likely that rhythm (which in Schleef's performance was generally a clearly accentuated rhythm) played a key role.

Since Georg Fuchs' work at the beginning of the century, rhythm became extremely important in performance – whether in Reinhardt's performances or the mass spectacle between the wars, Nitsch's 'Orgy Mystery Theatre' or Marthaler's choric theatre. In *The Mothers* – as in all Schleef's performances – rhythm was vital to the process of releasing, transferring and exchanging energy between actors and spectators, to allow energy to circulate in space. Such processes were not only triggered by the rhythmical movements of the actors in and through the space but also by rhythmic speaking. While it is true to say that energy circulating in the theatrical space can neither be seen nor heard, nonetheless, it is perceived. Rhythm is physical, a biological principle; it regulates our breathing as well as our heartbeat. In this sense, the human body is rhythmically tuned. That is why the human body is able to perceive rhythm as an external, as well as an internal principle. We see certain movements and perceive them as rhythmical; we hear particular sequences of words, tones, sounds and perceive them as rhythmical. However, as an energetic principle, rhythm can only have an impact if it is bodily sensed – in the same way that our own bodily rhythms are sensed.

In *The Mothers*, the energies released by the rhythmical movements and rhythmical speaking circulated among actors and spectators; that is to say, they caused a mutual release and intensification of energy. Such energies might confront each other so that a 'battle' between chorus and audience was fought. However, they could also unite, and in this way, bring forth a community of actors and spectators in a few moments of happiness which, however, individual spectators could evade. Which path the energies would take could neither be planned nor predicted. It depended on the intensity of the energy which the actors were able to summon up and homogenize in each performance as well as in each and every moment of the performance. It also depended on the individual spectator's responsiveness in terms of the energy floating in the space, on his capability to sense it by and with his body, and on his readiness to be affected by it and in this way, to mobilize his own energetic potential. Furthermore it depended on the relationship between responsive and less responsive spectators – as well as on many other factors. Thus, the circulation of energy cannot be interpreted as a manipulative device – as some critics suggest – but as an emerging phenomenon. The responsive spectators sensed the energy emanating from the chorus and being transferred to them physically; they accepted it and this caused more energy to emerge and be released in them. This energy was sensed by the actors and other spectators and did its work on them and so on. It was the permanent circulation of energy which brought forth the performance as well as a possible community of actors and spectators.

Such energy does not even require particular spatial arrangements. It can also be released and circulate where actors and spectators meet in and before a box-set stage. For his production of Elfriede Jelinek's *Sportstück* (*Sportplay*) which premiered in 1998 at the Burgtheater in Vienna, Schleef did not demand any reconstruction of the traditional theatrical space. He simply placed the leader of the chorus on the balcony, at the back of the audience. Jelinek's play deals with the special transformations experienced by human bodies in post-industrial societies and, in particular, by bodies of competitive athletes – transformations that would have far transcended Coubertin's imagination. In one scene, the chorus of men and women, dressed in sportswear, performed the same stressful exercises with highest possible intensity for 45 minutes repetitively until physical exhaustion. At the same time, they also repeated the same sentences with varying volume, pitch, stress and tone of voice over and over again with no less intensity. The release of energy and circulation of it in space could be physically sensed. Several spectators seemed offended after only a few minutes and left the auditorium. Those who remained exposed to what was happening on stage, sensed how an energetic field came into being between actors and spectators which intensified the longer the repetitions lasted. Here, a community of actors and spectators was brought forth solely by the circulation of energy among them which, in the exchange of forces, allowed a kind of union, sometimes even harmony to emerge, although the tension remained. At the end of the scene, when the actors fell to the floor, the spectators jumped up from their seats and gave them a standing ovation, acting out in this way the own energy mobilized during the scene.

Since Schleef's theatre was a choric theatre – like the *Thingspiel* plays – since the impact of the chorus was quite often experienced as an act of violence, as an attack on the spectator, and since each and every performance was carried out as a negotiation of the relationship between individual and community, some critics denounced it as fascist – in particular those critics who had fervently advocated political theatre in the 1960s and early 1970s as a theatre of enlightenment. They regarded Schleef's choruses as a relapse into barbarism. They completely ignored that here, a new tragic theatre was emerging, a theatre that dealt with the *conditio humana* as a tragic condition and yet negated the need for sacrifice. In Schleef's theatre, individual and community cannot be conceived independently of each other. There is an ongoing battle between the two but it is a battle which can never be won. It must continue for ever – i.e. as long as human society exists. Thus, no one should claim that the conflict could be solved by the mechanism of sacrifice, by directing the violence of all onto one victim. A sacrifice is unable to uphold the community. Society can only exist as a permanent conflict between individual and community. Such a conflict may only be settled temporarily – in rare moments when there is harmony between all members of the community. But such a harmony will not be brought about by sacrifice. It cannot be planned. It emerges unforeseen and unpredictably – as a result of fortuitously uniting energies which may split up again and confront each other the very next moment. It is not sacrifice, nor common beliefs, ideologies, convictions, ideas, commonly performed actions, nor shared experiences that are able to bring forth a community. It is, according to Schleef, an anthropological necessity which drives individuals to form a community as well as uphold their own individuality at the same time. The one cannot do without the other, although both are constantly threatened by the existence of the other. There is no way out of this constellation. A 'viable dialectic between solitude and being-with-others' is inconceivable. Thus, the position realized and suggested by Schleef's theatre radically opposed the rather naïve utopian visions of communities of former epochs – from the turn of the century until *Dionysus in 69*.

The *conditio humana*, as embodied by Schleef's theatre, also entails a particular relationship between body and language, body and mind. One might assume that since a shared rhythm generally synchronized the bodily movements and the vocal recital of the choral passages, there was, if not harmony, at least a correspondence between body and language. The shared rhythm, however, functioned as the site and means of another battle. On the one hand, language tried to force its rhythm on the bodies, to inscribe it onto the bodies and thus to subordinate the bodies to its own symbolic order. On the other hand, the bodies rebelled against such an attempt. They tried to force a rhythm which often distorted the syntactical order onto the language, so that the sentences did not make sense any more and the symbolic order of language was destroyed. Neither came off as the winner in this battle; rather, there was a permanent shift between the symbolic order of language and the ecstatic order of the body. While language tried to subordinate the ecstatic body to its symbolic order, the body strove to undermine and to subvert the symbolic order of language by dissolving it in the maelstrom of its ecstasy.

This battle between body and language was also reminiscent of Nietzsche's ideas about the birth of tragedy. What was performed by the choruses might be seen as the battle between the Dionysian principle (embodied by ecstatic dancing, running, falling bodies) and the Apollonian principle (embodied by the symbolic order of language). However, in the case of Schleef's choruses, the outcome of the battle was never predictable. As long as the performance continued, the battle moved back and forth without generating a winner.

Since, in Western tradition, language is usually related to the mind, the battle between body and language can also be grasped in terms of the relationship between body and mind. It seems that it is also conceived as a permanent conflict which can be settled only temporarily. In the chapter on Reinhardt, I have argued that the energy that emanated from the actors' bodies caused in the spectators a sense that the actors were present in an unusual and uniquely intense way and that this conferred the spectators with the ability to sense their own presence in an especially intense way. This is to say that in experiencing the energetic actors' bodies, the spectators seem to experience the performers as well as themselves as embodied minds, i.e. as human beings in an emphatic sense of the word.[2] As we have seen, in Schleef's production of *Sportstück* – as in all his productions – energy emanated from the chorus, circulated in the space, was transferred onto the spectators and mobilized in them their own energetic potential. Therefore, we can conclude that they sensed the performers as well as themselves as embodied minds.

Thus, we have to differentiate between two positions. The chorus was performing an ongoing, never-ending battle between body and mind, with changing dominances that allow for no permanent supremacy of the one over the other. What was happening between the chorus and the spectators, however, was the experience of the other and oneself as an embodied mind. As there were only rare moments of harmony between individuals and community on stage and between chorus and spectators, there were also rare moments when the spectators experienced the actors and themselves as embodied minds. These were moments of fulfilment that granted something that, because of the human condition, cannot last, but must remain transitory and ephemeral despite the utopian visions at the beginning of the century or the *promesse de bonheur* of the mass spectacles between the wars – and in *Dionysus in 69*. Even the new performative culture will be unable to change the *conditio humana* although it might contribute to understanding it better.

With *The Mothers*, Einar Schleef laid the foundation of his tragic theatre based on the chorus. He continued to develop this concept further, without ever returning to Greek tragedy, until his very last production *Verratenes Volk* (Betrayed People), (performed at the Deutsches Theater Berlin, in 2001), in which he himself appeared on stage as Nietzsche, reciting from *Ecce Homo* for 45 minutes. In his once scandalous book, Nietzsche had developed a theory about the origin of Greek theatre from sacrificial ritual in order to lay the foundations for a new theatre, the theatre of the future which he saw already partly realized in Richard Wagner's musical theatre. Einar Schleef turned to ancient Greek theatre and, in particular, to the chorus, in order to establish a contemporary form of tragic theatre, a theatre which featured the complicated and ever-changing relationship between individual and community, between mind and body, a relationship which can only be transferred momentarily into a state of harmony or even balance. The tragic theatre reborn here out of the chorus was a theatre of violence which also did violence to its spectators, a theatre which physically and spiritually hurt, and yet, fiercely opposed the idea of sacrifice. Schleef did not resort to ancient Greek theatre in order to construct and convey a new image of Greek culture or theatre, nor to emphasize its fundamental strangeness and inaccessibility nor did he attempt to topicalize it by making references to current social and political problems. He resorted to it because he saw the chorus as the indispensable condition of tragic theatre. And this was what he was striving for – unfortunately in times which had completely lost any sense of the tragic.

Epilogue
Renouncing sacrifice

Neither Schleef's theatre nor Grüber's *The Bacchae* can be regarded as a fusion of theatre and ritual of whatever kind. They did not borrow ritual elements and patterns either from familiar religions (as did the mass spectacles between the wars) or from foreign cultures (as did *Dionysus in 69*). Nonetheless, they opened up the possibility of transformation for individual spectators by transferring them into a state of liminality – as did all the performances under investigation here. Does this mean that they transgressed the boundary between theatre and ritual as I have stated with regard to *Electra*, proceeding from the concept of theatre as was common in Western culture at the turn of the century? This conclusion would seem hardly plausible when considering Max Herrmann's reconceptualization of theatre as performance. He redefined theatre out of the relationship between spectators and performers as well as out of the impact both parties have on each other – i.e. he redefined theatre as a transformative performance. In this, he revived an old idea of theatre for the purposes of modern society.

In the *Poetics*, Aristotle describes the impact of tragic theatre as bringing about *éleos* and *phóbos*, compassion and fear, as well as *catharsis*, purification from just these emotions. He implies in this a transformation of the spectator caused and enabled by the act of looking on in a performance. When the patristic writers in late antiquity and other opponents of the theatre in the Middle Ages and early modern times warned against the danger entailed by a visit to a theatre performance to the salvation of a spectator's soul or, quite the contrary, the physician serving the Emperor in 1609 expressly recommended such a visit because the spectator's health would be improved by the process of watching a comedy, they all understood theatre's transformative potential as something to be avoided or sought after. Interestingly, in all these cases, both the risk and opportunity offered by transformation were assumed to be located in the particular communicational conditions and means of theatre, i.e. in the bodily co-presence of actors and spectators. This holds true until the second half of the eighteenth century. Rousseau (1987: 210) condemned the theatre because 'the constant outbursts of different emotions to which we are subjected in the theatre, disturb and weaken' the spectator and make him 'even less able to control' his 'own passions'. Henry Home, Diderot, Lessing and many other theoreticians of the eighteenth century, however, praised it for its capacity 'to make us so open to emotion that we are moved by and empathise with the unlucky in whatever form whenever he appears' (Lessing 1757; 1973: 163). By the end of the eighteenth century, however, the idea that theatre as a transformative performance and the concept of looking on could be a contagious process was lost or at least, banned from advanced theatre aesthetics. It was replaced by concepts of autonomous art and empathy. It was the performative turn at the end of the nineteenth century, early twentieth century, and the proclamation of a body culture that brought the old idea of theatre as a transformative performance back to theoretical discourse on theatre, albeit in a particular context: in the context of a shift from myth to ritual and from text to performance. Both ritual and theatre were redefined as transformative performances – this is what encouraged the different fusions of theatre and ritual which we have studied – although Herrmann himself never applied the term ritual to theatre.

Nonetheless, the idea of transformation entails the idea of liminality. Although, it arose and was developed in the context of ritual theory, there is no reason why it should not be applied to theatre even if theatre is *not* identified with ritual. Thus, we have to distinguish between different kinds of liminal experience. In ritual, liminal experience is characterized by the criteria irreversibility and social acceptance. That is to say, that here, through/in liminal experience a transformation from status/identity A into status/identity B is accomplished which is accepted by the other members of that community later on. In theatre, however, the transformation brought about by liminal experience does not come to a definite end. What happens in the course of the transformative process is, in principle, reversible and does not need public acclaim. In distinguishing this kind of liminal experience from ritual experience I call it aesthetic experience – thereby redefining the concept of aesthetic experience in a specific way. It is no longer understood in the sense of Kantean 'detached pleasure' but as a liminal experience, as a process of transformation undergone while participating in a theatre performance.

Whereas we can suppose the liminal experience made possible by Reinhardt's performances can be regarded as aesthetic experience, the liminal experience triggered and enabled by the mass spectacles between the wars came much closer to ritual experience. It is not always easy or possible to delineate one clearly from the other – not even within one performance. While spectator X may feel the liminal experience s/he undergoes in a performance as aesthetic experience, it might be a rather more ritual experience for spectator Y. Nonetheless, general tendencies can be identified. The mass spectacles between the wars – as even the early pageants – did, in fact, strive for a ritual experience. They aimed for transformation from identity A to a particular collective identity B which should be accepted and publicly acclaimed at least by all those participating in the performance, even if they not always succeeded, as we have seen.

Although Nitsch's *Orgy Mystery Theatre*, the self-violating performances by Abramović and other artists, even Schechner's so-called ritual theatre of *Dionysus in 69* referred to ritual elements and patterns, the liminal experience they allowed for was not a ritual but an aesthetic experience – as was that which spectators underwent in *The Bacchae* and in Einar Schleef's performance. Here, the emphasis was on the transformative process itself and not on a particular ending to it.

All the fusions of theatre and ritual of twentieth century under consideration here – from the early English and American pageants onwards through the mass spectacles between the wars to the so-called ritual theatre of the late 1960s, early 1970s – strove to regain the transformative potential of theatre. Since the 1970s, however, theatre and performance art have invented and developed so many new artistic devices which enable liminal experience that the transformative power of theatre – which, in fact, is based on and granted by the bodily co-presence of actors and spectators – could no longer be ignored. Hence, by the end of the twentieth century there no longer seems to be any need for fusing theatre and ritual in order to give theatre back its transformative potential. When theatre artists take recourse to rituals today, they do it for very different artistic purposes.

Over the twentieth century, the rediscovery of theatre's transformative potential to be released by particular fusions of theatre and ritual went hand in hand with a desire for new communities, with a deep yearning for communal experience. Theatre's transformative potential was sought after and exploited in order to bring about such communities. Therefore, theatre was held to be the place where the imagined new communities could come to life – it was hoped, as anticipations of a later state of future societies which have become communities again. Theatre, thus, was thought of as a kind of laboratory in which to find out how to bring about a community, and the communities which came into existence here, both onstage as well as between actors and spectators, were held as models for future social and political communities – which, in the long run, turned out to be nothing but an illusion.

While religious studies at the turn of the century as well as in the 1970s unanimously explained that the evolution of a community was something based on a sacrifice, the communities brought forth in and by theatre performances were related to the issue of sacrifice in quite a different way.

Reinhardt's Theatre of the Five Thousand and the early pageants before World War I provided a model of a community between actors and spectators that did not demand a radical change but seemed to be possible under the existing social and political conditions. It did not ask for a sacrifice, either. It seemed to suffice that an action was unfolding on stage that also entailed sacrifices. The community that evolved in the case of Reinhardt's theatre – and in this respect unlike the pageants – was conceived as a temporary community which would not outlast the end of the performance – a theatrical community.

By applying the Reinhardtean devices, the mass spectacles between the wars brought about communities that were not only ideologically determined and conceived as long-lasting, but also were regarded as resulting from radical social and political changes – such as the Bolshevik revolution, the seizure of power by the Nazis or the foundation of a Jewish state. The communities presented on stage were, in fact, based on sacrifices, on the self-sacrifice of members or those who wanted to bring about community, and they also asked the spectators to be ready to offer sacrifice for the common cause they shared.

Without taking recourse to the Reinhardtean devices but by inventing and developing strikingly new ones instead, *Dionysus in 69*, Grüber's *The Bacchae*, the performances of Schleef's theatre returned, in a way, to the model of community first provided by Reinhardt's theatre. The community between actors and spectators they promoted was also a theatrical community, a community that is unable to survive the performance. However, while Reinhardt used devices to cast a spell on the spectators from which they seemed unable to escape before the end of the performance, theatre after the 1970s employs devices that open up the possibility for spectators to reject any community of actors and spectators that might come into being, and to distance her/himself from or oppose it in some way. These are communities that do not require sacrifice – although a sacrifice is often symbolically, even actually, performed on stage.

Such theatrical communities appear as a model for a new type of community brought about by the new performative culture of post-industrial societies during the last years of the twentieth century. Contemporary modern festivals, sports matches, rock and pop concerts, demonstrations and many other newly invented genres of cultural performance allow such temporary, ephemeral communities that do not ask for any longer-lasting commitment nor for a collective identity to emerge. They leave it to the individual whether and when to join or leave the community without the threat of sanctions, thus allowing individualists as well as conformists to participate. Such communities may, in fact, provide a 'viable dialectic between solitude and being-with-others' for members of post-industrial societies. Here, a bond is temporarily established by performing certain actions together and by sharing specific experiences. Such communities are not based on common ideologies and beliefs – let alone on sacrifice. While the theories on sacrifice from the turn of the century until almost the end of the twentieth century insist that there is an indissoluble connection between the evolution of a community and sacrifice, contemporary communities conceived as temporary, ever-changing communities demonstrate that such a connection is not mandatory.

In post-industrial societies this type of community may be welcomed as the most suitable since it does not restrict the individual's freedom and yet serves his/her needs for communal experience. In traditional societies, however, it might be seen as a threat posed by Western culture in the process of globalization. To some, it might seem attractive to draw from and revive the old cultural pattern of sacrifice and self-sacrifice in order to confirm the own traditional community, in order to prove its supremacy over the Western model – to become a 'martyr' for the sake of the traditional community and its values. But this is quite another story.

Looking back at twentieth century Western culture – an age of extremes abundant with war, catastrophe and all kinds of violence in crimes and madness – the utopian vision of a community theatre devised and realized not only in the 'religious' plays between the

wars, but even in Reinhardt's performances, stands out as an ambivalent shining star, spreading light and hope in a world of darkness
and partly even supporting dangerous political strategies. In any
case, it highlighted two characteristics of a possible community
which theatre, in particular, is able to bring out. First, to be self-
organizing and self-organized, and second, as something that lasts
only temporarily. As we have seen, a performance is able to bring
forth a community of actors and spectators by processes of self-
organization that do not demand any kind of sacrifice, *per se.* In the
mass spectacles between the wars, it was the underlying ideologies,
the secular religions and their semiotic background that asked for
sacrifices. However, in the performance itself it was the performative
enactment of shared experiences that allowed for a community to
come into existence, that inspired a communal experience to
emerge.

That is to say that two features are characteristic of all theatrical
communities: they result from processes of self-organization and can
last only temporarily. Thus, in retrospect, such performances show
theatre to be a kind of laboratory in which a new concept of
community was developed and tried out – a concept that could be
fruitfully applied to modern societies, irrespective of whether they
were industrial or post-industrial ones. It is the reconceptualization
of theatre which emphasizes the relationship between actors and
spectators, i.e. the autopoietic feedback loop, through which any
performance comes into being, that allows for such communities. As
long as scholars continued to identify a particular ideology, to dis-
cover a particular symbolic meaning, a message, conveyed in these
performances; as long as the semiotic level was stressed, this particular potential of theatre to develop a new concept of community
remained hidden and concealed. Or if it was discovered, it seemed
contaminated by the particular ideology that went with it. Only when
focusing on the performative level does this potential come to the
fore and unfold before our eyes. The concept of community which
Reinhardt's theatre already developed, the concept of a theatrical
community in modern and especially, in post-industrial societies,
seems to be the only conceivable one. It is a community that comes
into being in and through processes of self-organization and therefore cannot last but for a very limited time span only. Whether this
kind of community will suffice to stabilize our societies, remains to
be seen.

Notes

Prologue – Electra's transgressions

1 dt., *Vorwärts*, 1 November 1903.
2 Fritz Engel, *Berliner Tageblatt*, 31 October 1903.
3 Richard Nordhausen, review from the archive of the Theatre Museum in Cologne, missing more detailed information.
4 H.E., *Freisinnige Zeitung*, 3 November 1903.
5 Paul Goldmann, unspecified review from the archives of the Theatre Museum Cologne.
6 dt., *Vorwärts*, 1 November 1903.
7 W.T., *Neue Hamburger Zeitung*, 1 November 1903.
8 dt., *Vorwärts*, 1 November 1903.
9 Unidentified review from the archives of the Theatre Museum Cologne.
10 Fritz Engel, *Berliner Tageblatt*, 31 October 1903.
11 Concerning the new concept of embodiment underlying Eysoldt's performance, see Fischer-Lichte 2000: 65–75.
12 J.S., *Hannoverscher Courier*, 1 November 1903.
13 Fritz Engel, *Berliner Tageblatt*, 30 October 1903.
14 Unidentified review from the archives of the Theatre Museum Cologne.
15 W.T., *Neue Hamburger Zeitung*, 1 November 1903.
16 *Berliner Morgenpost*, 1 November 1903.
17 dt., *Vorwärts*, 1 November 1903.
18 *Freisinnige Zeitung*, 1 November 1903.
19 Julius Hart in an unidentified review from the archive of the Theatre Museum Cologne.
20 *Berliner Morgen Zeitung*, 1 November 1903.
21 J.I., *Berliner Börsen Courir*, 31 October 1903.
22 See Didi-Huberman 2003 and Gauld 1992.
23 See Chapter 1.
24 I shall not interpret the two sacrifices in terms of the tragedy, for that would be beyond the point I want to make. For such an interpretation see Wilson 1991, Martens 1987, Robertson 1986, Newiger 1969, Doswald 1969, Baumann 1968, Ward 2000, Bremer 1994.
25 I do not only use the term 'sacrifice' as a technical term from religious studies or the Classics which can also be applied to sacrifice represented in Greek tragedy. I rather tend to exploit the term's ambiguity in

everyday language which makes it possible to use it in a metaphorical sense as well.

26 Regarding the concept of ritual see Chapter 1: Redefining 'ritual'.

27 It seems it was not only a small part of Goethe's audience who were opposed to such an attitude. After a performance of Friedrich Schlegel's adaptation of Euripides' *Ion*, Karoline Herder wrote in a letter on 1 March 1802 to the writer Johann Wilhelm Ludwig Gleim. 'We are supposed to sit in the pit as wooden puppets and to look at the wooden puppets on stage and listen to their declamation; moreover, we are to go home unmoved, empty and cheerless' (von Herder 1861/62: 301).

28 It is not the place here to describe and determine both styles in detail. For my purposes, a somewhat crude outline of general differences, which does not consider each and every concrete deviation, alteration and the like, will suffice.

29 Regarding the concept of liminality, see Chapter 1, especially the passages on van Gennep.

1 Reconceptualizing theatre and ritual

1 Alfred Klaar, 'Bühne und Drama. Zum Programm der deutschen dramatischen Gesellschaft von Prof. Max Herrmann', in *Vossische Zeitung*, 30 July 1918.

2 Max Herrmann, 'Bühne und Drama, Antwort an Prof. Dr Klaar', in *Vossische Zeitung*, 30 July 1918.

3 The term 'performative' was coined by John L. Austin. In his lectures on *How to do Things with Words*, held at Harvard University in 1955, he introduced it into the philosophy of language.

4 In my view, it is a fundamental error to equate European cultural history from the invention of print to the hypertext with the ideology of print, or, even worse, to deduce it from this ideology. Not only does the material history of print differ significantly from it (see Briston and Marotti 2000: 1–29), but also many performative practices of popular, as well as *élite* culture. By the end of the eighteenth century, the ideology of print was by no means 'inscribed' into the bodies governing their behaviour.

5 See Tait 1999, Chemers 2002. A very good selection of various essays on the treatment of abnormality, monstrosity and freak shows is given in Thomson 1996 and 1997.

6 Regarding the Colonial Exhibition (*Völkerausstellungen*) see Goldman 1985 and Hagenbeck 1909.

7 Regarding striptease shows see Barthes 1957, Bloom 1990 and Liepe-Levinson 1993.

8 It is rather surprising that although no one believes in the '*grands récits*' any more nor in the linearity of historical processes, attempts are still made to explain European cultural history from the invention of print until the arrival of the hypertext by referring to the ideology of print.

9 Such a performative turn can also be deduced from the change of the attitude towards the body taking place at the turn of the century. Various movements came into being such as the physical culturists, the Garden City Association, the *Lebensreform* and *Wandervogel* movements, which claimed to liberate the body from its existing constraints. These, they

believed, stemmed from an inappropriate sense of shame and from external conditions brought about by increasing urbanization and industrialization. Thus, such movements propagated a thorough reform of lifestyles in all spheres – in nutrition, hygiene, clothing, housing, leisure activities, sexuality. They believed vegetarianism and abstinence from alcohol and nicotine were as much a prerequisite for the development of a new attitude towards the body as was natural care of the body: bathing, taking a shower, massage, gymnastics, sports, clothes which did not restrict movement. A new culture, a body culture was proclaimed and hailed, featuring the vital, energetic body moving in and through space. See also Fuchs 1906.

10 Other theatre scholars went even further. While Herrmann's foremost concern was theatre as an art form, Arthur Kutscher (1878–1960) who taught in Munich, took a deeper interest in 'folk' theatre in southern Germany and other parts of Europe where the tradition of Passion plays or folk theatre was still alive. Carl Niessen (1890–1969) from Cologne University even directed his attention to festivals, processions, ceremonies, plays, dances, funerals and other rituals in different cultures. He conceived theatre studies as a discipline not only devoted to theatre but to all genres and kinds of cultural performance of all cultures and times. Accordingly, he demanded an enormous expansion of the field of theatre studies, an expansion into what today we would call Performance Studies. But instead of elaborating a theory of performance, as Herrmann did, Kutscher and Niessen referred to the *mimus* which they understood as an anthropological given, as an inborn human urge to act out all kinds of psychic and mental states physically. Since they only cited the *mimus* without actually theorizing it, the concept of *mimus* did not provide such a strong impulse towards further research as Herrmann's performance theory did.

11 Herrmann's idea of something not only as 'psychic' re-enactment – as in empathy – but of 'a shadowy repetition of the actor's performance', of a 'hidden urge to execute the same movements, to produce the same sounds in the throat', has been supported by the fascinating theory of the so-called mirror neurons, which Vittorio Gallese and Alvin Goldman have developed in the 1990s. This is based on the assumption that neurons which, in the observer of a bodily action – like in a soccer game – trigger a similar impulse which, however, is usually impeded, so that it will not be completely acted out. See Gallese and Goldman 1998: 493–501.

12 See for his catalogue of conditions Austin 1975: 14–27.

13 See Part III of the study.

14 After being sued for heresy and having lost his position, Smith was offered a Professorship of Arabic Language at Cambridge University. Here, Frazer was Fellow of Trinity College.

15 At the time Durkheim published the book, the usage of the term had become deeply problematic. In 1910, A.A. Goldenweiser published an article in the *Journal of American Folklore* that undermined the construct of totemism in a way and to a degree that serious anthropologists would not refer to it any more as a 'social fact'.

16 See for the following, van Gennep 1960.

17 Van Gennep points to this correspondence himself in chapter 9, footnote 489.
18 Therefore, it could be expected that van Gennep's findings would be met with some enthusiasm, in particular by Durkheim and his school. Surprisingly enough, the contrary was the case. Marcel Mauss, a nephew of Durkheim tore it to pieces in the year of the appearance of *The Rites of Passage*, in his review in *L'Année Sociologique*, the journal of the Durkheim school. One year later, J.P. Lafitte followed his example in his review in *L'Anthropologie*. One cannot ignore that both critics quite maliciously provided a false report and a distorted summary of van Gennep's argumentation. In Great Britain – as well as in the USA – the book was more favourably received. However, even there it did not become very influential until the appearance of its English translation in 1960. Thanks to Victor Turner, in particular, nowadays his ideas are basic for any research into ritual and transformation processes.
19 See Schlesier 1991.
20 See among others Rozik 2002.

2   Re-inventing a people's theatre

1 In 1901, i.e. one year later, Peter Behrens rebuilt the so-called Arnims Festsäle from Unter den Linden into Reinhardt's Kleines Theater.
2 The fact that it was not 'the people' who flocked to the first Bayreuth festival in 1876, but the rich and the powerful – the emperor, kings and princes, dukes, landowners, industrialists, factory owners, bankers and the like – is quite another matter. It was largely due to the financial circumstances and conditions which, to Wagner's great dismay, could not escape the rules of capitalism.
3 In Vollmoeller's translation, the second part of the trilogy, *The Libation Bearers* bore the title *Sacrifice for the Dead.*
4 Regarding the interpretation of *King Oedipus* and the *Oresteia*, see Fischer-Lichte 2002: 8–25.
5 The reviews to which I refer mainly derive from productions in Berlin, or Munich.
6 Paul Goldmann, *Neue Freie Presse*, November 1910.
7 Julius Keller, *Berliner Lokal-Anzeiger*, 8 November 1910.
8 J.L., *Berliner Börsen-Courier*, 8 November 1910.
9 E.v.B., *Berliner Börsen-Courier*, 8 November 1910.
10 Julius Keller, *Berliner Lokal-Anzeiger*, 8 November 1910.
11 Siegfried Jacobsohn, *Die Schaubühne*, 17 November 1910, p. 1177.
12 See Poizat 1992.
13 *Vossische Zeitung*, 8 November 1910.
14 See Baier 2001.
15 Fire, for example, was a traditional element of European festive culture. Since the French Revolution which inaugurated the first modern political festival, fire has been a permanent element of festivals. In early nineteenth century Germany, the so-called 'sacred flame' served as a somewhat ambivalent symbol of a vague idea of the Germanic, in particular for patriotically oriented male choirs, gymnastic clubs (Turnvereine) and fire-arms clubs (Schützenvereine). Later on, student fraternities

made frequent use of the symbolism of fire. The flickering flame represented either the victory of light over darkness, of day over night, or spring over winter. However, it was never used as a clear, unambiguous symbol. See Mosse 1977.

16 The term 'theatrical community' was coined by Matthias Warstat (2004) in his brilliant PhD dissertation (Free University Berlin, 2002), which deals with the festive culture of the German workers' movements in the Weimar Republic.

17 Fritz Engel, *Berliner Tageblatt*, 8 November 1910.

18 Ibid.

19 Siegfried Jacobsohn, *Die Schaubühne*, 17 November 1910, p. 1178.

20 E.v.B., *Neue Preussische Kreuz-Zeitung Berlin*, 8 November 1910.

21 See Danto 1981.

22 Regarding this concept see Csordas 1994, M. Johnson 1987 and Varela et al. 1991.

23 See regarding the performance in detail Berg 1988 and Buckle 1971.

24 Philipp Scheidemann was a member of the Social Democratic Party. On 9 November 1918, he proclaimed the Republic. In February 1919, President Ebert appointed him as the Parliament's President. Scheidemann resigned in June 1919 in protest against the Versailles Peace Treaty. Gustav Roethe was a distinguished Professor of German literature at Berlin University who propagated nationalist views on literature and science. Gerhard Hauptmann was a German writer, playwright and poet who wrote the first German naturalistic plays and Dr Cohn was a Union leader.

3 Re-inventing ritual

1 In 1874, Ernst Curtius came to an agreement with the Greek government. The German side agreed to bear all costs and to leave all finds to Greece (a quite novel provision at a time when most archaeologists felt entitled to take artefacts and the like home) and the Greek side, in return, granted exclusive excavation rights in Olympia to the Germans. See Drees 1968.

2 Regarding his precursors, see MacAloon 1984a: 146–53.

3 The year 776 BC, which the Greeks later calculated to be the date of the first Olympic Games, probably has more to do with the introduction of Greek writing than with the foundation of the *agones olympikoi*.

4 See Philostratus 1936.

5 See Burkert 1990.

6 It is not the place here to deal with Coubertin's olympism at great length, considering his elitist ideology, his sexism, even racism – the last sentence of the quotation, for instance, reads: '[...] symbol of the endurance of the race and the hopes of the nation', and in an article on 'The Philosophical Foundations of Modern Olympism' (1935) we read: '[...] the modern athlete exalts his country, his race, his flag' (de Coubertin 1966: 131). A number of contradictions in Coubertin's olympism seem to coexist peacefully alongside each other. Regarding a thorough account as well as interpretation of it see Alkemeyer 1996, especially pp. 41–223 and MacAloon 1984a.

7 Regarding these paradoxes see J.G. Frazer 1994, in particular the chapter on the Saturnalia, and Douglas 1966, especially pp. 176–8.

8 In his fine article 'Olympic Games and the Theory of Spectacle in Modern Societies', John MacAloon (1984b) distinguishes four major genres of cultural performance which overlap, partly even merge in the Olympic Games: spectacle, festival, ritual, game and clarifies each contribution to this particular type of cultural performance. It is for good reason that I do not draw on this distinction which, no doubt, is very useful with a view to the Olympic Games of the last fifty years. Instead, I shall work with the categories of festival, ritual and theatre. On the one hand, the fact that the competition and the ceremonies were performed before an audience is characteristic of theatre. Therefore, I subsume spectacle here under theatre – and also because I deal with the early Olympic Games only, i.e. the Games until Coubertin's death. With the exception of the Los Angeles Games in 1932, and, especially, the Berlin Games in 1936, they did not abound in spectacle as did the more recent Games. On the other hand, I am more interested in the particular fusion of theatre and ritual, as accomplished by the festival, and in how it redefined the two relationships.

9 Since the Olympic Games in Amsterdam in 1928 women also participated in the competition. Coubertin never fully agreed. In the above quoted article on the 'Philosophical Foundations of Modern Olympism' from 1935, he still objects to their participation: 'I personally do not approve of the participation of women in public competitions, which is not to say that they must abstain from practising a great number of sports, provided they do not make a public spectacle of themselves. In the Olympic Games, as in the contests of former times, their primary role should be to crown the victors' (de Coubertin 1966: 133).

10 See Dyreson 1995.

11 There has been a fierce, still ongoing debate on whether the Games in 1936 have abused the Olympic idea or, in consideration of the fact that Coubertin very much approved of the Berlin Games as fully in agreement with his idea of olympism, in which respect Coubertin's olympism and Nazi-fascism shared a common ideology. That such an alternative is much too simple is shown by Alkemeyer 1996.

12 Regarding the topography of the Reichssportfeld which, in many respects, was a copy of the topography of ancient Olympia, see Alkemeyer 1996: 305–439. On the site where the Temple of Zeus was erected in ancient Olympia, the Hall of Langemarck was placed. In this Hall, the 'Youth of Langemarck' were worshipped. Legend has it that in World War I, at Langemarck, a group of very young Germans who, in view of the doubtless superiority of the other side had no chance or hope for victory or even survival, nonetheless, went straight into the fire of the enemy artillery, while singing the German national anthem. Out of this, the myth of the 'Youth of Langemarck' was created celebrating the self-sacrifice of the young people for their fatherland. Soil from Langemarck was buried – almost enshrined under the floor of the Hall. The Hall was meant as a place of a cult of the dead, preparing another German youth for its sacrifice in the war to come.

13 For those who understood the words of the speaker which preceded the

agon: 'The holy meaning/of all play:/is the highest achievement/for the Fatherland./The highest commandment of the Fatherland/in need:/ sacrificial death!' A connection between the Hall of Langemarck, the myth of Langemarck and the *agon* suggested itself. For the others, the *agon* of the two protagonists as well as their death brought about a rather vague connection between sports and violence, as expressed in the *agon*; and thus, contributed to the solemn atmosphere of the whole opening ceremony.

14 See MacAloon 1984a, especially: 225–41.

15 In his very early writing, Coubertin hailed the idea of internationalism, sharply opposing it to cosmopolitanism which he found obnoxious, destroying the basis for any kind of international understanding. See de Coubertin 1898. Even after the war which had shown that sports were unable to prevent wars, he stuck to his position. In the article on 'The Philosophical Foundations of Modern Olympism' in 1935 he wrote: 'To celebrate the Olympic Games is to appeal to History. [...] To ask the peoples of the world to love one another is merely a form of childishness. To ask them to respect one another is not the least utopian, but in order to respect one another it is first necessary to know one another. Universal history [...] is the only genuine foundation for a genuine peace' (de Coubertin 1966: 134). Regarding Coubertin's opposition between internationalism and cosmopolitism see MacAloon 1984a, especially pp. 262–8.

16 In Athens, the award ceremony focusing on individual athletes was held at the end of the Games, not in the stadium, i.e. not in full public, but in a separate space. Coubertin was not quite satisfied with it. In 1910, he still complained that 'hitherto the distribution of awards' had 'taken place in the most vulgar and hideous fashion, with the laureates appearing in town clothes, in disorder and without concern for aesthetics. London innovated slightly. Most of the young people appeared in the costume of their respective events and this simple fact completely transformed the appearance of the ceremony' (de Coubertin 1910; 1966: 35). It took quite a while before the award ceremony was designed in its final form.

17 It was not before the Olympic Games in Melbourne in 1956 that the final procession of athletes into the stadium lost its national segmentation. From now on 'the athletes "march" in a band, not segmented by nationality, dress, event, or degree of Olympic success. This is offered as a ritual expression of the bonds of friendship and respect transcending barriers of language, ethnicity, class and ideology that the athletes are said to have achieved during the festival. At the same time, it is a symbolic expression of the human kindness necessary and available for all men and women, a final display and emotional "proof" that patriotism and individual achievement are not incompatible with true internationalism but are rather indispensable to it' (MacAloon 1984b: 253).

Part II Introduction

1 See Eksteins 1990.

2 See for instance Lane 1981.

3 Parker (1928: 95) wrote that it was an 'epoch making experience' when Wagner came to London in 1877. He reports that he missed only one performance in Bayreuth. With regard to his first pageant, he expressly mentions Wagner's influence on his use of indigenous material and uniting the people in a communal experience.

4 Regarding the history of the strike as well as the pageant see Green 1988. In my description of the pageant I follow his version.

5 Review in *The Independent*, 19 June 1913: 1306.

6 *Survey*, 28 June 1913: 428.

7 Regarding this performance see Fischer-Lichte 1997.

8 *The Independent*, 19 June 1913.

9 Concerning the development of political mass spectacles in the 1930s see Denning 1996.

10 Concerning the history of American historical pageantry before World War I see also Prevost 1990. In an appendix, the author offers a chronology of American pageants between 1908 and 1917 as they are listed in the APA (American Pageant Association) bulletins.

4 Times of revolution – times of festival

1 The putting down of the rebel sailors at Kronstadt on 18 March 1921 demonstrated clearly that the revolution had finally come to an end.

2 The October Revolution took place on 25/26 October 1917 according to the old Russian (Gregorian) calendar. By the end of January 1918, this calendar was replaced by the Western Julian calendar. This means the anniversary of the October Revolution was now celebrated on 7/8 November.

3 See van Geldern 1993: 85.

4 See Glebkin 1998.

5 Industrialization cannot be regarded as the main source of the crisis in Russia. For here, progress had not yet advanced very far. Nonetheless, in many respects, the situation in Russia was even more precarious than in Western countries. This led to the outbreak of the revolution in 1905 which was brutally put down shedding the blood of hundreds of people.

6 See also his essay 'The Essence of Tragedy', in Senelick 1981.

7 Nietzsche's *Birth of Tragedy* translated into Russian in 1903, 'had the effect of a veritable "bomb" in Symbolist circles'. See Kleberg 1979: 183.

8 In 1919, Granovsky opened the Jewish Studio in Petrograd. In 1920, it moved to Moscow where it became 'The State Jewish Theatre' (GOSET). Whereas the 'Habimah Theatre' tried to revive Hebrew, the GOSET played in Yiddish.

9 See also the descriptions on pp. 38, 42, 46.

10 See Piotrovsky 1926: 64.

11 Proletkult leader Pavel Kerzhentsev in his influential book *The Creative Theatre*, which appeared in 1918, suggested different models of a new people's theatre to be created after the revolution. He not only draws on Wagner and Rolland but also on first hand experience of English and American pageants, discussing the St. Louis Pageant of 1914, the Yale Pageant of 1916, the New Jersey Pageant of 1916, and the community masque Caliban in New York in 1916 in detail. That is not to suggest that

affinities between the mass spectacles and the pageants listed above resulted from Kerzhentsev's descriptions and propositions. However, they might have had a certain impact.

12 It was Marina Dalügge who drew my attention to the analogy between the orthodox Easter liturgy and the dramaturgy of the mass spectacles. I have also greatly profited from her collection of research material. See Dalügge 2004.

13 The Mobile-Popular Theatre was founded in 1903 as the Popular Theatre by Pavel Gaideburov and his wife, Nadezhda Skarskaia. Its repertoire mainly consisted of the Classics; its first production in 1903 was Ostrovsky's *Storm*. Regarding the history of this theatre and its significance in the development of mass spectacles see van Geldern 1993.

14 In my description of the performance, I shall principally follow that given by Vinogradov-Mamont (1972).

15 One review reports another sequence of eight scenes 'with apotheosis': '1) 9 January 1905; 2) the family of a Moscow student; 3) revolt in a military prison; 4) the arsenal; 5) at the Police Headquarters; 6) on the barricades; 7) at the front; 8) in the headquarters' (O.A. 1919).

16 See Feltz 1999, Morowitz 2002 and Johnson 2001.

17 See Fischer-Lichte 2004a.

18 When it was shown in the square in front of the Winter Palace in July 1919, it had lost some of its impact. This was due, in particular, to the fact that the most important device, the occupation of the space, did not work in this huge square. The 10–12,000 spectators did not even fill one third of it. Even the firing of 500 guns disappeared in the vastness of the space (see Piotrovsky 1919: 2) – Piotrovsky was particularly critical of the performance because he competed with Vinogradov-Mamont and wanted to replace him in the directorship of the Red Army Studio which, in fact, he did shortly afterwards.

19 This is how van Geldern (1993) argues, which seems to me highly plausible. The historical event, in fact, was very different from the myth. On the one hand, it was a rather chaotic action and on the other, all the regiments with the exception of the Women's Battalion, surrendered (see Reed 1919). John Reed died in 1920 in Moscow, one day before the 'Storming of the Winter Palace'.

20 Regarding the course of the performance in more detail see Deak 1975, Evreinov 1924, Holitscher 1924 and Shubsky 1920.

21 See Getty 1985 and Riegel 1998.

5 Producing the *Volk* community – the *Thingspiel* movement 1933–36

1 See Benn 1962.

2 Rainer Schlösser, 'Das Spiel von Job dem Deutschen', in *Völkischer Beobachter* 326/7, 22/23 November 1933.

3 See Goertz 1974: 92.

4 See Warstat 2004.

5 See Biccari 2001.

6 See Raabe 1965: 305.

7 In my description of the celebration I follow the description of the festivities as they were held in the year 1935, as given in Behrenbeck 1998.

8 Here, it was expressly pointed out that the route of the procession was a 'sacrificial route' and the procession itself a 'sacrificial procession'.

9 In the *Völkischer Beobachter* 29 October 1934, the ceremony was explained as follows: 'The eternal renewal and rejuvenation of the National Socialist Front took place in the spirit of the martyrs (*Blutzeugen*) and a new generation of Hitler Youth stepped into the shoes of the SA'.

10 See chapter 3; note 42.

11 A cultural programme was also planned for the Olympic Games in Los Angeles in 1932. It was elaborated by Max Reinhardt but not realized because of financial shortcomings.

12 Möller made this utterance in 1970 in an interview with Glen Gadberry. It seems that Möller had forgotten Reinhardt's productions, in particular his performances of his new people's theatre in the Circus Schumann and in the *Großes Schauspielhaus*.

13 In fact, the return to bourgeois traditional theatre was accomplished much earlier in 1934/35, i.e. at a time when the *Thingspiel* movement seemed at its peak, but liminal times were already over. By the beginning of the 1934/35 season, the political director of Berlin theatres assigned by the government in 1935 were replaced by artists: Gustaf Gründgens was appointed director at the Staatstheater and Heinz Hilpert director of the Deutsches Theater. In 1935, particular attention and subsidies were being paid to the traditional theatre. The most representative theatre buildings in Berlin such as the Deutsche Oper, the Schillertheater, the Staatstheater and Reinhardt's Großes Schauspielhaus, renamed The Theatre of the People were completely renovated. Thus, it was only for a very short time that the interest shifted from the traditional theatre to the *Thingspiel* movement.

6 Towards the rebirth of a nation – American Zionist pageants 1932–46

1 Regarding the description of the performance see Citron 1989.

2 Regarding his biography as well as the circumstances that inspired him to the idea of such a pageant see his autobiography: Weisgal 1971.

3 Regarding the history of Zionism see in particular Laqeur 1972.

4 See with regard to this reinterpretation – as well as my following deliberations – Don-Yehiya 1992.

5 See in particular Raider 1998, esp. pp. 69–124 as well as Berkowitz 1997, esp. pp. 91–124.

6 See Don-Yehiya 1992: 11.

7 It seems to be a particular characteristic of the Zionist pageants that they all feature a narrator.

8 For a description of the performance see Citron 1989.

9 See Reinhardt 1979: 248.

10 Brooks Atkinson, *New York Times*, 8 January 1937.

11 Douglas Gilbert, *New York World Telegram*, 8 January 1937.

12 Robert Coleman, *New York Daily Mirror*, 8 January 1937.

13 John Mason Brown, *New York Post*, 8 January 1937.

14 Gilbert W. Gabriel, *The New York American*, 24 January 1937.

15 Brooks Atkinson, *New York Times*, 8 January 1937.

16 Burns Mantle, *New York Daily News*, 8 January 1937.
17 Richard Watts Jr., *New York Herald Tribune*, 8 January 1937.
18 Joseph Wood Krutch, *The Nation*, 23 January 1937.
19 Brooks Atkinson, *New York Times*, 8 January 1937.
20 Ibid.
21 Richard Watts Jr., *New York Herald Tribune*, 8 January 1937.
22 Brooks Atkinson, *New York Times*, 8 January 1937.
23 John Anderson, *New York Evening Journal*, 8 January 1937.
24 It was not the New York Philharmonic Orchestra, as Rundt states, but the Philadelphia Orchestra.
25 Virgil Thomson, *Modern Music*, January/February 1937, 14 (2), pp. 103–5.
26 Translation of Werfel's text: Ludwig Lewisohn; translation of Reinhardt's handwritten directions, here appearing in italics, by Jo Riley. A clef means: music, singing (Weill), ∩ a pause.
27 Gilbert Gabriel, *The New York American*, 22 January 1937.
28 Richard Watts Jr., *New York Herald Tribune*, 8 January 1937.
29 *Time Magazine*, 8 January 1937.
30 See Virgil Thomson, *Modern Music*, January/February 1937, 14 (2), pp. 103–5.
31 Brooks Atkinson, *New York Times*, 8 January 1937.
32 See Citron 2000 and Whitfield 1996.
33 Regarding the background and the events that led to the decree of the White Paper see also Berman 1990.
34 Regarding American politics since its entry in the war see Berman 1990: 96–183 and Wyman 1984.
35 See Wyman 1984: 90.

Part II Conclusion

1 The fact that American Zionists tended to understand the death of six million European Jews as a sacrifice for the common cause explains why the term 'holocaust' was introduced and became almost generally accepted. 'Holocaust' means, as is well known, a burnt offering as it is described at great length in Moses, Book 3, Chapter 1. For those, who do not follow the Zionist interpretation, the term seems rather inappropriate. See for instance Petuchowski 1992: 146. Therefore I use the term 'Shoah'.

7 Bringing about a crisis

1 It was also in 1968 that a military dictatorship took over in Greece.
2 See Girard 1977.

8 *The Bacchae* – dismembering the text

1 Regarding Soyinka's version see Fischer-Lichte 1992.
2 Regarding Suzuki's production see Mcdonald 1992, especially pp. 59–74. Suzuki reworked his production several times. The last version came out in 2001.
3 Regarding ritualistic theatre see Aronson 2000: 42–107, Innes 1981, Innes 1993: 125–92.

4 The performance, which I have not seen myself, is very well documented. As well as Schechner's long deliberations on it in *Environmental Theater* see also Schechner 1970, n.p. (approx. 350 pp.) as well as the film by Brian de Palma which is also available on video. Bill Shephard (1990), who played the part of Pentheus most of the time, has written his PhD dissertation on the performance. Recently, a very fine article appeared on the performance written by Froma I. Zeitlin (2004), a scholar of Greek Language and Literature, who saw the performance.

5 As Schechner's own deliberations on various performances of *Dionysus in 69* as well as the *Commune* show, the democratic model did not always work. Spectators sometimes tended to exploit the situation or initiate a power struggle. Thus, the 'democratic model' has to be taken with care.

6 See Burkert 1983, especially pp. 1–48.

7 Regarding the *Exercises for Actors* see Fischer-Lichte 2004b, especially pp. 332–7.

8 For the description of the beginning see also Jäger 1974. I saw the performance myself thirty years ago. In order not to rely exclusively on my memory, I have also used a video recording of the performance.

9 The rebirth of tragedy out of the chorus

1 Regarding the production see Theater Neumarkt Zürich 1997 and Kurzenberger 1998.

2 See chapter 2.

Bibliography

Adler, G. (1964) *Max Reinhardt, Sein Leben*, Salzburg: Festungsverlag.

Alkemeyer, T. (1996) *Körper, Kult und Politik, Von der 'Muskelreligion' Pierre de Coubertins zur Inszenierung von Macht in den Olympischen Spielen von 1936*, Frankfurt a.m.: Campus.

Aronson, A. (2000) *American Avant-Garde Theatre*, London/New York: Routledge.

Astruc, G. (1929) *Le pavillon des fantômes*, Paris: Grasset.

Atkinson, B. (1974) *Broadway*, rev. ed., New York: Macmillan.

Austin, J.L. (1975) *How to do Things with Words*, Oxford: Clarendon Press.

Bahr, H. (1907) *Glossen zum Wiener Theater*, Berlin: Fischer-Verlag.

Baier, G. (2001) *Rhythmus, Tanz in Körper und Gehirn*, Reinbek: Rowohlt.

Barthes, R. (1957) 'Striptease', in R. Barthes (ed.) *Mythologies*, Paris: Èd. du Seuil, pp. 165–8.

Bauer, J. (1935/36) 'Natürlicher Aufbau der werkhaften Feier', in *Das deutsche Volksspiel* 3, pp. 243–9.

Baumann, G. (1968) 'Hugo von Hofmannsthal: Elektra', in S. Bauer (ed.) *Hugo von Hofmannsthal*, Darmstadt: Wissenschaftl. Buchgesellschaft, pp. 274–310.

Beck, E. (1926) *Die russische Kirche, Ihre Geschichte, Lehre und Liturgie*, Bühl: Unitas.

Behrenbeck, S. (1998) 'Gefallenengedenken in der Weimarer Republik und im "Dritten Reich"', in S.R. Arnold, C. Fuhrmeister and D. Schiller (eds) *Politische Inszenierung im 20. Jahrhundert: Zur Sinnlichkeit der Macht*, Wien/Köln/Weimar: Böhlau, pp. 35–55.

Behrens, P. (1900) *Feste des Lebens und der Kunst*, Leipzig: Diederichs.

Benn, G. (1962) 'Reden und Essays 1933/4', in D. Wellershoff (ed.) *G. Benn, Gesammelte Werke*, Bd. 1, Wiesbaden: Limes.

Bercovici, K. (1946) 'Foreword', in B. Hecht (ed.) *A Flag is Born*, New York: American League for a Free Palestine.

Berg, S.C. (1988) *Le Sacre du Printemps, Seven Productions from Nijinsky to Martha Graham*, Ann Arbor/London: UMI Research Press.

Berkowitz, M. (1997) *Western Jewry and the Zionist Project, 1914–1933*, Cambridge: Cambridge University Press.

Berman, A. (1990) *Nazism, The Jews and American Zionism, 1933–1948*, Detroit: Wayne State University Press.

Biccari, G. (2001) *'Zuflucht des Geistes'? Konservativ-revolutionäre, faschistische und nationalsozialistische Theaterdiskurse in Deutschland und Italien 1900–1944*, Tübingen: Gunter Narr.

Bloom, M.P. (1990) *The Bawdy Politics, Strips and Culture and the Culture of Strip*, Ottawa: National Library of Canada.

Böhme, G. (1995) *Atmosphäre, Essays zur neuen Ästhetik*, Frankfurt a.M.: Suhrkamp.

Braumüller, W. (1935a) 'Kritische Gedanken zur Thinghandlung auf dem Heiligen Berg', in *Bausteine zum deutschen Nationaltheater* 3, pp. 219–21.

—— (1935b) 'Kurt Heynicke: "Der Weg ins Reich" ', in *Deutsche Bühnenkorrespondenz* 58, pp. 1–3.

Bremer, J.M. (1994) 'A daughter fatally blocked: von Hofmannsthal's Electra', in H. Hillenaar and W. Schönau (eds) *Fathers and Mothers in Literature*, Amsterdam: Rodopi, pp. 113–21.

Breuer, J. and Freud, S. (1991) *Studien über Hysterie*, Frankfurt a.M.: Fischer.

Briston, M.D. and Marotti, A.F. (eds) (2000) *Print, Manuscript and Performance*, Columbus: Ohio State University Press.

Buckle, R. (1971) *Nijinsky*, London: Weidenfeld & Nicholson.

Bukharin, N. (1971) 'Die eiserne Kohorte der Revolution', in *Marxismus und Politik*, vol. 1, pp. 319–32.

Burkert, W. (1983) *Homo Necans, The Anthropology of Ancient Greek Sacrificial Ritual and Myth*, trans. P. Bing, Berkeley/Los Angeles/London: The University of California Press.

—— (1990) 'Heros, Tod und Sport, Ritual und Mythos der Olympischen Spiele in der Antike', in T. Alkmeyer and G. Gebauer *et al.* (eds) *Olympia-Berlin, Gewalt und Mythos in den Olympischen Spielen von Berlin 1936*, Berlin: Universitätsdruck, pp. 87–110.

Butler, J. (1990a) *Gender Trouble*, New York: Routledge.

—— (1990b) 'Performative acts and gender constitution: an essay in phenomenology and feminist theory', in S.E. Case (ed.) *Performing Feminism, Feminist Critical Theory and Theatre*, Baltimore/London: Johns Hopkins University Press, pp. 270–82.

Charcot, J.M. (1991) *Clinical Lectures on Diseases of the Nervous System*, London: Tavistock/Routledge.

Charcot, J.M. and Richer, P. (1988) *Die Besessenen in der Kunst*, (ed.) M. Schneider, Göttingen: Steidl.

Chemers, M.M. (2002) 'Monsters, myths, and mechanics', in *DAIA* 62 (8), pp. 2632–3.

Citron, A. (1989) *Theatre and Pageantry in the Service of Jewish Nationalism in the United States, 1933–1946*, PhD Dissertation, New York University.

—— (2000) 'Art and propaganda in the original production of "The Eternal Road" ', in H. Loos and G. Stern (eds) *Kurt Weill – Auf dem Weg zum 'Weg der Verheißung'*, Freiburg i.B.: Rombach Verlag, pp. 203–8.

Cornford, F.M. (1914) *The Origin of Attic Comedy*, London: Edward Arnold.

Csordas, T.J. (1994) 'The body as representation and being-in-the-world', in T.J. Csordas (ed.) *Embodiment and Experience, The Existential Ground of Culture and self,* Cambridge: Cambridge University Press, pp. 1–26.

Dalügge, M. (2004) 'Die Manöverinszenierungen der Oktoberrevolution in Petrograd – Theatralität zwischen Fest und Ritual', PhD dissertation, Freie Universität Berlin.

Danto, A.C. (1981) *The Transfiguration of the Commonplace, A Philosophy of Art,* Cambridge/MA: Harvard University Press.

Darnley, Earl of (1932) *Frank Lascelles: 'Our Modern Orpheus',* Oxford: Oxford University Press.

Das Deutsche Theater (ed.) (1920) *Das Große Schauspielhaus,* Berlin: Verlag der Bücher des Deutschen Theaters.

Deak, F. (1975) 'Russian Mass Spectacles', in: *TDR* 19, no. 2, pp. 7–22.

de Coubertin, P. (1898) 'Does cosmopolitan life lead to international friendliness?', in *American Monthly Review of Reviews* 17, pp. 429–34.

—— (1931) *Memoirs olympiques,* Lausanne: Bureau international de pédagogie sportive.

—— (1966) *The Olympic Idea, Discourses and Essays,* trans. J.G. Dixon, ed. The Carl-Diem-Institut Köln, Schorndorf: Hofmann.

—— (1986) *Textes Choisis,* 3 vols, vol. II, ed. Comité International Olympique, Zürich/Hildesheim/New York: Weidmann.

de Man, H. (1932) *Wir! Ein sozialistisches Festspiel,* Berlin: Arbeiterjugendverlag.

Denning, M. (1996) *The Cultural Front, The Laboring of American Culture in Twentieth Century,* London/New York: Verso.

Deutsche Bühnenkorrespondenz (DBK) (1934) 'Die Eröffnung des ersten Thingplatzes bei Halle', in *DBK* (3) 45, p. 2.

Diderot, D. (1902) *Le paradoxe sur le comédien, edition critique avec introduction, notes, fac-simile par Ernest Dupuy,* Paris: Societé Francaise d'imprimerie et de libraire, Ancienne Librairie Lecéne.

Didi-Huberman, G. (2003) *The Invention of Hysteria, Charcot and the Photographic Iconography of the Salpêtrière,* trans. A. Hartz, Cambridge/MA: MIT.

Domarus, M. (1965) *Hitler, Reden und Proklamationen 1932 bis 1945, Kommentiert von einem deutschen Zeitgenossen,* München: Süddeutscher Verlag.

Don-Yehiya, E. (1992) 'Hanukkah and the myth of the Maccabees in Zionist ideology and in Israeli society', in *The Jewish Journal of Sociology,* vol. 34, pp. 5–23.

Doswald, H. (1969) 'Nonverbal expression in Hofmannsthal's Elektra', in *Germanic Review (New York)* 44, pp. 199–210.

Douglas, M. (1966) *Purity and Danger,* London: Macmillan.

Drees, L. (1968) *Olympia: Gods, Artists, and Athletes,* New York: Praeger.

Dürr, D. (1935) 'Die Lage', in J. Goebbels (ed.) *Unser Wille und Weg, Die parteiamtliche Propagandazeitschrift für die politischen Leiter der NSDAP, Monatsblätter der Reichspropagandaabteilung,* ed. B, München, p. 399.

Dürre, K. (1933/4) 'Praktische Erfahrungen im Thingspiel', in *Das deutsche Volksspiel* 1, pp. 280–2.

Durkheim, É. (1912) *Les formes élémentaires de la vie religieuse,* Paris: Alcan.

—— (1914) 'Le dualisme de la nature humaine et ses conditions sociales', in F. Jonas (ed.) *Geschichte der Soziologie* 2, *Sozialwissenschaft,* Reinbek: Rowohlt, pp. 368–91.

—— (1933) *The Division of Labor in Society,* trans. G. Simpson, New York: Free Press.

Dyreson, M. (1995) 'Marketing National Identity: The Olympic Games of 1932 and American culture', in *Olympika, The International Journal of Olympic Studies,* vol. IV, pp. 23–48.

Eggers, K. (1933) *Das Spiel von Job dem Deutschen, Ein Mysterium,* Berlin: Volkschaftverlag.

Eichberg, H., Dultz, M., Gadberry, G. and Rühle, G. (1977) *Massenspiele, NS-Thingspiel, Arbeiterweihespiel und Olympisches Zeremoniell,* Stuttgart-Bad Cannstatt: frommann-holzboog.

Eicher, T., Panse, B. and Rischbieter, H. (eds) (2000) *Theater im 'Dritten Reich': Theaterpolitik, Spielplanstruktur, NS-Dramatik,* Seelze-Velber: Kallmeyer.

Eksteins, M. (1990) *Rites of Spring, The Great War and the Birth of the Modern Age,* London: Black Swan.

Engel, J.J. (1804) *Schriften,* vol. 7: *Mimik,* First Part, Berlin: Myliussche Buchhandlung.

Esty, J.D. (2002) 'Amnesia in the fields, late modernism, late imperialism, and the English pageantry-play', in *ELH* 69 (1), pp. 245–76.

Euringer, R. (1936) *Deutsche Passion 1933,* Berlin: Volkschaft Verlag.

Evans, G. (1937/38) 'Toward a new drama in Germany: a survey of the years 1933–37', in *German Life and Letters 1937/8,* vol. 2, Oxford: Blackwell, pp. 188–200.

Evreinov, N. (1920) 'Vziatie Zimnego dvortsa' ('The Storming of the Winter Palace'), in V.E. Rafalovich, E.M. Kuznetsov, A.A Gvozdev and A.I. Piotrovsky (ed.) *Istoriia sovetskogo teatra. Tom pervyi. Petrogradskie teatry na poroge Oktiabria i v epokhu Voennogo kommunizma 1917–1921 (The History of Soviet Theatre. Vol. 1. The Petrograd Theatres on the eve of October and at the time of communism of war 1917–1921),* Leningrad 1933, Leningradskoe otdelenie gosudarstvennogo izdatel'stva khudozhestvennoi literatury (Leningrad Department of the National Publisher of Fiction), p. 279.

—— (1923) *Apologiia teatralnosti (Apologia of theatricality),* Berlin: Academia, pp. 23–31.

—— (1924) ' "Vziatie Zimnego dvortsa", Vospominaniia ob instsenirovke v oznamenovanie 3 – i godovshchiny Oktiabr'skoi revoliutsii ("The Storming of the Winter Palace", Memories of a production commemorating the third anniversary of the October Revolution)' in *Zhizn' iskusstva (Life of the Art)* 45, 4 November 1924, pp. 7–9.

—— (1927) *The Theatre in Life,* trans. A.I. Nazaroff, New York: Brentano's.

Feltz, B. (1999) *Auto-organisation et émergence dans les sciences de la vie,* Paris: Vrin.

Fetting, H. (1973) *Max Reinhardt über Schauspielkunst, Material zum Theater,* ed. Verband der Theaterschaffenden der DDR, Material zum Theater 32, Reihe Schauspiel, issue 11, Berlin, n.p.

Fiedler, L.M. (1991) '"Bleiben doch die ewigen Juden . . .", Max Reinhardts Exil', in E. Koch and F. Trapp (eds) *Exiltheater und Exildramatik 1933–1945*, vol. 2, Maintal: Exil special, pp. 41–62.

—— (ed.) (1996) *Der Sturm Electra, Gertrud Eysoldt, Hugo von Hofmannsthal, Briefe*, Salzburg/Wien: Residenz-Verlag.

Figes, O. and Kolonitsky, B. (1999) *Interpreting the Russian Revolution of 1917*, New Haven/London: Yale University Press.

Fischer-Lichte, E. (1992) 'Wiedergewonnene Mündlichkeit: Praktiken des Ritualtheaters', in U. Schild (ed.) *On Stage, Proceedings of the Fifth International Janheinz Jahn Symposium on Theatre in Africa*, Göttingen: Ramaswany, pp. 1–20.

—— (1997) 'From theatre to theatricality: how to construct reality', in E. Fischer-Lichte (ed.) *The Show and the Gaze of Theatre*, Iowa City: University of Iowa Press, pp. 61–72.

—— (2000) 'Embodiment – from page to stage: the dramatic figure', in *Assaph, Studies in the Theatre*, no. 16, pp. 65–75.

—— (2002) *History of European Drama and Theatre*, trans. J. Riley, London/New York: Routledge.

—— (2004a) *Ästhetik des Performativen*, Frankfurt a.M.: Suhrkamp.

—— (2004b) 'Thinking about the origins of theatre', in E. Hall, F. Macintosh and A. Wrigley (eds) *Dionysus Since 69, Greek Tragedy at the Dawn of the Third Millenium*, Oxford: Oxford University Press, pp. 329–61.

—— (2004c) 'Ritual und/oder Theater? Anmerkungen zu den geistlichen Spielen des Mittelalters', in E. Fuhrich and H. Haider (eds) *Theater, Kunst, Wissenschaft, Festschrift für Wolfgang Greisenegger zum 66. Geburtstag*, Wien/Köln/Weimar: Böhlau, pp. 143–54.

Franken, P. (1930) *Vom Werden einer neuen Kultur, Aufgaben der Arbeiter-, Kultur- und Sportorganisation*, Berlin: Laub.

Fraser, R. (1994) 'Introduction', in J.G. Frazer, (ed.) *The Golden Bough, A New Abridgement, from the Second and Third Edition*, ed. with an introduction by R. Fraser, London/New York: Oxford University Press, pp. IX–XXXIX.

Frazer, J.G. (1994) *The Golden Bough, A New Abridgement, from the Second and Third Edition*, ed. with an introduction by R. Fraser, London/New York: Oxford University Press.

Friedlaender, I. (1917) 'The significance of Palestine for the Jewries of the world', in *American Hebrew*, 4 May 1917, p. 888.

Fuchs, G. (1905) *Die Schaubühne der Zukunft*, Berlin: Schuster & Loeffler.

—— (1906) *Der Tanz*, Stuttgart: Strecker & Schröder.

—— (1909) *Die Revolution des Theaters*, München/Leipzig: Georg Müller.

—— (1911) *Die Sezession in der dramatischen Kunst und das Volksfestspiel*, München: Müller.

Gallese, V. and Goldman, A. (1998) 'Mirror neurons and the simulation theory of mind-reading', in *Trends in Cognitive Sciences* 2, pp. 493–501.

Gauld, A. (1992) *A History of Hypnotism*, Cambridge: Cambridge University Press.

Geldern, J. van (1993) *Bolshevik Festivals 1917–1920*, Berkeley/Los Angeles/London: University of California Press.

Gennep, A. van (1960) *The Rites of Passage*, trans. M.B. Virdon and G.L. Coffee, Chicago: University of Chicago Press.

Getty, J.A. (1985) *Origins of the Great Purges, The Soviet Communist Party Reconsidered 1933–1938*, New York: Cambridge University Press.

Gilman, S.L. (ed.) (1971) *NS-Literaturtheorie, Eine Dokumentation*, Frankfurt a.M.: Athenäum.

Girard, R. (1977) *Violence and the Sacred*, trans. P. Gregory, Baltimore: Johns Hopkins University Press.

Glassberg, D. (1990) *American Historical Pageantry, The Uses of Tradition in Early Twentieth Century*, Chapel Hill/London: The University of North Carolina Press.

Glebkin, V.V. (1998) *Ritual v sovetskoi kul'ture (Ritual in Soviet Culture)*, Moscow: Ianus-K.

Goebbels, J. (1933) 'Der Sinn unserer großen Feiern', in *Eine olympische Kundgebung deutschen Geistes, Das Fest der deutschen Schule*, Völkischer Beobachter 12. September 1933, p. 2.

—— (1935) 'Kunst und Kultur im Dritten Reich', in *Autor* 10, vols 5/6, pp. 11–12.

Goertz, H. (1974) *Erwin Piscator in Selbstzeugnissen und Bilddokumenten*, Reinbek: Rowohlt.

Goes, G. (1933) *Aufbricht Deutschland!*, Berlin: Traditions-Verlag.

Goethe, J.W. (1901) 'Regeln für Schauspieler', in *Gesammelte Werke, Weimarer Ausgabe*, vol. 40, Weimar: Hermann Böhlaus Nachfolger, pp. 139–68.

Goldenweiser, A.A. (1910) 'Totemism: an analytical study', in *Journal of American Folklore* 23, pp. 179–293.

Goldman, S. (1985) 'Wilde in Europa, Aspekte und Orte ihrer Zurschaustellung', in T. Theye (ed.) *Wir und die Wilden, Einblicke in eine kannibalische Beziehung*, Reinbek: Rowohlt, pp. 243–69.

Gosling, N. (1980) *Paris 1900–1914*, München: Südwest-Verlag.

Green, M. (1988) *New York 1913, The Armory Show and the Paterson Strike Pageant*, New York: Charles Scribner's and Sons.

Gregor, J. and Fülöp-Miller, R. (1928) *The Russian Theatre, its Character and History with Especial Reference to the Revolutionary Period*, trans. P. England, Philadelphia: J.B. Lippincot.

Hagenbeck, C. (1909) *Von Tieren und Menschen: Erlebnisse und Erfahrungen*, Berlin: Vita Deutscher Verlag.

Harrap, G.G. (1927) *Das russische Theater, Sein Wesen und seine Geschichte mit besonderer Berücksichtigung der Revolutionsperiode*, Zürich: Amalthea.

Harrison, J.E. (1890) *Mythology and Monuments of Ancient Athens*, London/New York: Macmillan.

—— (1962) *Themis, A Study of the Social Origins of Greek Religion*, Cleveland/New York: Meridian Books.

Hecht, B. (1946) *A Flag is Born*, New York: American League for a Free Palestine.

—— (1954) *A Child of the Century*, New York: Simon and Schuster.

Herder, J.G von (1861/62) *Von und an Herder: ungedruckte Briefe aus Herders Nachlaß*, 3 vols, vol. 1, ed. H. Düntzer & F.G. von Herder, Leipzig: Dyk.

Herrmann, M. (1914) *Forschungen zur deutschen Theatergeschichte des Mittelalters und der Renaissance*, Berlin: Weidmannsche Buchhandlung.

—— (1931) 'Das theatralische Raumerlebnis', in *Bericht vom 4. Kongreß für Ästhetik und Allgemeine Kunstwissenschaft 1930*, insert of *Zeitschrift für Ästhetik und allgemeine Kunstwissenschaft* 25, vol. II, Stuttgart: Ferdinand Enke, pp. 152–63.

Herzl, T. (1946) *The Jewish State, An Attempt at a Modern Solution of the Jewish Question*, New York: American Zionist Emergency Council.

Heynicke, K. (1935) 'Neurode, Ein Spiel von deutscher Arbeit', in K. Heynicke (ed.) *Der Weg ins Reich*, Berlin: Volkschaft Verlag, pp. 5–56.

Hobsbawm, E. (1994) *Age of Extremes. The Short Twentieth Century 1914–1991*, London: Joseph.

Hofmannsthal, H. von (1979a) 'Electra, Tragödie in einem Aufzug', in H. von Hofmannsthal (ed.) *Gesammelte Werke in zehn Einzelbänden*, ed. B. Schoeller, vol. II (1892–1905) Frankfurt a.M: Fischer, pp. 185–234.

—— (1979b) 'Letter of Lord Chandos', in H. von Hofmannsthal, *Gesammelte Werke in zehn Einzelbänden*, ed. B. Schoeller, vol. II (1892–1905) Frankfurt a.M.: Fischer, pp. 451–65.

Holitscher, A. (1924) *Das Theater im revolutionären Rußland*, Berlin: Volksbühne Verlag.

Innes, C.D. (1981) *Holy Theatre: Ritual and the Avant-Garde*, Cambridge: Cambridge University Press.

—— (1993) *Avant-Garde Theatre, 1892–1992*, London/New York: Routledge.

Ivanov, V.I. (1909): *Po zvezdam (To the Stars)*, St. Peterburg: Izdanie Ory.

—— (1981) 'The essence of tragedy', in L. Senelick (ed.) *Russian Dramatic Theory from Pushkin to the Symbolists*, Austin: University of Texas Press.

Jacobsohn, S. (1912) *Das Jahr der Bühne*, Berlin: Osterheld.

Jäger, G. (1974) '... wie alles sich für mich verändert hat', in *Theater heute*, March 1974, pp. 12–20.

Johnson, M. (1987) *The Body in the Mind, The Bodily Basis of Meaning, Imagination and Reason*, Chicago/London: University of Chicago Press.

Johnson, S. (2001) *Emergence*, New York: Scribner.

Kahane, A. (1928) *Aus dem Tagebuch eines Dramaturgen*, Berlin: Bruno Cassirer.

Kleberg, L. (1979) ' "People's Theatre" and the Revolution. On the history of a concept before and after 1917', in N.A. Nilsson (ed.) *Art, Society, Revolution, Russia 1917–1921*, Stockholm: Almqvist & Wiksell International, pp. 179–97.

Klier, H. (ed.) (1981) *Theaterwissenschaft im deutschsprachigen Raum*, Darmstadt: Wissenschaftliche Buchgesellschaft.

Kloss, W. (1981) *Die nationalsozialistischen Thingspiele, Die Massenbasis des Faschismus 1933–35 in seinem trivialen Theater, Eine parataktische Darstellung*, PhD dissertation, Universität Wien.

Kowalke, K. (2002) *'Ein Fremder ward ich im fremden Land ...'* – Max

Reinhardt's Inszenierung von Franz Werfels und Kurt Weills 'The Eternal Road (Der Weg der Verheißung)' 1937 in New York, *Entstehungsgeschichte und Regiebuchanalyse*, PhD dissertation, Freie Universität Berlin.

Kuhnt, C. (2000) 'Drei "pageants" – ein Komponist. Anmerkungen zu The Eternal Road, We Will Never Die und A Flag is Born', in H. Loos and G. Stern (eds) *Kurt Weill – Auf dem Weg zum 'Weg der Verheißung'*, Freiburg i.B.: Rombach Verlag, pp. 218–43.

Kurzenberger, H. (1998) 'Chorisches Theater der neunziger Jahre', in E. Fischer-Lichte *et al.* (eds) *TRANSFORMATIONEN, Theater der neunziger Jahre*, Berlin: Theater der Zeit, pp. 83–91.

Lane, C. (1981) *The Rites of Rulers*, Cambridge: Cambridge University Press.

Laqeur, W. (1972) *A History of Zionism*, London: Weidenfeld and Nicholson.

Laubinger, O. (1934) 'Theater der Nation', in *Deutsche Mitte, Mitteldeutsche Hefte f. Kultur u. den Sinn d. Wirtschaft* 4, Halle: Brandt, pp. 25–30.

Lazarus, E. (1982) *Selections from Her Poetry and Prose*, ed. M.U. Schappes, New York: Emma Lazarus Federation of Jewish Women.

Lepenies, W. (1989) 'Gefährliche Wahlverwandschaften', in W. Lepenies (ed.) *Gefährliche Wahlverwandschaften, Essays zur Wissenschaftsgeschichte*, Stuttgart: Reclam, pp. 80–110.

Lessing, G.E. (1973) 'Brief an Nicolai vom November 1757', in *Werke*, vol. IV, ed. H.G. Göpfert, München: Hanser.

Liepe-Levinson, K. (1993) *A Striptease Poetics*, New York: City University of New York.

Lipstadt, D.E. (1986) *Beyond Belief: The American Press and the Coming of Holocaust, 1933–1945*, New York: Free Press.

Liskowsky, O. (1934) 'Passion oder Epos', in *Deutsche Bühnenkorrespondenz* 3 (63), pp. 1–2.

Lotman, J. (1992) ' "Dogovor" i "vruchenie sebia" kak arkhetipicheskie modeli kul'tury ("Contract" and "self-transfer" as archetypical cultural models)' in J. Lotman (ed.) *Izbrannye stat'i v trëkh tomakh (Selected Papers in three volumes)*, vol. I, Tallin: Aleksandra, pp. 345–55.

Lunacharskii, A. (1918) 'Vstuplenie (Foreword)', in R. Wagner (ed.) *Iskusstvo i revoliuciia (Art and Revolution)*, Petrograd: Narkompros.

MacAloon, J.J. (1984a) *This Great Symbol, Pierre de Coubertin and the Origin of Modern Olympic Games*, Chicago/London: Chicago University Press.

—— (1984b) 'Olympic Games and the theory of spectacle in modern societies', in J.J. MacAloon (ed.) *Rite, Drama, Festival, Spectacle, Rehearsals Towards a Theory of Cultural Performance*, Philadelphia: Institute for the Study of Human Issues, pp. 241–80.

McDonald, M. (1992) *Ancient Sun, Modern Light*, New York: Columbia University Press.

MacKaye, P. (1912) *The Civic Theatre in Relation to the Redemption of Leisure, A Book of Suggestions*, New York/London: Mitchell Kennerley.

Mannhardt, W. (1875/76) *Wald- und Feldkulte*, 2 vols, Berlin: Borntraeger.

Marcuse, H. (1973) 'Kunst und Revolution', in H. Marcuse, *Konterrevolution und Revolte*, Frankfurt a.M.: Suhrkamp, pp. 95–148.

Martens, L. (1987) 'The theme of repressed memory in Hofmannsthal's Elektra', in *German Quarterly* 60 (1), pp. 38–51.

Möller, W.E. (1974) 'Das Frankenburger Würfelspiel', in G. Rühle (ed.) *Zeit und Theater, Diktatur und Exil*, 3 vols, vol. 3, Berlin: Propyläen Verlag, pp. 335–78.

Morowitz, H.J. (2002) *The Emergence of Everything, how the World Became Complex*, Oxford: Oxford University Press.

Mosse, G.L. (1977) *The Nationalization of the Masses: Political Symbolism and Mass Movements in Germany from the Napoleonic Wars through the Third Reich*, New York: New American Library.

Newiger, H.-J. (1969) 'Hofmannsthals Elektra und die griechische Tragödie', in *Arcadia* 4, pp. 138–63.

Nietzsche, F. (1960) 'Unzeitgemäße Betrachtung, viertes Stück', in F. Nietzsche (ed.) *Werke*, vol. 1, ed. K. Schlechta, München: Hanser, pp. 367–434.

—— (1995) *The Birth of Tragedy out of the Spirit of Music*, trans. S. Whiteside, ed. M. Tanner, London: Penguin Books.

Nitsch, H. (1979) *Das Orgien Mysterien Theater, Die Partituren aller aufgeführten Aktionen 1960–1979*, vol. 1, Neapel/München/Wien: Studio Morra.

—— (1990) 'Die Realisation des O.M. Theaters', in H. Nitsch (ed.) *Das Orgien Mysterien Theater, Manifeste, Aufsätze, Vorträge*, Salzburg/Wien: Residenz Verlag, pp. 69–109.

O.A. (1919) 'Chronika. Truppa improvizatorov (Chronicle. A group of improvisers)', in *Zhizn` iskusstva, (Life of the Art)* 110, 3 April 1919, p. 3.

—— (1920) 'Na repetitsii instsenirovki "Vziatie Zimnego Dvortsa" (At the rehearsal of "The Storming of the Winter Palace")', in *Petrogradskaia pravda* 248, 4 November 1920, p. 2.

—— (1968) 'Libretto instsenirovki "Vziatie Zimnego dvortsa" (Libretto of the production of "The Storming of the Winter Palace")', in A.Z. Iufit (ed.) *Russkii sovetskii teatr 1917–1921, Dokumenty i materialy (Russian soviet theatre 1917–1921), Documents and materials)*, Leningrad: Iskusstvo, pp. 272–3.

Parker, L.N. (1928) *Several of My Lives*, London: Chapman and Hall.

Petuchowski, J.J. (1992) *'Mein Judesein', Wege und Erfahrungen eines deutschen Rabbiners*, Freiburg i.B.: Heller.

Philostratus, F. (1936) *Concerning Gymnastics*, trans. T. Woody, Ann Arbor/MI: UMI Research Press.

Piotrovsky, A. (1919) 'Sverzhenie samoderzhaviia – Predstavlenie na Dvortsovoi ploshchadi (The overthrow of the autocracy – performance on Palace Square)', in *Zhizn' iskusstva (Life of the Art)*, 199–200, 26/27 July, p. 2.

—— (1926) 'Khronika Leningradskikh prazdnestv 1919–1922 (Chronicle of the Leningrad festivals 1919–1928)', in A. Gvozdev, A. Piotrovsky and N.P. Izvekov (ed.) *Massovye prazdnestva (Mass festivals)*, Leningrad: Gosudarstvennyi Institut Istorii iskusstv, pp. 53–84.

Plessner, H. (1970) *Laughing and Crying, A Study of the Limits of Human Behaviour*, Evanston, Il: North Western University Press.

Poizat, M. (1992) *The Angel's Cry, Beyond the Pleasure Principle in Opera*, trans. A. Duner, Ithaca/London: Cornell University Press.

Prevost, N. (1990) *American Pageantry, A Movement for Art and Democracy*, Ann Arbor: UMI Research Press.

Raabe, P. (ed.) (1965) *Expressionisms, Der Kampf um eine literarische Bewegung*, München: Deutscher Taschenbuch Verlag.

Raider, M.A. (1998) *The Emergence of American Zionism*, New York/London: New York University Press.

Reed, J. (1919) *Ten Days That Shook the World*, New York: Boni and Liveright.

Reinhardt, G. (1979) *The Genius: A Memoir of Max Reinhardt*, New York: Knopf.

Riegel, K.-G. (1998) 'Die Inszenierung von Verbrechen. Die Moskauer Schauprozesse (1936–1938)', in H. Willems and M. Jurga (eds) *Inszenierungsgesellschaft, Ein einführendes Handbuch*, Opladen/Wiesbaden: Westdeutscher Verlag, pp. 235–52.

Robertson, R. (1986) '"Ich habe ihm das Beil nicht geben können": The heroine's failure in Hofmannsthal's Elektra', in *OL*, vol. 41, no. 4, pp. 312–31.

Rousseau, J.J. (1987) *Discours sur les sciences et les artes/Lettre á d'Alembert*, ed. and introd. J. Verloot, Paris: Éditions Gallimard.

Rozik, E. (2002) *The Roots of Theatre, Rethinking Ritual and Other Theories of Origin*, Iowa City: University of Iowa Press.

Rühle, G. (1977) 'Die Thingspielbewegung', in H.M. Eichberg *et al.* (eds) *Massenspiele*, Stuttgart-Bad Cannstatt: frommann-holzboog, pp. 181–97.

Schebera, J. (2000) 'Awakening America to the European Jewish tragedy . . .', in H. Loos and G. Stern (eds) *Kurt Weill – Auf dem Weg zum 'Weg der Verheißung'*, Freiburg i.B.: Rombach Verlag, pp. 255–63.

Schechner, R. (1969) 'The Politics of ecstasy', in *Public Domain* 1969, pp. 209–28.

—— (ed.) (1970) *Dionysus in 69*, New York: Farrar, Strauss and Giroux.

—— (1973) *Environmental Theater*, New York: Hawthorne Books.

Schiller, F. (1980) 'Die Braut von Messina', in *Werke*, vol. 10, ed. N. Oellers and S. Seidl, Weimar: Böhlau, pp. 9–125.

Schleef, E. (1997) *Droge Faust Parzifal*, Frankfurt a.M.: Suhrkamp.

Schlesier, R. (1991) 'Prolegomena to Jane Harrison's Interpretation of Ancient Greek Religion', in W.M. Calder III. (ed.) *The Cambridge Ritualists Reconsidered*, Atlanta, GA: Scholars Press, pp. 185–226.

Schlösser, R. (1935) *Das Volk und seine Bühne*, Berlin: Langen-Müller.

Senelick, L. (ed.) (1981) *Russian Dramatic Theory from Pushkin to the Symbolists*, Austin: University of Texas Press.

Shephard, W.H. (1990) *The Dionysus Group, American University Studies*, Series 26, *Theatre Arts*, vol. V, New York: Peter Lang.

Shklovsky, V. (1923) 'Drama i massovye predstavleniia (Drama and mass performances)', in *Khod konia* (*The Knight's Move*), Moscow/Berlin: Gelikon, pp. 59–63.

Shubsky, N. (1920): 'Na ploshchadi Uritskogo (Vpechatleniia moskvicha) (On Urickii Square (Impressions of a moscower))', in *Vestnik teatra* (*Theatre Messenger*) 75, pp. 4–5.

Simmel, G. (1923) *Soziologie, Untersuchungen über die Form der Vergesellschaftung*, München/Leipzig: Duncker & Humblot.

Smith, W.R. (1957) *The Religion of the Semites, The Fundamental Institutions, Burnett Lectures 1888–89*, New York: Meridian Books.

Stommer, R. (1985) *Die inszenierte Volksgemeinschaft, Die 'Thing-Bewegung' im Dritten Reich*, Marburg: Jonas Verlag.

Stravinsky, V. and Craft, R. (1978) *Stravinsky*, New York: Simon and Schuster.

Styan, J. (1982) *Max Reinhardt*, Cambridge: Cambridge University Press.

Tait, P. (1999) 'Circus bodies as theatre animals', in *ADS* 35, pp. 129–43.

Theater Neumarkt Zürich (1997) *'Top Dogs', Entstehung – Hintergründe – Materialien*, Zürich: Kontrast Verlag.

Thomson, R.G. (ed.) (1996) *Freakery: Cultural Spectacles of the Extraordinary Body*, New York: New York University Press.

—— (1997) *Extraordinary Bodies*, New York: Columbia University Press.

Turner, V. (1969) *The Ritual Process, Structure and Anti-Structure*, Chicago: Aldine.

Uspensky, B.A. (1994) 'Tsar'i samozvanets: samozvanchestvo v Rossii kak kul'turno-istoricheskii fenomen (Tsar and usurpation in Russia as cultural historical phenomenon)', in B.A. Uspensky (ed.) *Izbrannye trudy (Selected Works)*, vol. I, Moscow: Gnozis, pp. 75–109.

Varela, F.J., Thompson, E. and Rosch, E. (1991) *The Embodied Mind*, Cambridge: MIT Press.

Vattimo, G. (1992) *Die transparente Gesellschaft*, Wien: Edition Passage.

Vechten, C. van (1915) *Music after the Great War*, New York: Schirmer.

Vinogradov-Mamont, N. (1972) *Krasnoarmeiskoe chudo (The miracle of the soldiers in the Red Army)*, Leningrad: Isskusstvo.

Vischer F.T. (1922) Article on the 'Symbol', in R. Vischer (ed.) *Kritische Gänge*, vol. 4, München: Meyer & Jessen, pp. 420–56.

Ward, P.M. (2000) 'Elektra and the representation of women's behaviour through myth', in *German Life and letters*, vol. 53, no. 1, pp. 37–55.

Warstat, M. (2004) *Theatrale Gemeinschaften, Zur Festkultur der Arbeiterbewegung 1918–1933*, Tübingen/Basel: Francke.

Weisgal, M.W. (1971) *So Far ... An Autobiography*, London: Weidenfeld and Nicholson.

Whitfield, S.J. (1996) 'The Politics of pageantry 1936–1946', in *American Jewish History*, vol. 84, no. 3, pp. 221–51.

Wilson, J. (1991) *The Challenge of Belatedness*, Lanham: UP of America.

Withington, R. (1963) *English Pageantry: A Historical Outline*, 2 vols, vol. 2, New York: Benjamin Blom.

Wittgenstein, L. (1979) *Notebooks 1914–1916*, second edition, ed. G.H. von Wright and G.E.M. Anscombe, Oxford: Blackwell.

Wyman, D.S. (1984) *The Abandonment of the Jews: America and the Holocaust, 1941–1945*, New York: Panthea Books.

Zeitlin, F.I. (2004) 'Dionysus in 69', in E. Hall, F. Macintosh and A. Wrigley (eds) *Dionysus Since 69, Greek Tragedy at the Dawn of the Third Millenium*, Oxford: Oxford University Press, pp. 49–75.

Subject index

Author index